NEWTON

MASSACHUSETTS

BY

M. F. SWEETSER

AUTHOR OF "ARTIST BIOGRAPHIES," "TICKNOR'S GUIDE-BOOKS," "KING'S NAHANT,"
"KING'S BOSTON HARBOR," "KING'S UNITED STATES," ETC.

TWO HUNDRED  ILLUSTRATIONS

BOSTON, MASS.
MOSES KING CORPORATION
1889

This is a public domain book re-published in 2014 by Power of Upper Falls Press

To order more copies (locally) contact:

    Power Of Upper Falls Press
    12 Spring St
    Newton MA 02464
    617-999-5300
    books@PowerOfUpperFalls.com

or purchase on-line at:

    PowerOfUpperFalls.com

Maurian,
Thanks for sharing your magical house for the afternoon
Jerry Reilly

FOREWARD

I stumbled on this book while poking around the Internet looking for some historical information about my neighborhood (Upper Falls).

This book is long, long out of print and in the public domain. Thanks to the wonderful work of Google Books (and others) this book and many thousands of others are available for free to everyone on-line.

There's something about the style of the writing here that I love. The combination of optimistic exuberance and over-wrought poetry gives a 19th century booster's view of our town.

I've decided to publish the book in print as a way to help raise funds for the re-building of the Emerson Playground in Upper Falls. 100% of the proceeds from the sale of the book will go to that effort.

So thanks for your purchase of the book. You are contributing to a civic good in today's Newton - something your 19th century Newton predecessors would certainly approve of.

Jerry Reilly
Power of Upper Falls Press

Introduction.

THIS book has been prepared as a popular household companion for all the families who make their homes in any of the fifteen villages which together form "The Newtons," the garden city of Massachusetts.

Although it abounds with historical and statistical matter, it does not claim to be a history, nor a book of statistics, nor a directory; but it is merely one of "King's Handbooks," and as such it will be found to contain the most notable and interesting facts pertaining to Newton, told in a simple, entertaining, and trustworthy manner, and at the same time illustrated so profusely and appropriately as to become at once attractive and enjoyable.

The text has been enriched with a great number of memorable historical facts, anecdotes of noted residents, fragments of poetry, and other piquant and interesting features. The form of treatment is in simple geographical order. The book opens with two or three preliminary chapters of a general nature about the town and the city, and then continues with sixteen chapters, each describing one of the villages or well-marked neighborhoods. Thus in each chapter a village is discussed, with its chief streets and parks, public and private buildings, famous natives and residents, bits of legend and poetry, stories of the colonial, Revolutionary, and modern days, and some local history. In this compact form a conception of each locality is presented, bringing into view all its phases, and yet without confusing references to other places. A clear, vivid, and individual idea is thus gained of each of the component parts of the whole city.

The author wishes to acknowledge his obligations to many people who have been moved — partly by local pride and partly by the prevailing courteousness — to read over and add to and correct the material here used, both in the manuscript and in the proof-sheets. It is not possible to enumerate all, but among them were ex-Governor Alex. H. Rice, ex-Governor William Claflin, the late Rev. Dr. Increase N. Tarbox, the Rev. Dr. Samuel F. Smith, the Rev. Dr. D. L. Furber, Colonel

Edwin B. Haskell, Dr. Charles F. Crehore, Dr. J. F. Frisbie, Dr. E. A. Whiston, Otis Pettee, William E. Sheldon, William C. Bates, and many other well-known citizens.

The publishers, too, have their acknowledgments to make to those well-to-do and generous citizens by means of whose pecuniary aid it is possible to offer this large and costly volume, with its one hundred and fifty illustrations, at a price so low that each and every resident can easily afford to own one copy at home and perhaps to send one or many copies to distant friends, or to present to guests, as a memento of their visits, or to place in the hands of acquaintances who are seeking suburban homes. It is hoped that the elaborate text, the great number of pictures, and the attractive mechanical make-up produce a volume useful and ornamental enough to be acceptable to all interested in Newton.

This volume is one of the now well-known series of "King's Handbooks," some of which have been in popular use for many years, while others are now in preparation. The crown and culmination of the series is "King's Handbook of the United States," covering between 500 and 600 pages, embellished with fifty full-page maps in colors, and illustrated with upwards of 1,200 original engravings.

MOSES KING CORPORATION,

Publishers " King's Handbooks," Guides, and Maps,

BOSTON, MASS.

Contents.

	PAGE
NEWTON OF THE PAST.— A Glimpse at the Old Days; the Refractory Colony of New Cambridge; Newtown at Last; Wars and Rumors of Wars; the Rise of the City, ...	15
NEWTON OF THE PRESENT.— Its Gifts from Nature; Streams and Hills; a Land of Good Health; the Villages; Municipal Expenses; Police and Fire Department, ...	29
NEWTON.— Boston and Worcester Railroad in 1834; an Old-Time Inn; the Morse Field; Revolutionary Memories; the Jackson Clan; the Free Library; Farlow Park and its Churches; the Cradle of Newton; the Eliot Church; Mount Ida; the Old Cemetery, ...	39
NONANTUM HILL.— Kenrick Park; the Apostle Eliot; the First Protestant Mission in the World; a Revolutionary Hero; One of Cromwell's Riders; the First Unitarian of New England, ...	101
NEWTONVILLE.— Hull's Crossing; Old-Time Scholars; the Village Square; the Newton Club; Washington Park; the High School; the Claflin Estate; General William Hull; Slavery in Newton; Bullough's Pond; the Newton Cemetery; Heroes of the Last American War, ...	131
NONANTUM.— The Old North Village, or Tin Horn; Fuller's Corner; the Bemis Factories; the First Gas-Lighting in America, ...	157
WEST NEWTON.— A Famous Old School; Bell-Hack and Squash-End; the Second Church; the Centenarian Dominie; the Blithedale Romance; the Pine-Farm School, ...	161
AUBURNDALE.— The Pretty Railway Station; Pioneer Farms; Pigeon's Battery; Saints' Rest; Sweet Auburn; a Noted Artist; Village Notables; Famous Schools; a Trio of Churches; a Provincial Inn; Islington; the Winslow Affair, ...	189
WOODLAND.— The Woodland-Park Hotel; William Dean Howells; the Short Hills; Burgoyne's Route; Vista Hill; Edwin B. Haskell; Newton Cottage Hospital, ...	205
RIVERSIDE.— The Newton Navy; the Placid River Charles; a Few Bits of Poetry; the Boat-Clubs; County Rock; the Carnival in September: an Old-Fashioned Apostrophe, ...	211

	PAGE
NEWTON LOWER FALLS.— A Paper-Making Glen; Newton's First Post-Office; Famous Paper-Mills; a Massachusetts Magnate; Old St. Mary's; a Fine Old Country-Seat; Outer Beacon Street, ...	217
WABAN.— The Red Chieftain's Hunting-Park; the Intruding Anglo-Saxon Deacon; a Merchant-Prince; Strong's Nurseries; Beacon Hill; the Collins Estate; a Landscape-Park, ...	231
ELIOT.— The Clark, Ellis, and Cheney Places; Hickory Cliff and its Poet; the Place of a Vanished Lake; Famous Trees; an Arcadia of the Future,	245
NEWTON UPPER FALLS.— An Indian Fisherman; Ancient Manufactures; Churches and Shrines; the Water-Works; Echo Bridge; the Sudbury Aqueduct; Turtle Island; Canoe Voyages, ...	249
NEWTON HIGHLANDS.— A Group of Modern Homes; the Sanitarium; Ancient Taverns; the Two Churches; a Colonial Family; Well-known Citizens, ...	267
NEWTON CENTRE.— Charles Dickens; the Ancient Common and its Churches; Noon-Houses; the National Song; Beacon Street; the Mother Church of Newton; an Old-Time Dominie; Master Rice; the Baptist Society; "Baptist Pond," Crystal Lake; Newton Theological Institution; Thompsonville; Johnsonville, ...	271
CHESTNUT HILL.— The Essex Colony; a Group of Villas; the Chapel; Waban Hill; Hammond's Pond; Ancient Worthies, ...	311
OAK HILL.— A Land of Highlands and Forests; the Old-Time Farmers; Modern Country-Seats; Oak Hill and Bald Pate; Holbrook Hall; Kenrick's Bridge, ...	321

List of Illustrations.

Allen, Bethuel, House, 267.
Allen, N. T., School of, 163.
Allen, The Misses, School of, 73.
Associates' Hall, Newton Centre, 279.
Auburndale Congregational Church, 199.
Auburndale Station, B. & A. R. R., 190.

Baptist Church, Newton, 77.
Baptist Church, Newton Centre, 273.
Bartlett, Dr. James W., Residence of, 51.
Barton, Charles C., Residence of, 291.
Becker, John, Residence of, 83.
Bell, Albert D. S., Residence of, 317.
Boat Club House, Riverside, 213.
Brackett House, The, 101.
Bray, Mellen, Residence of, 293.
Bridge connecting Weston and Auburndale, 202.
Bridge, The, Farlow Park, 65.
Brooks, Francis A., Residence of, 95.
Brown, Samuel J., Residence of, 147.
Burial Ground, The Old Centre-Street, 21.
Burr, Isaac T., Residence of, 113.
Buswell, Charles H., Residence of, 119.

Cemetery Gateway, 153.
Chaffin, John C., Residence of, 63.
Channing Church, Newton, 69.
Chapel and Conservatory, The Cemetery, 155.
Chestnut-Hill Station, B. & A. R. R., 311.
Church of the Messiah, Auburndale, 201.
City Hall, West Newton, 33 and 169.
City Seal, 38 and on front cover.
Claflin, Ex-Gov. William, Residence of, 133.
Cobb, Henry E., Residence of, 79.
Coburn, Nathan P., Residence of, 111.
Collins, Edward Jackson, Estate, 237.
Congregational Church, Auburndale, 199.
Congregational Church, First, Newton Centre, 277.
Converse, Edmund W., Residence of, 85.
Converse, Edmund W., Jun., Residence of, 80.
Cook, George, Residence of, 177.
Cottage Hospital, Newton, 210.
Cotton, John, Facsimile of Receipt, 16.
Crehore, Dr. Charles Frederic, Residence of, 223.
"Crow's Nest," Lasell Seminary, 189.
Curtis, Charles, Residence of, 141.
Cutter, Frederic R., Residence of, 185.

Davidson, Alexander, Residence of, 238.
Dresser House, The New, Waban, 240.
Dresser, William R., Residence of, 239.
Echo Bridge, Newton Upper Falls, 255 and on front cover, and also on title page.
Edmands, A. Lawrence, Residence of, 97.
Edmands, J. Wiley, Estate, 97.
Eliot Church, The Old, 25.
Eliot Church, The New, 75.
Eliot Memorial, Kenrick Street, 15, 39, 110, and on front cover.
Eliot Station, B. & A. R. R., 245.
Ellis, George H., Residence of, 265.
Elms, James C., Residence of, 105.
Emerson, Darius R., Residence of, 57.

Facsimile of John Cotton's Receipt, 16.
Facsimiles of Town Records, 18, 19.
Farlow, Hon. John S., Residence of, 109.
Farlow Park, 65.
Farquhar, David W., Residence of, 107.
Field, Dr. Henry M., Residence of, 121.
First Congregational Church, Newton Centre, 277.
First Locomotive, the "Meteor," 24.
First Settlers' Monument, 21; Tablet on, 100.
First (Unitarian) Church, West Newton, 164.
Fitch, Ezra C., Residence of, 93.
Fitz, Thomas B., Residence of, 171.
Free Public Library, 35.

Gate of Waban-Hill Reservoir, 313.
Gateway, E. B. Haskell's Residence, 209.
Gateway to Cemetery, 153.
Gay, Charles M., Residence of, 117.
Gay, Edwin W., Residence of, 102.
Gould, William H., Residence of, 241.
Grace Church, Newton, 65, 67.

Harwood, George S., Residence of, 127.
Harwood, Seth K., Hotel of, 47.
Haskell, Edwin B., Residence of, 209.
Hayward, Albert F., Residence of, 269.
Heath, Daniel C., Residence of, 139.
"Heathcote, The," 139.
Henshaw, Frederic H., Residence of, 235.
"Hickory Cliff" (William Peirce's Residence), 247.

LIST OF ILLUSTRATIONS.

High School, Newtonville, 145.
Hose and Hook-and-Ladder House, Newtonville, 37.
Hotel Hunnewell, 47.
Houdlette, Fred A., Residence of, 49.
Hull, General, House of, 131.
Hunter, Stephen V. A., Residence of, 305.

Interior of Grace Church, 67.

Jackson Estate, 61.
Johnson, Charles E., Residence of, 129.

Kenrick House, 108.
King, Moses, Residence of, 106.
Kingsbury House, Chestnut Hill, 315.

Lake, The, Farlow Park, 65.
Langford, John T., Residence of, 59.
Lasell Seminary, Auburndale, 189, 197.
Lasell Seminary Boat-House, Riverside, 215.
Lasell Seminary Grounds, 195.
Lasell Seminary, View from, 29.
Lee's Woodland Park Hotel, 207.
Library, Free Public, 35.
Lovell, Wallace D., Residence of, 125.
Lower Falls, Bird's-eye View, opp. p. 217.

Map of Newton, 1831, 23.
Map of Newton, 1889, 31.
Mason School, Newton Centre, 285.
McGee, Chauncey B., Residence of, 243.
"Meteor," The, Locomotive, 24.
Methodist Church, Newtonville, 149.
Methodist Episcopal Church, Newton, 99.
Methodist Episcopal Church, Newton Centre, 283.
Mitchell, Austin R., Residence of, opp. p. 144.
Monument, The Soldiers', 27.
Monument to First Settlers, 21; Tablet on, 100.

Names on First Settlers' Monument, 100.
Newton Club-House, 131.
Newton Theological Institution, 281.
Nichols, J. Howard, Residence of, 89.
Nickerson's Block, West Newton, 166.
Nonantum Congregational Church, 157.
Nonantum House, 41.
North Evangelical (Nonantum Cong.) Church, 157.

Oak-Hill School, 325.
Old Burial Ground, Centre Street, 21.
Old Wales Bridge, 225.

Page, Charles J., Residence of, 235.
Parker, Joseph W., Residence of, 287.
Partelow's Boat-Houses, 216.
Peirce, William, Residence of, 247.
Petersilea, Prof. Carlyle, Residence of, 103.
Pine Farm School, 188.

Pony-Track, E. B. Haskell's Residence, 209.
Pope, Col. Albert A., Residence of, 51.
Potter, John C., Residence of, 55.
Powers, Samuel Lee, Residence of, 105.
Prescott, John R., Residence of, 332.
Prescott, Mrs. Charles B., Residence of, 91.
Public Library, 35.
Pumping-Station, Newton Water-Works, 259.

Rice, Hon. Thomas, Residence of, 227.
Rice, J. Willard, Residence of, 193.
Rice, Marshall O., Residence of, 301.
Riley, Charles E., Residence of, 81.
"Rosedale" (John C. Chaffin's Residence), 63.

Schoolhouse, A, in Newton in 1800, 17.
Seal, The City, 38.
Seaver, Edwin P., Residence of, 234.
Second Baptist Church, Upper Falls, 251.
Second (Cong.) Church, West Newton, The Old, 161.
Second (Cong.) Church, West Newton, The New, 169.
Shannon, Mary, Estate, 87.
Sheldon, William E., Residence of, 173.
Snow, Daniel E., Residence of, 105.
Soldiers' Monument, 27.
Spaulding, Rev. Henry G., Residence of, 99.
Springer, Elestus M., Residence of, 115.
Square, The, Newtonville, 149.
St. Mary's Church, Lower Falls, 219.
Strong, George, Residence of, 72.
Swedenborgian Church, 135.

Tablet in Eliot Memorial, 15, 110.
Taylor, Bertrand E., Residence of, 289.
Theological Institution, The Newton, 281.
Tomb, The Soldiers', in Newton Cemetery, 27.
Town Records, Facsimiles of, 18, 19.

Underwood Primary School, 71.
Universalist Church, Newtonville, 143.

View from Lasell Seminary, 29.

Waban-Hill Reservoir, Gate at, 313.
Waban Station, B. & A. R. R., 233.
Wade, Levi C., Residence of, 323.
Wales Bridge, The Old, 225.
Walworth, Arthur C., Residence of, 295.
Warren, H. Langford, Residence of, 232.
Washington Street, Newton Lower Falls, 221.
Webster, William E., Residence of, 307.
Wesleyan Home, Newtonville, 5.
Weston, Bridge between Auburndale and, 202.
Wetherell Estate, The, 265.
White, T. Edgar, Residence of, 123.
Wilbur, George B., Residence of, 181.
Woodland Park Hotel, Woodland, 207.
Woodward Street, Waban, 231.

Index to Text.

Abbott, Holker W., 228.
Acacia-Tree, A Large, 60.
Adams Family, 182.
Adams, Phineas, 179.
Adams, Rev. J. Coleman, 138.
Adams, Seth, 59.
Alcott, Dr. William A., 193.
Allen, Bethuel, House, 267.
Allen, George, 53.
Allen, James T., 186.
Allen, Miss Hannah, 72.
Allen, Miss Julia G., 72.
Allen, Nathaniel T., 167, 170, 172, 179.
Allen, Phineas, 179.
Allen, Rev. J. A., 173.
Allen, Rev. N. G., 198.
Allen, Rev. Ralph W., 257.
Allen, The Misses, School for Girls and Young Ladies, 72, 73.
Allen, Walter, 268.
"America," 276, 278.
American Magnesium Company, 58.
American Watch Company, 182.
Ames, Fisher, 186.
Amory, Hon. Thomas C., 252.
Amos-Lawrence Farm, The, 318.
Anderson, Cyrus J., 80.
Anderson, Rev. Galusha, 308.
Anderson, Rev. Martin B., D.D., 309.
Andrews, Rev. Elisha B., D.D., 308.
Angier, Ensign Oakes, 40.
"Angier's Corner," 40.
Appleton, William S., 325.
Arch, A Great, 262.
Arnold, Rev. Albert N., D.D., 308.
Athenæum, The West-Newton, 174, 178.
Atkinson Place, The, 206.
Auburn, Mount, History of the Name, 147.
AUBURNDALE, 189-204.
Auburndale Congregational Church, 199.
Auburndale, History of the Name, 32, 34, 36, 38, 191, 192.
Auburndale Home School, 194.
Avann, Rev. J. M., 198.
Axtell, Seth J., 308.
Ayres, Helen, 172.
Ayres, Rev. William M., 136.
"Baby Ghost," The, 252.
Bacon, Daniel, 40, 45.
Bacon Family, 40, 74.
Bacon, George W., 41, 64, 66.
Bacon, Joseph N., 42, 45.
Bacon, Rev. Joel S., D.D., 308.
"Bacon's Corner," 40.
Bacon's Tavern, 268.
Badger Will Case, The, 176.
Bailey, Charles J., 53.
Bailey, Rev. Augustus F., 257.
Bailey, Rev. Jonas, 257.
Baker, Rev. Henry, 136.
Baldwin, Aaron, 82.
Baldwin, Enoch, 82.

Banks, Savings and National, 45.
Bannister, Rev. D. K., 257.
Banvard, Rev. Joseph, D.D., 308.
Baptist Churches, 76, 77, 183, 251, 257, 273, 275, 296.
"Baptist Pond," 147, 299-303.
Barber, John, 166, 182.
Barden, Frederic, 256.
Barnard, Rev. Charles F., 132, 168.
Barnes Estate, The, 206.
Barnes, Fred P., 58.
Barnes, Rev. Lemuel C., 297.
Barstow, Rev. E. H., 292.
Bartlett, Dr. James W., 53.
Bartlett, General William Francis, 303.
Bartlett, Joseph, 304.
Barton, Charles C., 291, 303.
Bashford, Rev. J. W., 198.
Bates, William Carver, 2, 44, 104.
Baury, Miss Elizabeth P., 224.
Baury, Rev. Alfred L., D.D., 224, 226, 229.
Baylies, Rev. A., 229.
Beacon Hill, Waban, 240, 242.
Becker, John, 80, 83.
Beecher, Catherine, 168.
Belgravia of Boston, The, 32.
Bell, Albert D. S., 316, 317.
"Bell-Hack," 175.
Bellows, Albert F., 192, 193.
Bellows, Dr. H. P., 193.
Bemis Family, 158.
Bemis, Seth, 158, 159, 179.
Benyon, Abner I., 64, 203.
Bigelow, Dr. Henry F., 151, 152.
Bigelow, Dr. Henry J., 324.
Bigelow Mortuary Chapel, 151, 152.
Billings, Charles E., 106.
Billings, Dr. Frank S., 172.
Binney, Rev. Joseph G., D.D., 308.
Bird, James, A.M., 194.
Bishop, Hon. Robert R., 172, 260, 280.
Bishop, Rev. T. W., 136.
Bixby Family, 270.
Black-Bass Club, The Newton, 299.
Blake, Mrs. Mary, Quotation from Essay, 262-264.
Blanden, Francis, 302.
Blood, Rev. Caleb, 296.
Boat-houses, 213, 215, 216.
Bourne Family, 192.
Bowditch, Ernest W., 244.
Bowles, Rev. R. H., 183.
Bowman, Dexter D., 104.
Brackett, Captain George F., 136.
Brackett Family, 285.
Brackett, Hon. J. Q. A., 324.
Bragdon, Prof. Charles C., 196.
Braislin, Rev. Edward, 297.
Bray, Mellen, 293, 309.
Brayton, Rev. Durlin L., 308.
Bremer, Fredrika, at Newton, 188.
Bridges, 65, 202, 225, 234, 262.

Bridgman, Raymond L., 203.
Brooks, Francis A., 90, 95.
Brooks, Rev. Phillips, D.D., 76.
Brown, Rev. Charles Rufus, 303.
Brown, Rev. Nathan, D.D., 308.
Brown, Samuel J., 137, 147, 151.
Buckingham, Rev. John A., 315.
Bullens, George S., 64, 66, 102, 208.
Bullough's Pond, 148, 150.
Bullough, Tom, 150.
Bunker, Major David T., 194.
Burbank, Moses, 303.
Burgoyne's Army, Prisoners from, 164, 165.
Burnham, Clara Louise, 59.
Burr, Deacon C. C., 193.
Burr, Heman M., 315.
Burr, Isaac T., 64, 66, 106, 113.
Burrage, Charles H., 315.
Burrell, Rev. Jacob, 183.
Burroughs, Rev. Henry, 228.
Burton, Rev. Ernest DeWitt, 303.
Bushnell, Rev. William, 272, 286.
Buswell, Charles H., 106, 119.
Burial Ground, 21, 153, 155.
Butler, Charles S., 298.
Butler Estate, The, 206.
Butler, Rev. Dr. William, 298.
Cabot Family, The, 86, 88, 147, 285.
Cabot, John, 86.
Caldwell, Rev. A., 229.
Caldwell, Rev. Samuel L., D.D., 309.
Calkins, Rev. Wolcott, 74, 80.
Campbell, F. J., 132.
Carpenter, Rev. C. H., 292.
Carpenter, Vernon E., 183.
Carrier, Rev. Augustus H., 198.
Carruth, Captain W. W., 136.
Carter, Henry H., 137.
Cate, Edward W., 175.
Cemetery, The Old, 96; the Present, 151-156.
Centenary (M. E.) Church, Auburndale, 198.
Central Congregational Church, 134.
Chaffin, John C., 63, 64, 66.
Chandler, Hon. Parker C., 172.
Channing Church, 58, 69, 70-72.
Channing, Rev. William Ellery, D.D., 70.
Chapin, Rev. Solomon, 198.
Chaplin, Rev. Jeremiah, 76.
Charles River, 29, 54, 56, 204, 211-216, 252, 253, 261.
Chase, Chief-Justice S. P., 141.
Chase, Rev. Irah, 304, 306.
Cheesecake Brook, 161, 162.
Cheney House, The, 245, 256.
Cheney, John, 304.
Cheney, Mrs. Ednah D., 84.
Cheseborough, E. S., 167.
CHESTNUT HILL, 311-320.
Chestnut Hill, 96.
Chestnut Hill Station, 311.
Chestnut-Tree, A Famous, 292.
Child, David Lee, 168; Epitaph composed by, 98.
Child, Lydia Maria, 168, 187, 188.
Chism, Samuel, 42.
Church of the Messiah, 201.
City Hall, West Newton, 33, 173-175.
City Seal, 29.
Claflin Estate, 84, 141-148.
Claflin, Ex-Gov. William, 133, 141.
Claflin Guard, 28, 58.
Claflin, Henry, 53.
Clark, Charles P., 278.
Clark, John, 250.

Clark, Rev. Edward W., 198.
Clark, Rev. F. E., 194.
Clark, Rev. Joseph B., 134.
Clark, Rev. Joseph S., D.D., 167, 168.
Clarke, Hon. Julius L., 168.
Clarke, Joseph T., 172.
Clarke, Rev. James Freeman, 122, 141, 146, 147, 187, 191, 278.
Clarke, Rev. W. N., 297.
Clarke, Rev. William R., D.D., 274.
Clement, Charles F., 242.
Clements, William, Jr., 45.
Clinton, De Witt, 180.
Cobb, Darius, 268.
Cobb Family, 74.
Cobb, Henry E., 80.
Coburn, Nathan P., 104, 106, 111.
Cochituate Aqueduct Tunnel, 130.
Coffin House, The, 54.
Coffin, Langdon, 78.
Colby, Gardner, 90, 92, 94, 294, 297, 298.
Cole's Block, 45, 67.
Collins, Edward Jackson, 237, 244.
Collins, Edward L., 240.
Collins Family, 243, 244.
Conant, D. A., 136.
Conant, Marshall, 167.
Congregational Churches, 25, 74, 75, 134, 157, 161, 169, 175, 196, 199, 268, 277, 282.
Converse, Edmund W., 82, 85.
Converse, Edmund W., Jr., 80.
Cook, George, 177, 182.
Cooke, Rev. Dr. Edward, 298.
Cooke, Robert, 250.
Coolidge, Charles, 126.
Coolidge, Joseph, 126.
Coolidge, Nathaniel, 56.
Coolidge, Rev. John Wesley, 229.
Coolidge Tavern, 56.
Copeland, Charles, 280.
Cordingley, W. S. and F., 220.
Cottage Hospital, The Newton, 208, 210.
Cotton, Dr. John, 16, 86, 98, 302.
Cotton, Rev. John, 84, 86, 88, 98, 290.
Cotton, Rev. Nathaniel, 86.
Crafts House, The, 320.
Cramer, Rev. M. J., 193.
Crane, Rev. Origen, 257.
Crane, William H., 194.
Crawley, Rev. Arthur R. R., 308.
Creasy, Professor, 164.
Crehore, Dr. C. F., 2, 220, 223.
Crehore Family, 224, 230.
Crocker, Rev. William, 308.
Cromack, Rev. J. C., 78.
Croswell, Rev. Andrew, 228.
Crystal Lake ("Baptist Pond"), 299-303.
Cunningham, Rev. L. T., 258.
Curry, Samuel S., 303.
Curtis, Alice, 172.
Curtis, Charles, 137, 141.
Curtis, Daniel Sargent, 314.
Curtis Family, 122, 128, 220, 222, 224.
Curtis, Obadiah, 122, 128, 130.
Cushing, Professor C. W., 196.
Cushing, Rev. C. W., 198.
Cutler, Nathan P., 227.
Cutler, Rev. Calvin, 198.
Cutler, Rev. Lyman, 74, 98.
Cutler, Frederic R., 185.
Cutshamekin, 15.
Dall, Rev. William, 183.
Dall, William H., 172, 183.

INDEX TO TEXT.

Dana, Henshaw, 168.
Dana, Rev. S. H., 268.
Danforth, Rev. James R., 134.
Davidson, Alexander, 238, 242.
Davis, Charles S., 278.
Davis, Goody, 321, 322.
Davis, Harriet, 168.
Davis, Hon. John, 78, 172.
Davis, John, 48, 173.
Davis, Joseph P., 172.
Davis, Seth, 165, 170, 173, 179–182.
Dearborn, Dr. A. D., 256.
De Costa, Rev. B. F., 228.
Dedham, Controversy with, 253.
Deer-Reeves, 151.
Degen, Rev. Henry V., 198.
De Gruchy, Rev. Thomas, 257.
Dennison, Rev. Charles W., 257.
Dennison, Rev. Joseph, 257.
Derby, Elias Hasket, 104.
"Devil's Den," 266.
Dewson, Francis A., 137.
Dickens, Charles, 271, 272.
Dickinson, Hon. John W., 140.
Dike, Rev. S. W., 194.
Division of Newton, 166, 167.
Dix, Jonathan, 165.
Dodge, Rev. Ebenezer, D.D., 309.
Dolan, Father Michael, 183, 258.
Dolby, George, 271, 272.
Dom Pedro II. entertained in Newton, 316.
Dorchester, Rev. Daniel, Jr., 136.
Downs, Lieutenant H. W., 136.
Dresser, William R., 239, 240, 242, 243.
Druce, Vincent, 320.
Drummond, Rev. Joseph Payson, 178.
Dummer, Richard, 45.
Dudley Hosiery Company, 220, 224.
Dupee Family, 280.
Durant Family, 108, 225, 282.
Eames, Charles, 41.
Earle, Rev. Dr. Absalom B., 54.
Earle, James H., 54.
Eastman, Rev. C. L., 136.
Eaton, Henry P., 222.
Eaton, Rev. Arthur Wentworth, 315.
Echo Bridge, 1, 234, 255, 262.
Edes, Benjamin, 56.
Edmands Estate, 84, 90, 97.
Edmands, A. Lawrence, 97.
Edmands, General J. Cushing, 135, 153.
Edmands, J. Wiley, 64, 90, 97.
Education, Expenditures on, 36.
Edwards, Rev. B. A., 183.
Eel-Weirs, 249.
Eldredge, Mrs. Elizabeth Trull, 70, 208.
ELIOT, 245–248.
Eliot Church, 25, 74, 75.
Eliot, John, the Apostle, 16, 39, 60, 96, 98, 110–122.
Eliot, President Charles W., 112.
Elliot, Gen. Simon, 250, 253.
Ellis, Charles, 246.
Ellis, Dr. Rufus, 187.
Ellis, George H., 2, 265.
Ellis, Rufus and David, 256, 266.
Ellison, Ex-Mayor William P., 72.
Elm, A Venerable, 166.
Elms, James C., 102, 105.
Emerson, Darius R., 57, 58.
Emerson, Ralph Waldo, 228, 261, 262, 267.
Emerson, William C., 136.
Emerson, William Ralph, 314.

Emery, William H., 122.
English, Rev. John M., 303.
Episcopal Churches, 67, 198, 217, 226, 270.
"Essex Colony, The," 311.
Esty, A. R., 70.
Evarts, Hon. William M., 124.
Fales, Rev. T. F., 68.
Farley, Alderman, 32.
Farlow, Hon. John S., 64, 66, 104, 109, 148, 151, 324.
Farlow Park, 65, 66, 70.
"Farm of the Governors," 142.
Farquhar, David W., 104, 107, 148.
Faxon, John Lyman, 297.
Fay, Rev. Eli, D.D., 71.
Fay, Rev. H. W., 198.
Female Academy, The Newton, 292.
Field, Dr. Henry M., 106, 121.
Field, George A., 180.
Field, Rev. Chester, 257.
Fields, James T., 271, 272.
Fire Department, 36.
Fireworks Company, The U. S., 256.
First Baptist Church, West Newton, 183.
First Congregational Church, Newton Centre, 277, 282, 287.
First Kindergarten in Massachusetts, 170.
First Normal School, 170.
First Permanent Settler, 17, 21, 100.
First Sermon to Indians, 112, 114.
First Settlers, Monument to, 21, 100.
First Unitarian Church, 164.
Fish-Culture in Crystal Lake, 299.
Fish-Reeves, 56.
Fisher, Theodore W., 195.
Fisheries, 56, 249.
Fiske, John, 78.
Fitch, Ezra C., 88, 93.
Fitz, Thomas B., 171.
Flagg, Sol, 166.
Flood, Father Bernard, 183, 258.
Fowle, Hon. W. B., 203.
Fowle, William B., Sen., 167.
Francis, Mrs. Julia F., 88.
Freeland, Rev. Samuel M., 74.
Freeman, Dr. James, 122, 124.
French, James W., 53.
Frisbie, Dr. J. F., 2, 76, 80.
Fuller Academy, 167, 170.
Fuller, Colonel Nathan, 182.
Fuller, Deacon Joel, 44, 182.
Fuller Family, 142, 144, 162, 188.
Fuller, John, 142, 162.
Fuller, Judge Abraham, 98, 144.
Furber, Rev. Dr. D. L., 44, 286, 292.
Gamewell Fire-Alarm Telegraph Co., 270.
"Garden City, The," 232.
Gardner, Elizabeth M., 194.
Gardner, Hon. William S., 102.
Garfield, Lieutenant Walter H., 230.
Garrison-House, Waban Hill, 317.
Gay, Charles M., 106, 117.
Gay, Edwin W., 102.
Gay, Levi B., 106.
Gibbs, Henry, 290.
Gilbert, Rev. Lyman, D.D., 167, 178.
Gilbert, Rev. Washington, 173.
Gill, Rev. J., 229.
Gilman, Gorham D., 66.
Gilman, Rev. N. P., 188.
Glover, General John, 165.
Goddard, Mrs. Mary T., 126.
Goddard, Rev. Joseph, 308.

INDEX TO TEXT.

Goddard, Rev. Josiah R., 308.
Gould, Rev. J. B., 78, 229.
Gould, William H., 241, 244.
Grace Church, 65, 67-70.
Grafton, Rev. Joseph, 98, 132, 288-290, 296-298.
"Grandmother Rose," The, 60.
Graves, Major F. D., 136.
Graves, Rev. Joseph M., 183.
Gray, Morris, 315.
Greene, Rev. J. S. C., 68.
Greenough Family, 175-178, 182.
Greenough, Mrs., Anecdote of, 176.
Greenwood, Thomas, 320.
Guiney, Louise Imogen, 203, 208.
Gunsaulus, Rev. F. W., 134.
Hackett Estate, The, 306.
Hackett, Rev. H. B., 304, 306.
Hagar House, The, 224.
Hagar, Professor D. B., 179, 230.
Hague, Rev. John B., 292.
Hague, Rev. William, D.D., 308.
Haley, John J., 104.
Hall, Charles W., 53.
Hall Family, 270.
Hall, George W., 73.
Hall, Rev. C. M., 229.
Hamblen, Ephraim S., 53.
Hammond Family, 92, 316.
Hammond, Thomas, 320.
Hammond's Pond and Woods, 309, 318-320.
Harbach Family, 126, 128, 130, 147.
Harding, Rev. Sewall, 198, 200.
Hardon, Henry C., 53.
Hardy, Edward E., 203.
Harlow, Louis K., 242.
Harrington, Abel, 48.
Harwood, George S., 64, 66, 122, 127.
Harwood, Seth K., 47; 53.
Haskell, Edwin B., 2, 200, 205, 208, 299, 242.
Haskell, William E., 172.
Hatch, George E., 122.
Haven, Rev. William Ingraham, 274.
Hawthorne, Julian, 184.
Hawthorne, Major Nathaniel, of Salem, 20.
Hawthorne, Nathaniel, 168, 184, 186.
Hayden, Henry C., 148.
Hayes, Ex-President R. B., 141.
Haynes, Gideon, 179.
Haynes, Gov. John, 300.
Hayward, Albert F., 269, 270.
Healthfulness of Newton, 32.
Heath, Daniel C., 137, 139.
Henshaw, Frederic H., 235, 242.
Hepworth, Rev. George H., 326.
Herrick, Rev. A. F., 257.
"Hickory Cliff," 246, 247.
High School, Newton, 140, 145.
Hills, Joel H., 64.
Hills, The Seven, 30.
History of Newton, A Singular, 182.
Hitchcock, Dr. (Harvard Dental School), 152.
Hoar, Hon. George F., 124.
Hobart, Rev. Nehemiah, 84, 94, 98.
Hobbs, Prentiss, 48.
Hodge, Rev. Elias, 136.
Hodges, Rev. C. E., 173.
Holbrook Hall, 325.
Holland, Rev. T. B., 183.
Hollis, Alderman J. Edward, 58.
Holman, Edwin S., 42.
Holmes, Oliver Wendell, 60, 215, 228, 272, 276-278.
Holmes, Rev. Theodore J., 286.

Holway, Rev. Raymond F., 136.
Homer, Rev. Dr. Jonathan, 60, 98, 146, 284-286, 288, 292-294.
Homes for Missionaries' Children, 200, 280.
"Horn-Breaker," A, 250.
Hornbrooke, Rev. Francis B., 72, 73.
Hosford, Professor E. N., 215.
Hosmer, Elbridge, 292.
Hosmer, Harriet G., 53, 54.
Hosmer, Rev. George W., D D., 71, 72.
Hotels: Hunnewell, 47, 53; Woodland Park, 205, 206, 207.
Houdlette, Fred A., 49, 50.
Houghton, Benjamin F., 165, 166, 179.
Houghton Family, 182.
Hovey, Rev. Dr. Alvah, 303-306.
Howard, Rev. E. A., 229.
Howe, Rev. E. Frank, 134, 152.
Howells, William Dean, 207, 249.
Howland, Otis Norcross, 122.
Hull, General William, 45, 98, 104, 131, 132, 136, 144-146.
Hunnewell, Jonathan, 52.
"Hunnewell Hotel," 47, 53.
Hunt, J. W., 302.
Hunter, Rev. Pleasant, Jr., 134.
Hunter, Stephen V. A., 303, 305.
Huntington, Bishop F. D., 151.
Huntington, Rev. W. E., 44, 78, 292.
Hutchins, Rev. Ben T., 228.
Hyde, Deacon Samuel, 17, 82.
Hyde Family, 17, 82, 92, 100, 146, 268, 270, 273.
Hyde, George, 45.
Hyde, Hon. J. F. C., 28, 44, 270.
Hyde, Jonathan, 273, 282, 288.
Hyde, Lieutenant Hosea, 136.
Hyde, Samuel the younger, 302.
Ihrie, General George P., 32.
Illuminating Gas first used, 159.
Illumination on Charles River, 213, 214.
Independence, Resolution of, 24; Centennial Celebration of, 44.
Indian Cemetery, An Ancient, 58.
Institution Hill, 303-310.
Inter-municipal War, An, 167.
Iron-Works Company, The Newton, 266.
Jackson, Deacon John, 17, 50, 67.
Jackson, Edward, 28, 84.
Jackson Family, The, 50-52, 60-62, 67, 74, 92, 96, 98, 285.
Jackson, Francis, historian of Newton, 62, 98.
Jackson, Hon. William, 42, 45, 59.
Jackson, Rev. S., 78.
Jackson, Samuel, 40.
James, Miss Hannah P., 66.
James, Rev. R. S., D.D., 183.
Jaynes, Rev. J. C., 173.
Jenckes, Rev. Joseph S., D.D., 68.
Jenison Family, 182.
Jenks, Joseph William, 132.
Jersey Stock Club, 326.
Jewett, David B., 66.
Jewett, Rev. Lyman, D.D., 308.
Johnson, Charles E., 122, 129.
Johnson Estate, The, 206.
Johnson, Rev. Charles T., 257.
Johnson, Rev. John W., 308.
Johnsonville, 309.
Jones, George H., 64-66.
Jones, Rev. E. H., 257.
Jones, Rev. John Taylor, D.D., 306.
Jones, Rev. S. F., 78.
Kapiolani, Queen, entertained in Newton, 66.

INDEX TO TEXT.

Kelley, Rev. Edmund, 183.
Kenrick Family, 92, 100, 106-110, 285.
Kenrick, John, Epitaph of, 98.
Kenrick, William, 104.
Kenrick's Bridge, 326.
Kidder, Rev. Joseph, 228.
Kimball, Hon. J. Wesley, 138.
Kimball, Rev. O. D., 183.
King, Dr. John, 98, 302.
King, Henry F., 186.
King, Hon. Horatio, 186.
King, Moses, 102, 104, 106.
King, Rev. John D., 136.
Kingsbury, Colonel Isaac F., 28, 58, 315, 316.
Kingsbury House, The Old, 315, 316.
Kinmonth, David, 236.
Knapp, Francis, 56.
Knapp, Rev. W. H., 173.
Knowles, Rev. J. D., 304, 306.
Knox, General Henry, 56, 62.
Lafayette in Newton, 180.
Lake, A Former, 248.
Lamb, Rev. William A., 158.
Lancaster, Charles B., 110.
Lancey, Dustin, 138.
Lane, Rev. Dr. S. Eliot, 194.
Langford, John T., 59.
Lasell, Edward and Josiah, 195, 196.
Lasell Seminary, 29, 189, 195, 196, 197, 215.
Lawrence, Amos, Farm, 318.
Leach, Miss (teacher Female Academy), 292.
Leavitt, Rev. William S., 74.
Lee, Francis L., 313, 314.
Lee, George C., 315.
Lee, Henry, 314.
Lee, Joseph, 205, 206, 207.
Lee, Thomas, 314.
Leeson, Joseph R., 208.
Leighton, Rev. Samuel S., 257.
Leland, Luther E., 222.
Lemon, Henry, 48.
"Lenticular Hill," A, 80, 82.
Leonard, Rev. J. M., 78.
Lester, Rev. C. S., 198.
Lewis, Edwin J., Jr., 194.
Lewis, Rev. Joseph W., 257.
Library, Newton Free, 35, 62, 64-66, 69, 76, 104.
Lincoln, John L., LL.D., 308.
Lincoln, Rev. Heman, D.D., 308.
Linder Estate, 296.
Linwood Park, 136.
Lisle, Rev. William M., 175, 183.
"Listener, The," Boston *Transcript*, 211, 212.
Little, Rev. George Barker, 178.
Lockwood, Rev. William L., 136.
Lord, Hon. George C., 104.
Lord's Prayer in Indian Tongue, 118.
Loring Estate, 296.
Loring, Joshua, 297, 298.
Lothrop, Rev. Dr. John, 175.
Lovell, Wallace D., 106, 125.
Lowell, Judge John, 318.
Lowry, Rev. Samuel E., 157.
Lucas, Rodney M., 136.
Luquiens, Professor Julius, 194.
Lyon, Dr. Henry, 230.
Machine Company, The Newton, 58.
Mackay, Rev. Henry, 44, 228.
Macreading, Rev. Charles S., 257.
Maginnis, Rev. John S., D.D., 308.
Magnesium Company, The American, 58.
Magoon, Rev. Elias L., D.D., 308.
Manly, Rev. Basil, D.D., 308.

Mann, Daniel P., 42.
Mann, Horace, 160, 170, 184.
Manning, Rev. E. A., 54.
Mansfield, Rev. G. W., 136.
Manufacturers' Hotel, 265, 266.
Manufacturers, 158, 160, 217, 250-256, 266, 270.
Maps, 23, 31.
March, Andrew S., 106.
Marshall, General J. F. B., 193.
Martin, Mike, Highwayman, 165.
Mason, Hon. David Haven, 275, 278.
Mason, Rev. Francis, D.D., 306.
Mason Schoolhouse, 285.
Massachusetts Baptist Education Society, 304.
Maugus, John, 249.
Mayer, Rev. Henry Christian, 68.
Mayhew Family, 52, 60, 84, 88, 142.
McCarthy, Father John, 258.
McCullough, Rev. J. P., 76.
McDonald, Rev. William, 198.
McGee, Chauncey B., 242, 243.
McKeown, Rev. Andrew, 198, 229.
McManus, Rev. M. T., 183.
Meacham, George F., 71, 74.
Means, Rev. Dr. James, 198.
Merriam, Rev. Jonas, 98, 283, 284, 293.
Merrill, Fannie Buss, 194.
Merrill, Rev. Joseph A., 257.
Messiah, Church of the, 198.
Metcalf, Rev. Henry A., 198.
"Meteor," The, Locomotive, 24, 42.
Methodist Churches, 78, 99, 136, 149, 229, 256, 274, 283.
Mills, Miss Frances Maria, 48.
Mills, Rev. Carlton P., 270.
Mineral Region, A, 309.
Mitchell, Austin R., 137, 148.
Mitchell's Tavern, 268, 302.
Monument to Soldiers, 27; to First Settlers, 21, 100.
Moorfield, Captain, 252.
Moraine, A Glacial, 207.
Morey, Rev. James W., 257.
Morse, George W., 148.
Morton, Rev. James F., 303.
Morton, William, 278.
Mother Brook, 253, 261.
Mount Ida, 30, 74, 78-82.
Mudge, Rev. James, 257.
Mudge, Rev. Z. A., 136, 257.
Municipal Statistics, 38.
Musical Association, The Newton, 43.
Muzzey, Rev. A. B., 315.
"My Country, 'tis of Thee," 276, 278.
Myrtle Baptist Church, 183.
Nahaton, 249.
Nanepashemet, 15.
Nash, Rev. C. Ellwood, 138.
Nash, Rev. Henry S., 315.
Naples the Newton of the Mediterranean, 326.
Nason, Dr. Elias, 32.
Natural-History Club, The Newton, 76.
New-Church Society, 137.
Newell, Josiah B., 256.
Newhall, Rev. W. Rice, 198.
"New Lights," The, 309.
Newspapers, 39.
NEWTON, 39-100.
NEWTON CENTRE, 271-310.
Newton Centre Associates, 279.
Newton Club-House, 131, 136, 137, 144.
"Newton Corner," 39.
Newton Female Academy, 292.

INDEX TO TEXT.

NEWTON HIGHLANDS, 267-270.
Newton, History of the Name, 20, 28, 40.
Newton in 1800, 320.
NEWTON LOWER FALLS, 217-230.
Newton Machine Company, 58.
NEWTON OF THE PAST, 15-28.
NEWTON OF THE PRESENT, 29, 38.
Newton Theological Institution, 281, 303-310.
NEWTON UPPER FALLS, 249-266.
NEWTONVILLE, 131-156.
Newton, William B., 41.
Nichols, J. Howard, 88, 89.
Nichols, Rev. Fayette, 78.
Nickerson, Thomas, 294.
Nickerson's Block, 166.
NONANTUM, 157-160.
Nonantum Congregational Church, 157.
Nonantum Dale Nursery, 110.
NONANTUM HILL, 101-130.
Nonantum Hill, 30, 53.
Nonantum House, 41, 45, 48.
Nonantum, Signification of the Name, 112.
Nonantum Worsted Company, 160.
Normal School for Girls, The First, 170.
Normal School removed from Lexington, 167, 170.
North Evangelical Church, 157, 158.
"Norumbega," Remains of, 215.
Nottage, Rev. W. A., 229.
OAK HILL, 321.
Oak Hill School, 325.
Oak Hill, View from, 324.
Oaks at Eliot, Two Venerable, 248.
O'Brien, Father Martin, 258.
Old Trees, Two Famous, 326.
Olmsted, Frederick Law, 311.
Ordway, J. L., 156, 175.
Orphan and Destitute Girls, Home for, 292.
Orrery, The First, in Massachusetts, 180.
Osgood, James R., 271, 272.
Otheman, Rev. B., 198.
Otheman, Rev. Edward, 257.
O'Toole, Rev. Laurence J., 183.
Our Lady Help of Christians, Church of, 60, 131, 134.
Page, Charles J., 235, 242.
Paine, Robert Treat, Jr., 187.
Paper Mills, Lower Falls, 218-222.
Park Family, 150, 162.
Park, Frank G., 58.
Park, Hon. John C., 80, 175.
Park, Richard, 76.
Park, W. H., 136.
Parker, Colonel Francis J., 48, 260.
Parker, John, 250.
Parker, John C., 302.
Parker, Joseph W., 287, 303.
Parker, Nathaniel, 250.
Parker, Noah, 250, 296.
Parker, Rev. John, 257.
Parker, Theodore, 86, 88, 168, 170.
Parker, William, 167.
Parkhurst, Rev. Charles, 198.
Parsons, William, 48.
Partelow's Boat-Houses, 212, 216.
Patrick, Rev. Henry Johnson, 178.
Paul, Deacon Luther, 302.
Paul, Henry, 297.
Paulson, Rev. John, 257.
Peabody, Miss Elizabeth P., 168.
Peck, John, 304.
Peirce, Mrs. Charles W., 78.
Peirce, Rev. Bradford K., 44, 66, 78, 274, 298.
Peirce, William, 246, 247.

Pelham, Charles, 86, 88.
Pemberton Estate, The, 206.
Pentecost, Rev. William, 229, 257.
Pepper, Rev. George D. B., D.D., 308.
Perkins, Rev. George H., 274.
Perry Family, 54, 67.
Perry, Bishop W. S., 54, 67, 68.
Petersilea, Carlyle, 102, 103.
Peterson, Rev. John, 257.
Pettee Manufacturing Company, 254.
Pettee, Otis, 2, 250, 253, 254, 272.
Phipps & Train, Messrs., 252.
Phipps, Rev. George G., 268.
Pickard Estate, The, 206.
Pickthall, Thomas, 136.
Pierce, Rev. Cyrus, 167.
Pigeon, Dr. J. C. D., 191, 192.
Pigeon Family, 191, 194, 273.
Pigeon, Rev. C. D., 198.
Pine-Farm School, 187, 188, 206, 279.
Plimpton, Joseph W., 167.
Police Department, 36.
Pomeroy, Rebecca R., 58, 292.
Pomfret, Rev. William J., 257.
Pope, Alexander, "Let Newton be," 326.
Pope, Colonel Albert A., 51, 53.
Pope, E. W., 53.
Population, Increase of, 30.
Post-Offices, List of, 34.
Potter, John C., 55, 59.
"Pound Lane," 298.
Powers, Samuel L., 102, 105.
Pratt, Charles S., 194.
Prentice, Captain Thomas, 128, 290, 322.
Prentice Family, 92, 94, 290.
Prentice, Rev. George, 136.
Prescott, Mrs. Charles B., 91.
Priest Estate, The, 206, 208.
Prisoners, British, March of, through Newton, 164, 165.
Prophecy, A Remarkable, 74.
Prospect Hill, View from, 317.
Pulsifer, Colonel Royal M., 28, 148, 200, 202, 205, 260, 315.
Pumping Station, 239.
Putnam, Rev. Richard F., 228.
Questions, Difficult, asked by Indians, 114, 116, 118.
Quincy, Hon. Josiah, 170.
Railway Stations, List of, 34.
Rand, Avery L., 275, 290.
Rand, George C., 290.
Randall Family, The, 246.
Ranlett, Captain Charles E., 203.
Ranlett, Miss S. Alice, 72.
Rawson, Madame Susanna, 46.
Rawson, Mrs. Susan C., 72.
Raymond Estate, 187.
Read, Charles A., 66.
Rebecca-Pomeroy Home for Orphan Girls, 58, 292.
Records, Old, 17-20.
Redpath, Ellis W., 137.
Resolutions, Theodore Parker's, 86.
Rice, Hon. Alexander H., 2, 44, 179, 180, 193, 228-230.
Rice, J. Willard, 179, 193.
Rice, Marshall O., 301.
Rice, Marshall S., 45, 256, 257, 274, 290, 292.
Rice, Professor John, 172.
Rice, Thomas, Jr., 220, 222, 224, 227, 229.
Richards Family, 270.
Richards, Rev. William C., 257.
Richardson Family, 270.

INDEX TO TEXT. 13

Richardson, Henry H., 76, 189, 231, 311.
Richardson, John, 48.
Richardson, Rev. W. S., 229.
Richardson, Squire Solon, 41.
Ricker Family, 102.
Riley, Charles E., 80, 81.
Ripley, Rev. Henry J., 304, 306.
RIVERSIDE, 211-216.
Riverside School (Mrs. D. T. Smith), 194.
Road-Makers, The Colonial, 217.
Roberts, C. S., 208.
Roberts, Mrs. John L., 136.
Robbins, Rev. Gilbert, 76.
Roberts, Rev. Kendall, D.D., 309.
Robins, Henry C., 308.
Robinson, Charles, Jr., 186.
Robinson, Luke, 56.
Robinson, Rev. Ezekiel G., D.D., 309.
Robinson, William, 190.
Robson, Stuart, 194.
Roche, James Jeffrey, 134, 135.
"Rocket," The, Locomotive, 42.
Rogers, John, 283.
Rogers, Rev. C. S., 78.
Rolfe, Dr. William J., 196.
Rolling Dam, The, 159.
Roman Catholic Churches, 60, 131, 134, 183, 258.
Roman Catholic Services, The First, 258.
Root, Dr. George F., 59, 60.
Round, Rev. J. Emery, 198.
Safford, Rev. Henry G., 257.
"Saints' Rest," 191.
Saltonstall Family, 280, 312, 314.
Samson, Rev. George W., D.D., 309.
Samson, Rev. Thomas S., 76, 175.
Sanborn, Rev. Jacob, 257.
Sargent, Frederick W., 122.
Savage, Captain Charles T., 167.
Savary, Rev. W. H., 173.
Sawtell, James A., 53.
Sawyer, J. Herbert, 316.
Sawyer, Rev. Artemas W., D.D., 308.
Schoff, Stephen A., 137.
School System, Honors awarded to, 141.
Schools, Private, 72, 136, 167-172, 193, 194, 292.
Scudder, Mrs. Marshall, 236.
Seal of the City, 38.
Sears, Rev. Barnas, D.D., LL.D., 304, 306, 308.
Sears, William B., 58.
Seaver, Hon. Edwin P., 234, 242.
Secession War, Newton in the, 153-156.
Second Baptist Church, 251.
Seger House, The, 54.
Seger, Nathaniel, 130.
Sever, Rev. Winslow W., 228.
Shannon Estate, The, 82, 84, 87, 88.
Shannon, Miss Mary Clarke, 82, 84, 87.
Shaw, Fayette, 140.
Shaw, Louis Agassiz, 313, 314.
Sheldon, Miss Marian, 184.
Sheldon, Rev. David N., D.D., 308.
Sheldon, William E., 2, 173, 184.
Shepard, Alexander, Jr., 190.
Shepard, Major Samuel, 162.
Sheppard, Samuel A. D., 102.
Sherman, Roger, 124.
Shillaber, B. P., 140.
Shinn, Rev. George Wolfe, D.D., 68, 208.
"Short Hills," 206.
Siedhof, Dr. Carl, 302.
Silk-Manufacturing, 252.
Skinner, Francis, 98, 122.
Skinner, Rev. Samuel P., 258.
Slack, Robert H., 228.

Slade, Dr. Daniel D., 316.
"Slate-Rock Woods," 319.
Sleeper, Hon. Jacob, 78.
Smallwood, Edwin, 50.
Smith, Miss Delia T., 193.
Smith, Rev. D. A. W., D.D., 308.
Smith, Rev. Eli B., D.D., 308.
Smith, Rev. Francis W., 198.
Smith, Rev. John, 136.
Smith, Rev. Joseph C., 71, 152.
Smith, Rev. Samuel Francis, D.D., 44, 132, 151, 152, 182, 257, 276-278, 297.
Soap-Manufacturing Company, The Warren, 58.
Social Library, The West-Parish, 178.
Societies, 44, 135, 168, 258, 275.
Soldiers' Monument, 27, 152.
Spaulding, Rev. Nathan B., 257.
Spaulding, Rev. Newell S., 257.
Speare, Hon. Alden, 44, 78, 90, 175, 274, 294.
Spring Family, 92, 132.
Springer, Elestus M., 106, 115.
Springer, Marcellus P., 102.
"Squash End," 167, 175.
St. Andrew's Church, Chestnut Hill, 315.
Starr, Dr. Ebenezer, 224, 230.
Starr, Horace, 224.
Statistics, 30-38.
St. Bernard's Church, West Newton, 183.
Stealing a River, 253.
Stearns Family, 268.
Stearns, Rev. Dr. Oakman S., 297, 303.
Stebbins, Rev. Dr. Rufus P., 298.
Steele, Rev. Daniel, 198.
Steenstra, Rev. Peter Henry, D.D., 68.
Stevens, Rev. Edward A., D.D., 308.
Stevens, Rev. Edward O., 308.
Stimson Mansion, 206.
St. Mary's Church, 217, 219, 226.
Stock Farm, Oak-Hill, 325.
Stocks, The, 284.
Stone, Dr. L. R., 66.
Stone Family, 324.
Stowe, Harriet Beecher, 141, 187, 188.
St. Paul's (Episcopal) Church, Newton Highlands, 270.
Strain, Father, 258.
Streets, List of, 30.
Strong, George, 72.
Strong, William C., 236-240.
Studley, Rev. W. S., 78.
Swedenborgian Church, 135, 137.
"Sweet Auburn," 147.
Sweet, Charles A., 193.
Sweetser, Isaac, 180.
Swimming-School, 172.
Sylvester, Austin T., 136.
Talbot, Rev. Samson, D.D., 308.
Tarbox, Rev. Dr. Increase N., 44, 184, 284.
Tax-Rate of Newton, 34.
Taylor, Bertrand E., 184, 280, 289, 305.
Tenney, Jonathan, 302.
Thaxter, Celia, 159.
Thayer, Rev. L. R., 136.
Theological Institution, Newton, 281.
Thomas, Rev. Benjamin C., 308.
Thomas, Rev. Jesse B., 303.
Thompson, the Hermit, 309.
Thompsonville, 309.
Thurber, Rev. Franklin, 256.
Thurston, Miss E. P., 66.
Thwing, Daddy, 270.
Tiffany, Hon. Francis, 172.
Tiffany, Rev. Francis, 173, 183.
Time-Table, B. & W. R. R., of 1834, 43.

"Tin Horn," 159.
Titus, Rev. H. F., 76.
Tomatoes, The first, in Massachusetts, 124.
Toulmin, Rev. William B., 257.
Tourjée, Dr. Eben, 194, 198.
Towne, W. J., 136, 279.
Trees, Some Noteworthy, 166, 180, 248, 326.
Trowbridge, Colonel William, 134.
Trowbridge Family, 74, 147, 148, 150.
Trowbridge, J. Eliot, 80.
Trowbridge, Professor John, 172.
True, Rev. Charles K., 257.
Tucker, Nathaniel, 88.
Tucker, Rev. J., Jr., 76.
Tuckerman Estate, 326.
Tuckerman, W. S., 48.
Turner, Job, 80.
Tyler, Warren P., 106.
"Underground Railroad," Former Station of, 183.
Underwood, General Adin B., 64, 66, 72, 135, 153, 154.
Underwood School, 66, 71.
Unitarian Churches, 70, 172, 298.
Universalist Churches, 138, 143, 258.
Upham, Rev. James, D.D., 309.
Urbino, S. R., 140.
U. S. Fireworks Company, 256.
Village-Improvement Associations, 168, 192, 275.
Villages in Newton, List of, 32.
Vista Hill, 16 Towns visible from, 209.
Vital Statistics, 38.
WABAN, 231, 244.
Waban Hill, View from, 313, 317.
Waban (Indian chief), 110-116.
Wade, Hon. Levi C., 297, 323, 324.
Wadsworth, Alexander, 104.
Wales Bridge, 225.
Walker, Mrs. Eliza H., 200.
Walker, Mrs. Nellie V., 53.
Walking-Match, A Notable, 271, 272.
Wallis, Mrs. William, 225.
Walton, George A., 184.
Walworth, Arthur C., 294, 295.
Ward, Charles, 274.
Ward, Colonel Joseph, 62, 124, 126.
Ward, Deacon Joseph, 182.
Ward Family, 94, 98, 124, 126, 147, 150, 282, 285.
Ware Family, 192, 224, 226.
Warren, General Joseph, 56.
Warren, H. Langford, 232, 242, 243.
Warren Soap Manufacturing Company, 58.
Washburn Family, 192.
Washington, George, 56, 225, 285.
Watch Company, The American, 182.
Waterhouse, Francis A., 137.
Water-Works, The Newton, 260; Sudbury-River, 262-264, 318.
Waters, Edwin F., 278.
Watson, Rev. E. R., 198.
Wear Lands, The, 54.
Webster, Daniel, Anecdote of, 176.
Webster, Rev. Amos, 257.
Webster, Rev. M. P., 257.
Webster, William E., 303-307.
Weir, Mrs., 136.
Wellman, Rev. Joshua, 74.
Wells, Artesian, 260.
Wells, Henry B., 53.
Wells, Professor Webster, 172.
Wells, Rev. William G., 228.
Wentworth, William P., 53, 70, 208.
Wesleyan Home, 5, 78.
West Church, 175.
West, Dr. George W., 312, 313.

WEST NEWTON, 161-188.
West-Newton Hotel, 173.
Weston, Rev. Henry G., D.D., 309.
Weston, Thomas, 106.
West-Parish Social Library, 178.
Wetherbee, W. A., 136.
Wetherell Estate, 265.
Wetherell, Horace R., 42.
Wheat, Dr. Samuel, 162, 164.
Wheedon, J. S., 136.
Wheeler, Rev. Horace Leslie, 298.
Wheeler, Rev. Melancthon, 198.
Whipple, Dexter, 42.
Whipple, E. P., 186.
Whiston, Dr. Edward A., 137.
White, Joseph, 302.
White, Ralph H., 314.
White, Rev. Rufus A., 138.
White, Rev. W. O., 172.
"White Swan," The, 214.
White, T. Edgar, 106, 123.
Whitefield, Rev. George, at Newton, 282, 283.
Whitman, Rev. B. L., 257.
Whitman, Rev. Freeman T., 257.
Whitmore, Charles E., 53.
Whitney, Anne, Birthplace of, 54.
Whitney, Dr. Allston W., 172.
Whitney, Dr. Samuel S., 256.
Whittemore, Samuel P., 53.
Whittier, John G., 141.
Whitwell, Elizabeth, 168.
Whitwell, Madam, 168.
Whitwell, Rev. William A., 315.
Whitwell, William S., 167.
Wiggin, E. D., 325.
Wilbur, George B., 181, 182.
Wilder, Marshall P., 104.
Willard, Jonathan, 296.
Willard, Rev. F. A., 297.
Williams College, 162.
Williams Family, 150, 162.
Williston's (Miss) Home, 195.
Wilmarth, Rev. Isaac M., 308.
Wilson, Edward B., 184.
Winchester Family, 270.
Winchester Hill, 325.
Winchester, Rev. Elhanan, 296.
Winslow, Ezra D., 200, 202, 208.
Winslow, John, 258.
Winsor, Ernest, 314.
Winthrop, Mrs., Description of British Prisoners, 165.
Wiswall, C. A. & H. M., 222.
Wiswall, Captain Jeremiah, 322.
Wiswall, Elder, 94.
Wiswall Family, 222, 236, 270, 273, 285, 296, 300, 302.
Wiswall's Pond, 299.
Wood, Deacon Bartholomew, 292.
Wood, Rev. Fred, 78.
Woodbridge, Rev. J. E., 198.
WOODLAND, 205-210.
Woodland Park Hotel, 205, 206, 207, 208.
Woods, Rev. Frederick, 136.
Woods, Rev. Henry W., 228.
Woodward, Deacon Ebenezer, 74, 270, 292.
Woodward Family, 74, 100, 231, 268, 270, 286.
Worcester, Rev. John, 137.
Worsted Company, The Nonantum, 160.
Wright, Rev. A. A., 78.
Yahveh, Church of, 258.
Young Estate, The, 206.
Young, Rev. Edward J., D.D., 71.
Zachos, Rev. John C., 173.

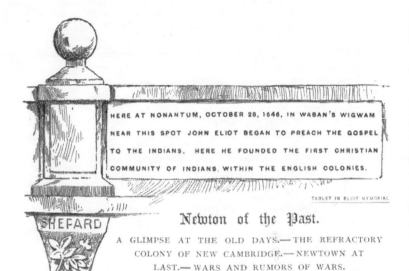

HERE AT NONANTUM, OCTOBER 28, 1646, IN WABAN'S WIGWAM NEAR THIS SPOT JOHN ELIOT BEGAN TO PREACH THE GOSPEL TO THE INDIANS. HERE HE FOUNDED THE FIRST CHRISTIAN COMMUNITY OF INDIANS, WITHIN THE ENGLISH COLONIES.

TABLET IN ELIOT MEMORIAL

Newton of the Past.

A GLIMPSE AT THE OLD DAYS.— THE REFRACTORY COLONY OF NEW CAMBRIDGE.— NEWTOWN AT LAST.— WARS AND RUMORS OF WARS. THE RISE OF THE CITY.

The first records of the Anglo-Saxon occupation of this region are closely connected with those of Cambridge, or Newtown, which was settled and fortified in 1631, less than a year after the foundation of Boston. The territory was duly bought from the Indians, in pursuance of the original instructions from England: "If any of the salvages pretend right of inheritance to all or any part of the lands granted in our pattent, wee pray you endeavour to purchase their tytle, that wee may avoyde the least scruple of intrusion." So the domain northward of the Charles was acquired from the Indian queen, the squaw-sachem, Nanepashemet's daughter, one of her perquisites being a new coat each winter as long as she lived. Allured by this promise of fair new gowns, she voluntarily put herself under the government and jurisdiction of the Massachusetts Colony in 1643, together with four other conspicuous Indian rulers. One of these was the famous Cutshamekin, John Eliot's friend, who lived at Neponset, and held some vague authority over the natives of Nonantum, the region of the present Newton.

The scattered condition of the Massachusetts Colony, straggling along the shore for several leagues, naturally caused the settlers to feel insecure; and the governor and assistants explored the country to find the best site for a fortified city, to serve as a rallying-point and refuge in case of overwhelming peril. They decided to build the *New-town* on the present site of Harvard College; and there was a general idea abroad that it would be the capital of the Colony, erected and fortified at the public cost. In fact, Massachusetts paid for the defences of the settlement, which consisted of a palisade and fosse a mile and a half long, surrounding the neat little rural hamlet of the Stuart era.

In 1632 the colonial authorities sent to settle at Newtown (Cambridge) the Rev. Mr. Hooker and forty-seven other men from English Essex; and when these pioneers desired to go away into the Connecticut Valley, because they had not land enough, the Government ceded to Cambridge, in 1635, the greater part of the present Brookline, Brighton, and Newton,

Facsimile of John Cotton's Receipt.

and the wilderness extending to the Merrimack River. But the Essex adventurers were not content, withal, and soon set up their valiant march for the Connecticut Valley,— Hooker and a hundred colonists and 160 cattle,— and after a fortnight of arduous pilgrimage reached and founded Hartford. They had grown weary and disappointed at finding that their settlement did not become the metropolis of the Colony; that the enemies of Massachusetts were not formidable enough to make their palisados a public benefit; and that their canal leading in from the shallow Charles could not help them in commercial competition with the sea-fronting bay of Boston. Their domains here were sold to the Rev. Mr. Shepard and his flock; and in 1638 the name of the place was changed from Newtown to Cambridge, in memory of the fair English city in whose ancient university so many of the founders of New England had been educated.

The savage wilderness across the river was at first vaguely called "The South Side of Charles River," by the Cambridge people; although it also bore the name of Nonantum, by which its apostle, the consecrated Eliot, had designated it. Pity it had not been retained to the present day, since the place is neither new nor a town. And Nonantum signifies REJOICING, which is the frame of mind of thousands of its contented inhabitants.

Of the twenty pioneers of this southside wilderness, four came from London, four from elsewhere in England, and the remainder from the Massachusetts towns. They were nearly all well-to-do persons, in the prime of life; and the exertions of opening a new country were so favorable to longevity that more than two-thirds of them lived to beyond the age of seventy. In the roll of the first-comers occur the names of Jackson, Hyde, Fuller, Wiswall, Park, Ward, Prentice, and Trowbridge, most of which still remain, filling out columns in the Newton City Directory. In 1645 there were 135 ratable persons in Newtown, with 90 houses, 551 head of cattle, 40 horses, 37 sheep, 62 swine, and 58 goats, the valuation of the settlement being £8,801.

The people came in family groups, at different times, and without the organized nomadism that characterized many other colonial establishments. There seems to have been a preliminary scattering inroad of now-forgotten settlers, who presently moved on farther into the country, leaving their half-begun farms to the chance of the next-comers. The first permanent settler was Deacon John Jackson, in 1639, on Brighton Hill; and he was followed, four years later, by his brother, Edward, the Whitechapel Vulcan. Deacon Samuel Hyde entered in 1640; John Fuller, in 1644; Jonathan Hyde and Richard Park, in 1647; Captain Thomas Prentice, in 1649; and in 1650 John Ward, James Prentice, Thomas Prentice, Jr., Vincent Druce, Thomas Hammond, and John Parker.

A School-house in Newton in 1800.

Among the quaint old town records we find such entries as these: —

"1649. It is ordained by the townsmen that all persons provide that their dogs may do no harm in cornfields and gardens, by scraping up the fish, under the penalty of three pence for every dog that shall be taken damage feasant, with all other just damages."

"1634. It was ordered that no person shall take tobacco publiquely, under the penalty of eleven shillings, nor privately, in his own house or in the house of another, before strangers, and that two or more shall not take it anywhere, under the aforesaid penalty for each offence."

"It was ordered that no person shall be allowed to sell cakes and bunns, except at funerals and weddings."

Voted march: y: 4: 1706 that a Commity take Care to provid a Schoolmaster for the town this year..

The persons that were Chosen were: Cap: Isaac Williames: Leiu: mason: Abraham Jackson

Voted march: y: 4: 1706: that a town Rate of 40 — 0 be made and Levied upon the town and paid into the town tresurey by mid Sumer: that is by the last of June.

Voted that a Small booke be bought for the Select mens use

Voted march: 3: 1707: that the Select men Shall be the Asesores to: ases the Contrey Reates

Voted march: 3: 1707. John mason Ebenezer Stone, Ephraim Wheeler be a Committey to provid a Schoolmaster for th: yere insuring

Voted march: 3 1707: that a town Rate be Levied upon the town of fifty pounds mony and that it be paid by the last of September

Voted march 3: 1707: that those that shall kill black birds from y: 1: of april til the Last of may and bring their heads to the Conts: or Select men Shall be allowed twelve pence for dosen out of the town rate

FACSIMILE OF TOWN RECORDS.

At a town meeting march: ye 4 1706 for the Choice of oficers

Surveighers of highway	town Clerk and tresar	Constables	Select men
Nath¹ Hamand			John Spring
thomas miller		thomas prown	Ebenezer stone
Samuel prentis	Edwd ickok	Edward hucd	John Ward
John Smith			Thomas wiswell
			Ephraim wheller

At a town meeting march: ye 3. 1707: for the Choice of oficers

Surveighers of Highways — town Clark Constables — Select men

Edward park
Joneth¹ Green   Edward park   Abraham Jackson
Nath¹ Seingly   free Edward Jaks Daniell hid   John Ward iun
John Kenrick   Nath¹ parker   Thomas Wiswell
John trowbridge   Jeremiah fuller
                                                  William Ward

Grand Jury man for: ye: Nath¹ Healy

Sealer of weights and mesurs: Lev¹ Spring
Sealer of Lether: Ebenezer Stone

fenes viewers: Jacob bakon John wooderd iun

Jonathan Coolidge and Richard wooderd Chosen
to take Care of hogs that they are yoked and ringed
according to Law

Voted march 3: 1707: that John Spring Nath¹
hamand Jonath Ward shall gather the
Schooler pole mony this yeare

tithing men Isaac: beech thomas hamad

FACSIMILE OF TOWN RECORDS.

"1660. None to be freemen but such as are in full communion with the Church of Christ."

In 1654 the Newtonians began to have religious services in their own neighborhood; and when the year 1656 came around, the people formed a religious society, and petitioned the General Court to be freed from helping to support the Cambridge church. This reasonable prayer was granted in 1662; and eleven years later they applied for entire absolution from their loyalty to the university town, desiring to set up a local government for themselves. The General Court responded by giving them a certain measure of exemption from Cambridge taxes; but this partial satisfaction they would not accept, and in 1678 fifty-two out of the sixty-five freemen made another similar demand. Cambridge heartily resisted this movement, but could not prevent important concessions being made, and in 1679 town-meetings began to be held here.

The Cambridge people had sturdily fought the attempts of their southern colony to secure self-government, but for twenty-five years the Newton farmers resolutely kept up the contest, refusing all compromises, and offering to pay for their municipal freedom with good lawful money. As the Cambridge authorities picturesquely remarked: "Those long-breathed petitioners rested not, but continued to bait their hooks, and cast their lines into the sea, tiring out the Courts with their eager pursuit, and obliging them to dance after their pipers for twenty-five years." Among the chief men of the General Court to officially consider and arbitrate upon this tranquil civil war was Major Nathaniel Hawthorne, of Salem, whose descendant, the greatest of American novelists, was a resident of Newton nearly two centuries later.

During this long contentious era, the domain of Newton was known as Cambridge Village, and sometimes as New Cambridge; but in 1691 the General Court christened it *Newtown*, in response to a petition of the people, to do away with the confusion arising from the irregular and interchangeable use of the two first-named titles. Concessions came but slowly from the Colony Government, in the matter of the political independence of this little rural state, and it was not until the year 1687, after over thirty years of spirited conflict, that Newton succeeded in securing her long-desired emancipation from Cambridge, and became a separate town, with a deputy to the General Court. The name bestowed upon it in 1691 was a revival of the ancient and abandoned name first given to Cambridge; and this again was without authority modified into NEWTON by Judge Fuller, who became town clerk in 1766.

42 freemen migrated into Newton between 1639 and 1679, and 30 of their sons grew up to man's estate during that period. Of this number, 5 had died and 2 moved away, leaving 65 freemen in the town at the time of its final and successful secession from Cambridge.

Meantime, the town had been threatened with the horrors of an Indian war, and the people resolved to fortify their little settlement, and bid defiance to the savage foe. To this end they prepared materials for a spacious defensive stockade, and their adventurous youth joined the colonial

Old Burial Ground, Centre Street.

forces campaigning among the hostile tribes, and marching against the strongholds of Canada. Two strong block-houses were erected in the town, as rallying-points in case of invasion; and the train-band stood ready to give a good account of any savage assailants. But the red-skinned skirmishers of Metacomet gave a wide berth to these grim yeomen of the Newe-towne; and for nearly a century the unmolested farmers, generation after generation, with their ploughs broke up the stubborn glebe, and slowly increased the humble wealth of the countryside.

First Settlers' Monument in the Old Burial Ground on Centre Street.

In the low red farm-houses among the marshalled cornfields, the sturdy republican virtues grew amain, under the influence of the minister and the schoolmaster, and the memories of Naseby and of Marston Moor. In 1765 the townsmen instructed their representative in the General Court to take vigorous action against the Stamp Act, saying: "We therefore think it our indispensable duty, in justice to ourselves and to our posterity, as it is our reasonable privilege, to declare our greatest dissatisfaction with this law; and we think it incumbent on you by no means to join in any public measures for countenancing and assisting in the execution of said act, but to use your best endeavors in the General Assembly to have the undeniable rights of the people of the Province asserted and vindicated, and left upon public record, that posterity may never have reason to charge the present time with the guilt of tamely giving them away. *Voted*, that the foregoing be recorded in the town book, that posterity may see and know the great concern the people at this day had for their invaluable rights, privileges, and liberties." But, while the men of Newton were tenacious of the liberties of Englishmen, they cherished a faithful loyalty to the Crown; and a year later they resented the lawless outbreaks in Boston against the Royal authorities, ordering that "the person who represents this town be directed and instructed, in his best discretion, to use what influence he may have, that such losses be made up in such a way and measure as may be most loyal and respectful to his Majesty, most safe relative to our invaluable rights, privileges, and liberties, and most kind and generous to the sufferers."

In 1772 a committee was appointed "to consider and report what it may be proper for the town to do relating to the present unhappy condition of the country," and as a result their representative was instructed to work against the payment by the Crown of the judges of the Supreme Court; and they officially urged the town of Boston "to persevere in all loyal, legal, regular, and constitutional methods for the redress of the grievances they felt, and for preventing those they had reason to fear." They also voted: "That we each and every one of us will not, directly or indirectly, by ourselves or any for or under us, purchase or use any India tea, while such tea is subject to a duty payable upon its arrival in America." Nevertheless, one or two of the villagers participated in the famous Boston tea-party, and, coming home late at night, were detected by their people with tea in their shoes.

By the year 1774 the selectmen were ordered by the town-meeting to provide fire-arms for such of the citizens as were too poor to get them for themselves; and raised a force of minute-men, and a light-artillery company. To the fatal field of Lexington, Newton sent three companies of minute-men, containing 218 soldiers, besides the 37 volunteers on the Alarm List, and many others, unbanded exempts and old men, who entered joyously

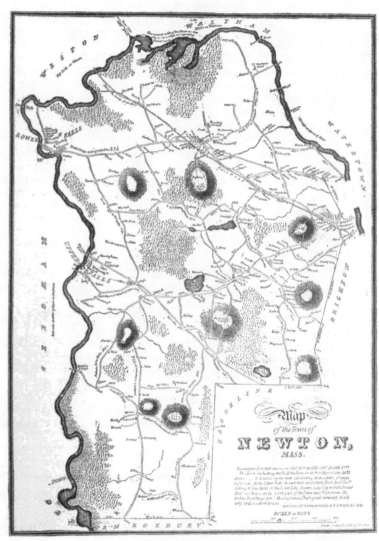

MAP OF NEWTON IN 1831.

into the fray. The West Company, Captain Amariah Fuller, turned out 105 men; the East Company, Captain Wiswall, 76; and the minute-men of Captain Phineas Cook, 37. All these rural heroes were in the battles of the 19th of April, marching twenty-eight miles, and scoring their determination to be free on the backs and fronts of King George's unhappy regulars.

As the clouds grew darker before the black storm of Revolution, the villagers resolved to prepare for troublous days betimes, and enrolled and equipped their gray old veterans of the French wars, and the brave lads from the farms along the Charles and the Cheesecake and Wiswall's Pond.

A company of minute-men was organized and set to drilling on the common; and the East and West Companies of militia assembled frequently under arms, making a little army of 218 soldiers which this town despatched against the British invaders in 1775. After the battle of Lexington, two companies of volunteers were sent from Newton to the American lines; and besides these the East and West Companies, numbering 113 men, marched to Dorchester Heights, at the request of Washington.

The "Meteor." First Locomotive between Boston and Newton.

It was within the walls of the town-house that the yeomen of Newton assembled, and passed their celebrated resolution of independence. Here is the transcript from the town records: —

"At a town-meeting of the Inhabitants of Newton duly warned and regularly Assembled at our meeting house on Monday the 17th day of June, A.D. 1776, to Act on Sundry Articles mentioned in the Warrant, reference thereto being had may more fully Appear. Capt. John Woodward was chosen Moderator of said meeting. After some debate on the Second Article in the Warrant the Question was put; that in Case the Hon[ble] Continental Congress Should for the Safety of the American Colonies declare them independent of the Kingdom of Great Britain, whether the Inhabitants of this Town would Solemnly Engage with their lives and fortunes to Support them in the measure, and the vote passed Unanimously in the Affirmative."

On the 5th of July, 1776, it was "*Voted*, to pay £6, 6s, 8d, to each person who passeth muster, and goeth into Newton's quota, in the expedition to Canada." "*Voted*, to authorize the treasurer to borrow the money to pay the bounty." "*Voted*, that tne money the treasurer shall borrow to pay the

THE ELIOT CONGREGATIONAL CHURCH AT NEWTON.
Destroyed by fire, Sunday morning, January, 1887.

bounty of the soldiers aforesaid shall be assessed on the polls and estates in Newton, and paid into the town treasury by the 1st of January next."

The town sent two full companies to the American army at Cambridge, one of which fought in Gardner's Middlesex regiment at Bunker Hill. Both companies stood in the line of battle along Dorchester Heights on that eventful March morning when Washington's new-made batteries, the growth of a single night, glowered and thundered down on the dismayed British garrison of Boston. When the forlorn and doomed American expedition was sent against the gray towers of Quebec, one of the Newton companies advanced with it, in solid ranks, and under the banners of freedom. Another company, of 96 men, fought in the Bennington and Lake-George campaigns against Burgoyne's magnificent army, whose panoply of glorious war fell before the yeomanry of New England and New York. Thereafter continual fresh contributions of men were called for, and at every levy a few more ploughs were left to rust in their furrows among the Newton glens, until there was not a single able-bodied man in the town who had not served under the colors at some time during the war. The little rural community of Newton, out of 1400 inhabitants, sent out 430 soldiers to do battle in the armies of the young Republic.

Nor did the martial spirit die out when the lords and gentlemen of England laid down their standards at Yorktown. During Shays's Rebellion, the town raised troops in defence of the State, voting them appropriate bounties; and on the approach of the war with France, in 1798, they urged the Government to firm and proud action, "pledging their lives and fortunes to support the absolute sovereignty thereof."

Two more generations arose and passed away among these fair valleys, and mile after mile of forest and of wilderness was reclaimed, and decently arranged in fruitful farms and pleasant estates. The tranquil and scanty annals of the region showed but an uneventful succession of sober and judicious selectmen, godly pastors, and thrifty representatives. Then the current of colonists from the crowded streets of Boston set in, creating among these fair hills new and populous villages of contented citizens, breathing here the purer and sweeter air of the open country.

But once again the loud drums of war sounded their long roll from Oak Hill to Silver Lake, when the young men went a-Maying in the torrid and blood-stained South. The quota demanded of Newton by the National Government, in the Secession War, was 1,067 men. Her actual contribution to the armies of the Union included 2 generals, 36 line and field officers, and 1,091 soldiers, many of whom went to the Walhalla of all heroes by way of dark Virginia and Louisiana, and never again saw these green and grassy hills of Newton.

After the war the people began to discuss the question of advancing their

SOLDIERS' MONUMENT AND TOMB IN NEWTON CEMETERY.
Erected in honor of those who fell in the Civil War.

community to the rank of a city, to which its population, wealth, and society seemed to give it a valid claim. At the town-meeting on April 7, 1873, Messrs. Hyde, Underwood, Pulsifer, Allen, Peirce, and other gentlemen warmly discussed the question as to whether the General Court should be petitioned for a city charter, and, although some favored instead a union with Boston, the majority voted for the motion introduced by J. F. C. Hyde, looking toward a city government. On October 13, the people assembled and voted, 1,224 to 391, to accept the change; and on the 4th of November the last town-meeting was held, and the simple form of government that had endured here for almost two centuries gave way to that more complex system demanded by the new conditions.

The first appearance of the word NEWTON as applied to this locality occurs in the following town-meeting record: —

"Newton May 18 1694"

"the select men then did meet and leavy a rate upon the town of twelve pounds six shiling. Eight pounds is to pay the debety for his service at the general Court in 93 and the other fore pound six shilling is to pay for Killing of wolves and other neseserey charges of the Town."

This is a true copy of the record, signed by Edward Jackson, town clerk, and copied for "King's Handbook of Newton" by Colonel Isaac F. Kingsbury, city clerk of Newton in 1889.

View from Lasell Seminary.

Newton of the Present.

ITS GIFTS FROM NATURE.— STREAMS AND HILLS.
A LAND OF GOOD HEALTH.— THE VILLAGES.
MUNICIPAL EXPENSES.— POLICE AND
FIRE DEPARTMENT.

The city of Newton occupies the south-eastern end of Middlesex County, which was incorporated in 1643, and named from the ancient metropolitan county of England. Its boundaries are Waltham and Watertown on the North, Brookline and the Brighton and West-Roxbury wards of Boston on the East, Needham on the South and West, and Wellesley and Weston on the West. The beautiful river Charles winds around the city for more than sixteen miles, providing valuable and fully utilized water-powers at its upper and lower falls, and adding greatly to the beauty of the country; and several minor streams and ponds still further adorn the face of Nature, giving eyes to the landscape, and points of brightness in the views. There are several well-marked plains and plateaus, marking probably ancient river-terraces of far-past geological periods, and affording fair locations for the villages which unite to form the municipality. In respect to hills, Newton claims the mystic and fortunate number of seven, like ancient Rome; and these bear the names of Nonantum Hill, Waban Hill, Chestnut Hill, Institution Hill, Bald Pate, Oak Hill, and Mount Ida. Less marked than these, but conspicuous features in their respective neighborhoods are Brighton Hill, Skinner's Hill, Moffat Hill, Sylvan Heights, and other eminences of local fame. In later years several of these highlands have been crowned with groups of modern villas, blest with abundance of pure air, and noble views over leagues of open country.

The roads and streets that connect these hills and plains are among the finest in the world, having been carefully constructed on scientific principles, and macadamized with the best and most durable materials. It therefore follows that driving or riding here is a positive pleasure, which appears to be participated in by a large proportion of the citizens, and many of the equipages are such as would do credit to Newport or Bar Harbor or the Bois de Boulogne. Here also are scores of the silent and swift bicycles, and many tricycles, which are in use by the younger ladies of the city. There are 110 miles of accepted streets (and 30 miles of streets constructed, but not accepted) within the municipal limits, and also a great extent of practicable but as yet unaccepted roadways.

The length of Auburn Street is $1\frac{3}{8}$ miles and 16 rods; of Auburndale Avenue, $\frac{3}{8}$ mile and 24 rods; of Beacon Street, $4\frac{1}{2}$ miles and 8 rods; of Boylston Street, 3 miles and 32 rods; of Brookline Street, $1\frac{1}{2}$ miles and 20 rods; of Cabot Street, $\frac{7}{8}$ mile; of California Street, $1\frac{1}{4}$ miles and 12 rods; of Centre Street, 3 miles and 24 rods; of Chestnut Street, 3 miles; of Crafts Street, $1\frac{1}{8}$ miles; of Dedham Street, $2\frac{1}{4}$ miles and 16 rods; Elliot Street, 1 mile; Grant Avenue, $\frac{1}{2}$ mile; Grove Street, $1\frac{5}{8}$ miles and 12 rods; Hammond Street, $1\frac{1}{4}$ miles and 32 rods; Homer Street, $1\frac{5}{8}$ miles and 8 rods; Mill Street, $\frac{3}{8}$ mile and 32 rods; Nahanton Street, 1 mile and 32 rods; Newtonville Avenue, 1 mile; Otis Street, $\frac{3}{4}$ mile and 36 rods; Park Street, $\frac{5}{8}$ mile and 16 rods; Parker Street, $1\frac{1}{4}$ miles and 12 rods; Pleasant Street, $\frac{1}{2}$ mile; Sargent Street, $\frac{3}{8}$ mile and 28 rods; Station Street, 1 mile; Ward Street, 1 mile and 40 rods; Washington Street (Boston line to Needham Bridge), $4\frac{7}{8}$ miles and 16 rods; Watertown Street, $1\frac{3}{4}$ miles; Waverley Avenue, $1\frac{1}{4}$ miles; Woodland Avenue, $\frac{3}{4}$ mile; Woodward Street, 1 mile and 23 rods.

The increase of population has been from 1,360 in 1790 to 1,491 in 1800, 1,709 in 1810, 1,856 in 1820, 2,377 in 1830, 3,351 in 1840, 5,258 in 1850, 8,382 in 1860, 8,978 in 1865, 12,825 in 1870, 16,995 in 1880, and 19,759 in 1885. In 1889 it is estimated to be 23,000. But much more notable has been the advance of the city in material prosperity and beauty, and in manifold attractions for the other thousands and tens of thousands who are to move hither in the next few decades. And so may come true the prophecy of ex-Governor Rice, that in the not-distant

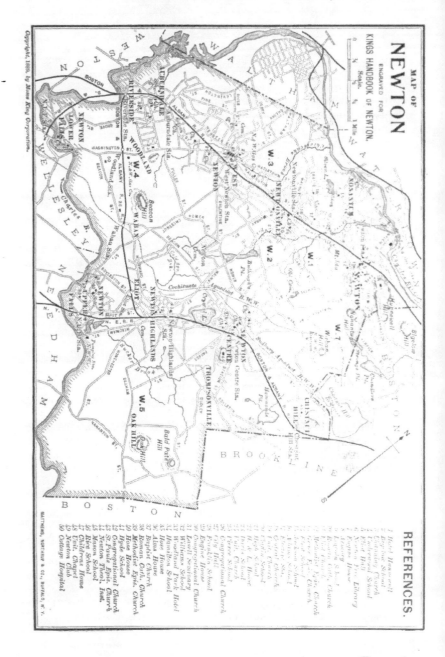

future Newton shall be the Belgravia of Boston, with her sunny hills and broad plains occupied by the happy homes of fifty thousand industrious, prosperous, and well-to-do citizens. The purity of the air among these rural highlands and glens, and the excellence of its water-supply, make Newton the healthiest city in Massachusetts, its annual death-rate being below fourteen in each thousand of population. Over and through all, there is a noticeable air of cleanliness and order. Alderman Farley says that one sees more fresh paint in the ten miles between Auburndale and Boston than in the seven hundred miles between Richmond and Jacksonville. A recent traveller from the West remarked that "the Boston host can take his guest such a drive from Cambridge through the Newtons to Auburndale as cannot be matched in the country, over twelve miles of roads smooth as a billiard table, shaded on either side by grand old trees, which stand like sentinels in front of an endless succession of the finest private estates in this country, and every one of them maintained in the highest degree of perfection. A stranger is at once impressed with the fact that they are homes in the best sense of the word, and the people who inhabit them do not live in their trunks five months in the year, as do all good New Yorkers." General George P. Ihrie, a gallant and accomplished officer on the western war staff of General Grant, and a very extensive traveller at home and abroad, says, "This nest of Newtons is one of the most beautiful spots on this earth, and reminds one of the suburbs of Paris."

A well-known Boston writer also says: "At the extreme easterly part of the city are Brighton Hill and Nonantum Hill; towards the west come Mount Ida, Newtonville Highlands, and the elevations in West Newton and Auburndale; opposite these is the magnificent range of hills commencing in Newton, including Prospect Hill in Waltham, and extending round to Waverley and Belmont; and then there is the basin between. One hardly needs to quote the valley of the Rhine or the bay of Naples, nor any part of the United Kingdom or Continental Europe, to express magnificent scenery, when such a scene as this and others of equal grandeur can be witnessed at home almost any day in the year." Or as old Dr. Elias Nason wrote: "Few towns in the Commonwealth present so many eligible sites for building, or more delightful prospects. The society is intelligent, refined, and elevated; the civic advantages are numerous; the railroad facilities excellent; the climate is healthful; and happy is the man who owns a homestead in this progressive town."

Newton contains ten villages, named as follows: Newton, Newtonville, Nonantum (or North Village), West Newton, Auburndale, Riverside, Newton Lower Falls, Newton Upper Falls, Newton Highlands, and Newton Centre; besides the populous neighborhoods around Nonantum Hill and Chestnut Hill, and the rural regions about Waban, Eliot, and Oak Hill,

CITY HALL.
Washington Street, corner Cherry, West Newton.

There are fourteen railway stations: Newton, Newtonville, West Newton, Auburndale, Riverside, Pine Grove, Newton Lower Falls, Woodland, Waban, Eliot, Newton Upper Falls, Newton Highlands, Newton Centre, and Chestnut Hill. The post-offices are nine in number: Auburndale, Chestnut Hill, Newton Lower Falls, Newton, Newton Centre, Newton Highlands, Newtonville, Newton Upper Falls, and West Newton.

The distances between the railway stations are as follows: Boston to Newton, 7 miles; thence to Newtonville, 1; thence to West Newton, 1; thence to Auburndale, 1; thence to Riverside, $\frac{3}{4}$; thence to Pine Grove, $\frac{3}{4}$; thence to Newton Lower Falls, $\frac{1}{2}$; Riverside to Woodland, $\frac{3}{4}$; thence to Waban, 1; thence to Eliot, 1; thence to Newton Highlands, $\frac{3}{4}$; thence to Newton Centre, $\frac{3}{4}$; thence to Chestnut Hill, $1\frac{1}{2}$; from Newton Highlands to Newton Upper Falls, $1\frac{1}{4}$ miles.

Newton is a compactly settled residence-quarter, the largest of the villages included within the city limits, with the two newspaper-offices and the Free Library and the handsomest churches. Newtonville is the seat of the High School and four churches. Nonantum contains several factories and an Evangelical church. West Newton is a busy village, with the City Hall and several churches. Auburndale has several important schools and many pretty dwellings. Riverside is on the Charles River, amid delightful scenery. Newton Lower Falls has several busy factories. Newton Upper Falls is known for its machine-shops and other works. Eliot, Waban, and Woodland are stations on the Circuit Railroad, the centres of future hamlets. Newton Highlands is a modern-residence village, on an elevated plain, with a rapid development. Newton Centre is a lovely upland village, near the Baptist Theological School. Chestnut Hill has many handsome villas, with ornamental grounds. Oak Hill is the rural and agricultural part of the city, in the southern part, toward the Charles River.

Access to these localities is made easy by the Boston and Albany Circuit Railroad, which traverses three sides of the city, with frequent trains of light and handsome cars, at low rates of fare, and with stations noticeable for their architectural beauty and convenience.

In the matter of politics, the citizens preserve a strong fealty to the Republican party, on National questions, while in their local elections they manifest a notable independence, somewhat akin to the aberrations of the Mugwumps.

For the practical persons who exult in statistics and names and titles, we add a few pages from the reports of the city government, in which the various defences of the people against fire and rogues and diseases are set forth in order. The tax-rate of Newton is $15.20 on each $1,000, which is less than those of Natick, Newburyport, Quincy, Salem, Stoneham, Wakefield, Winchester, Woburn, Weymouth, Arlington, Chelsea, Haverhill, Low-

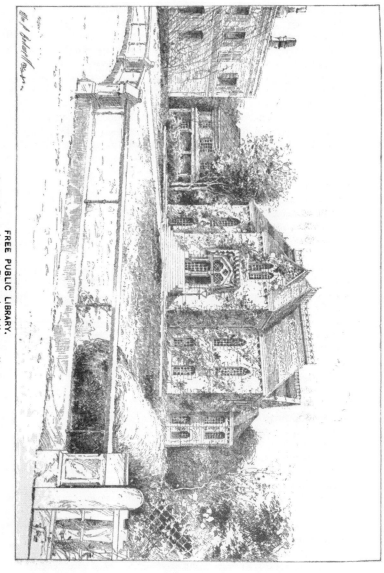

FREE PUBLIC LIBRARY.
Centre Street, between Elmwood and Vernon, Newton.

ell, Lawrence, Lynn, and other cities and towns, many of which have much less to show for their money, in roads, schools, water-supply, and public guardians. The annual expenditures of the city government reach about $600,000, and the net public debt of town and city is not far from $300,000, with a waterworks liability of over $900,000. Frequent attempts are made to reduce the scale of the municipal outlays; but the necessity of preserving and improving the highways, and increasing the public provision for schools, water-supply, etc., for a rapidly increasing population, renders rigid economies difficult of application. Latterly, the property valuation of the city has increased at the rate of about $1,000,000 a year, making adequate provision for larger future outlays, with lower rates of taxation.

The last report of the State Board of Education shows that Newton stands at the head of the cities and towns of Massachusetts in the matter of expenditures on public education. It has 3,611 school-children, and spends for them $103,691 a year, being an average of $28.71 for each one. Brookline and Boston come next in the amount spent on each of their children.

The police force numbers 3 officers and 20 patrolmen. Of the latter, 4 are stationed at Newton, 3 each at Nonantum, West Newton, and Newton Centre, 2 at Newtonville, and 1 each at Auburndale, Newton Lower Falls, Newton Upper Falls, Newton Highlands, and Chestnut Hill. There are also 6 police officers subject to call for special service. This vigilant civic force makes between 500 and 600 arrests each year, about one-third of which are of persons who have imbibed too freely, while perhaps 100 are incarcerated for disturbances of the peace, and 50 or more for larcenies. Most of these rueful culprits are foreigners, some of whom are also represented among the 1,200 tramps that are yearly cared for by the city authorities. There are police stations at Newton, Nonantum, West Newton, and Newton Centre. The City Council has just provided for the introduction of a police electric signal alarm.

The Fire Department has 3 steam fire-engines,— 1 at Newton, 1 at Newton Centre, and 1 in reserve; 7 hose-companies, at Newton, Newtonville, West Newton, Auburndale, Newton Lower Falls, Newton Upper Falls, and Newton Centre; a hook-and-ladder carriage, at Newtonville; and a chemical engine, at West Newton. The force includes upwards of 75 officers and men, and is supplemented by a fire-alarm telegraph and 6 tower-bells.

The city has 8,649 white males, 10,919 white females, 71 black males, 65 black females, 20 mulatto males, and 34 mulatto females. There are 5,089 single males, 6,580 single females, 3,481 married men, 3,569 married women, 169 widowers, 857 widows, and 14 divorced persons.

There are 4,018 dwelling-houses, of which 3,980 are of wood, 22 of brick, and 16 of stone. Newton is the eighteenth city of Massachusetts in size.

HOSE AND HOOK AND LADDER HOUSE.
Washington Street, Newtonville.

Malden, Fitchburg, Waltham, Newburyport, Northampton, Quincy, and Woburn being smaller.

In the matter of vital statistics, Newton has, according to the census of 1885 (out of its 19,750 inhabitants), 10,950 natives of Massachusetts, 3,315 of other States, 2,891 of Ireland, 598 of England, 1,563 of British Colonies (853 of Nova Scotia, 292 of New Brunswick, 231 of Canada, 129 of Prince Edward Island, and 39 of Newfoundland), 121 of Scotland, 99 of Germany, 51 of Sweden, 15 of Denmark, 12 of France, 7 of Switzerland, 5 of the West Indies, 5 of Italy, 4 of Norway, 3 of Portugal, 2 each of China, Wales, and Poland, and 1 each of Spain, Russia, Holland, Turkey, and South America.

The following table gives further interesting details about the city, and is based upon the latest received municipal statistics : —

Wards.	Polls.	Personal estate.	Real estate.	Total valuation.
1. Newton, west of Centre Street, and Nonantum,	888	$989,855	$2,749,000	$3,738,855
2. Newtonville,	1,067	1,106,036	3,940,200	5,046,236
3. West Newton,	804	1,078,810	3,472,530	4,551,340
4. Auburndale and Lower Falls,	803	1,009,370	2,942,325	3,951,695
5. Highlands, Upper Falls, and Oak Hill,	789	416,871	2,400,775	2,817,646
6. Newton Centre and Chestnut Hill,	902	2,416,321	4,655,700	7,072,021
7. Newton, east of Centre Street,	617	2,128,749	3,972,100	6,100,849
Totals,	5,870	$9,146,012	$24,132,630	$33,278,642

With this short preliminary sketch, let us ramble away among the lovely villages of Newton, and over its breezy hills, studying more closely the local institutions and localities and legends as we reach their various habitats, and refreshing ourselves with the sweet air and tranquil peace of this most Arcadian of cities.

Seal of the City.

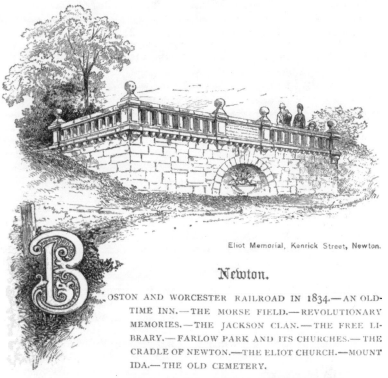

Eliot Memorial, Kenrick Street, Newton.

Newton.

BOSTON AND WORCESTER RAILROAD IN 1834.—AN OLD-TIME INN.—THE MORSE FIELD.—REVOLUTIONARY MEMORIES.—THE JACKSON CLAN.—THE FREE LIBRARY.—FARLOW PARK AND ITS CHURCHES.—THE CRADLE OF NEWTON.—THE ELIOT CHURCH.—MOUNT IDA.—THE OLD CEMETERY.

Newton is the first station and village that one meets in riding out from Boston on the main line of the Albany Railroad, as he enters the broad city of Newton. It is hemmed in between Brighton and Watertown, the Charles River, and Nonantum Hill and Mount Ida, miles away from the centre of the city; yet it claims the distinguished title of Newton *par excellence*, because it is much the largest of the numerous villages within the city's bounds, and has the finest churches, the chief hall, the Free Library, and the offices of the two city newspapers, the *Journal* and the *Graphic*. Sometimes it is spoken of as "Newton Corner," in allusion to its remote place on the confines of other towns; but there are grave citizens who resent this provincialism, and courteously correct the inadvertent blunderer.

It seems to be peculiarly a place of homes; and the local shops are fewer and smaller than a Western town a quarter of its size would have. The wants of the people are largely supplied from the emporiums of Boston merchants; and their needs in other respects are satisfied from the same little London of New England. At morning, a dozen trains bear eastward the working force of the place, the merchants, clerks, and what not; and at evening they come backward to their homes hereaway, tired with the anxieties and efforts of the day, and ready for the tranquil joys of their suburban domiciles amid the trees and flowers.

From such a peaceful and matter-of-fact present we turn to the gray past, to seek some tinge of romance with which to color the bland neutrality of the picture. If it be true that happy is the people whose annals are dull, then the condition of the Newtonians of the last two centuries must have been beatific. Fruitless is the search for Indian massacres, pestilences, conflagrations, or hostile invasions; and the grieved and disappointed annalist turns sadly away, to fill his pages with the inconsequent genealogies of hard-handed farmers, the road-making achievements of ancient selectmen, and the pragmatic theses of rural ministers.

It appears, then, that the first name of this locality was "Bacon's Corner," derived from an ambitious tailor, one Daniel Bacon, who migrated hither from the Old Colony, in 1669; bought up much land; and died intestate, in 1691, leaving his son Isaac to inherit the site of the Nonantum House, and other broad acres. Hither also came Ensign Oakes Angier, and bought from Samuel Jackson, in 1731, the tract near the present Nonantum House, where he opened a village inn, on the old Watertown and Roxbury turnpike. For more than fifty years this martial Boniface dispensed good cheer in his snug little tavern, and the up-country farmers and wagoners gratefully bestowed upon the locality the name of "Angier's Corner," which it bore for full half a century after he had entered into rest. Then the Worcester Railroad came along, and named their station here "Newton Corner"; and the old title faded into forgetfulness, like the joyous flip and foaming ale of which it had once been suggestive. Lastly, arose the strong civic spirit in the village, which looked askance at the "Corner" part of the name, and rejected it, as ill beseeming the destinies of a place where building-lots are held at fifty cents a foot. Waltham has its Piety Corner, and Hingham its Queen-Anne Corner, indeed; but to handicap a metropolitan ward with a suffix befitting a cross-roads hamlet was no longer allowable; and so the name of NEWTON was assumed, and has since been sturdily worn. By the year 1884, the village had attained to a population of 4,251, or nearly a quarter of the entire population of the city of Newton. Yet, only four-score years earlier, there were but twelve houses within a radius of half a mile hereabouts; and life moved slowly and tranquilly with the good farmers, wringing their subsistence painfully from the reluctant

Massachusetts soil. There was much teaming, on the great east-and-west route running through the place; and many a wagon from Berkshire or from the remote wilderness of the Genesee country creaked its slow way past the elm-embowered farm-houses that stretched from Little Cambridge to Needham, like beads on a long-drawn rosary. During the War of 1812, when His Britannic Majesty's tall line-of-battle ships and swift frigates blockaded our ports, and broke up our coasting-trade, much of the flour and other provisions used in Boston came from New York and Philadelphia, in four-horse wagons, great trains of which rumbled almost continuously along the main highway of Newton. The people called them "Madison's Ships,"

Nonantum House. Washington Street, Newton.

in unkindly allusion to the then Chief Executive of the Republic. Down this highway, in later years, passed the huge chain teams from Worcester County, laden with hogs, butter and cheese, dried apples, and apple-sauce, or with wood and hay, and returning westward with outward-bound freights of vast diversity, including everything, from tape and needles and calicoes to hogsheads of molasses and puncheons of rum.

The first aggrandizement of the Corner came in the year 1820, when Squire Solon Richardson made the long journey to Washington to induce the Government to establish a post-office here. Charles Eames, the village watchmaker, became the first postmaster, and had his office on the site of George W. Bacon & Co.'s dry-goods store. The annual revenue of the office was under $40. After some years Eames gave up his jewelry trade and his official commission to William B. Newton, his journeyman, who afterwards voluntarily resigned it to Joseph N. Bacon. About the year 1849 this gentleman left the solid phalanx of Whiggery, and became a Freesoiler, whereupon the official axe fell upon his functional neck. The next three incumbents were Daniel P. Mann, the apothecary, Horace R. Wetherell, and Dexter Whipple; and, on the accession of President Lincoln, the office was given to Samuel Chism. When Andrew Johnson became Chief Magistrate, he put Edwin S. Holman in charge.

As late as the year 1840, the village was composed of two stores, a blacksmith's shop, half-a-dozen dwellings, and a little wooden building, half of which was used by the local harness-maker, and the other half by the railway station. It has been pointed out, with great oratorical fire, that this station was the first one established on that colossal line of rail westward from Boston, which now reaches clear to the Pacific Coast, over the sealike prairies, and through the wild passes of the Rocky Mountains. The location of the Worcester Railroad through the unsettled farmlands of Newton was the result of the intense opposition of the more northerly towns — Watertown, Waltham, and Weston — to its passing through their centres, and alongside the old stage-road. When the railway officials found themselves confronted with this storm of dissent, they reluctantly resolved to alter the line of the road, abandoning Watertown and Waltham, and traversing the lonely fields of Newton. Through the efforts of the Hon. William Jackson, then the principal resident of Newton, the right of way was granted through the town, the land being then of but little appreciable value, except at Angier's Corner and Squash End.

The railroad service of the Worcester Railroad began on April 16, 1834, when the "Meteor," a locomotive built by George Stephenson, in England, made three trips each way daily between Boston and Newton, carrying from two to eight trembling passengers on each trip. This fiery little engine and its companion, the "Rocket," were constructed with great care and finish by the transatlantic machinists. As an eye-witness reported: "Placed upon the track, its driver, who came with it from England, stepped upon the platform with almost the airs of a juggler, or a professor of chemistry, placed his hand upon the lever, and with a slight move of it, the engine started at a speed worthy of the companion of the 'Rocket,' amid the shouts and cheers of the multitude. It gave me such a start that my hair seemed to start from the roots, rather than to stand on end." On the 7th of April, it ran as far as Davis's tavern in Newton, with the directors and fifty guests, making the run in thirty-nine minutes. The next day a train set out from Boston, with the directors and one hundred and thirty gentlemen; but the connecting-rod broke half-a-dozen times, and the party got home at evening, "quite cross." The cars were like old-fashioned stage-coaches, entered from the sides, and standing high on spoked wheels;

and the brakemen, sitting on coach-boxes, regulated the speed by pressing their feet on levers attached to the wheels, like the brakes on mountain wagons. Such were the first passenger-trains run in New England, the precursors of the meteor-like "Flying Yankees" and "Flying Dudes" of to-day. The Boston *Advertiser* of May 12, 1834, contained the following advertisement: "Boston & Worcester Railroad. The Passenger Cars will run daily from the Depot, near Washington Street, to Newton, at 6 and 10 o'clock, A.M., and at $3\frac{1}{2}$ o'clock, P.M., and Returning, leave Newton at 7, and a quarter past 11, A.M., and a quarter before 5, P.M. Tickets for the passage, either way, may be had at the Ticket Office, No. 617 Washington St., (Price $37\frac{1}{2}$ cents each), and for the return passage, of the Master of the Cars, Newton."

Compare this advertisement, if you please, with the time-table of trains now running between Boston and Newton.

The completion of the railway and the rapid growth of Boston caused the village to expand its boundaries, and multiply its streets and houses. The Hyde and Brackett and Kenrick estates were laid out into house-lots, and speedily occupied by comfortable and well-to-do settlers. The old block-houses and cornfields followed the Indian lords of the soil into forgetfulness, and were supplanted by the Italian villas and French-roofed houses of the Olympiads of Buchanan and Lincoln. During the period of the Secession War, the growth of the village went forward apace, though many of its citizens were campaigning in the South. From time to time, detachments of volunteers were sent away, amid great enthusiasm; and others were received home again, with joy. When Company B of the 44th Massachusetts Infantry returned from the Carolina campaigns, they were triumphantly welcomed here by the civic organizations and officials, with speeches and cheerings and banquets, as a band "that had never disgraced their flag or their native town."

Other interests arose in quick succession, and made their presence known in the growing town. The Newton Musical Association dates its origin from that most gloomy and unmusical of American years, 1861; and at the time of the second Peace Jubilee, in 1872, it sent a chorus of three hundred trained singers to the Coliseum. The association has several times rendered the "Messiah," the "Creation," "Elijah," "Samson," and Mendelssohn's "Hymn of Praise." The musical spirit has always been a marked feature of the town, from the days of the psalm-singing of the Massachusee converts at Nonantum Hill, and the Puritan colonists in their grim little seventeenth-century meeting-house. Seventy years ago St. David's Musical Society used to meet at Bacon's Hotel, and sing away the dark winter evenings, with long-drawn sacred melodies and forgotten Jacobite ballads.

Among the local societies are Waban Lodge, No. 156, of Odd Fellows; Channing Council, No. 76, of the Royal Arcanum, instituted in 1878; Branch No. 392 of the Order of the Iron Hall; Nonantum Colony, No. 77, of the United Order of Pilgrim Fathers; Newton Lodge, No. 21, of the Ancient Order of United Workmen; the Young Men's Christian Association, on Elmwood Street; the Newton Bicycle Club, with forty-five members; the Monday-Evening Club; the Tuesday-Evening Club; and the Channing Literary Union.

The centenary of the adoption of the Liberty resolutions by the town-meeting was celebrated in Eliot Hall, June 17, 1876. The Newton City Band opened with National airs; the people sang a patriotic hymn, to the tune of "Old Hundred"; the Rev. W. E. Huntington offered an invocation; the people sang "Hail Columbia"; the Rev. Dr. Furber led in prayer; the choir sang a hymn by Anna Eichberg; Mayor Alden Speare offered an address of welcome; Governor Alexander H. Rice delivered an oration; the Rev. Dr. Bradford K. Peirce read a hymn written for the occasion by the Rev. Dr. S. F. Smith; ex-Mayor James F. C. Hyde delivered an historical address; Whittier's "Centennial Hymn" was sung; an original poem by the Rev. Dr. Increase N. Tarbox, "Newton, June 17, 1776–1876," was read; William C. Bates made an address, presenting to the city a portrait of Colonel Joseph Ward; the people sang "America"; and the benediction was pronounced by the Rev. Henry Mackay, rector of St. Mary's. Many another joyous civic celebration has been held here, in which the beauty and fashion of Newton, and its plain old folks and broad-shouldered farmers, have met to commemorate some locally important event; and the records of all these are preserved with scrupulous accuracy in the village newspapers, and discourteously condensed in the Boston papers under the head of "Surburban Items," seemingly oblivious of the fact that Newton is a city of gardens and a garden of cities.

Let us turn from such displays of metropolitan superciliousness, and ramble slowly about this favored village, with here and there a reminiscence of its old times. Near the railway station are the chief public institutions of the village,— the Newton Free Library, the post-office, the newspaper offices, and the tall brick building of Eliot Hall. Here, on the arrival of the afternoon trains from Boston, is a scene of pleasing animation, when carriages start off from the station in every direction, to the villas about Nonantum Hill, and along Centre Street, and elsewhere in this comfortable nest of well-to-do homes. The public vehicles also fare away over the broad roads, occasionally occupied, but oftener empty, and bowling along with the cradlelike rumble that characterizes the genus hack, in Newton as well as in Moscow or Bombay. At such an hour, one can scarcely realize that at the beginning of the present century there were but three family carriages in town, those pertaining to General Hull, General Elliot, and Dr. Freeman.

A little way to the northward is the cheerless little square around which are aligned the small shops and markets of the village, with the dark brick building of the Savings and National Banks near the centre, overshadowed by magnificent trees. On the site of the bank in the old days stood Joseph Bacon's tavern, a long and narrow building with a vast black barn, into whose wide-expanding doors laden teams from the country used to be driven, to be put up for the night. The Newton Savings Bank was founded in the year 1829, by the Newton Temperance Society and Lyceum, "to promote the industry, economy, and prosperity of its members." It received incorporation in 1831. Its presidents have been William Jackson (1831-35 and 1848-55), Joel Fuller (1835-48), Marshall S. Rice (1855-58), and George Hyde. In 1858 it had 224 depositors, and $14,396 in deposits; in 1863, 224 depositors, and $26,467; in 1880, 3,035 depositors, and $764,779 in deposits; in 1889, 6,574 depositors, and $1,568,766 in deposits.

The Newton National Bank was founded in 1864, and Joseph N. Bacon is its president.

Murdock's ancient store, on the corner, near by the tavern, was devoted to the sale of a few groceries and much New-England rum, a comfortable commodity which then cost not more than fifty cents a gallon, and was esteemed as much a necessity in every farm-house as the inevitable and dyspeptic pork-barrel. At eleven in the morning and four in the afternoon, the farm-hands left their rural avocations, with great solemnity, and took their regular drams, whereby (as they averred) they were stimulated for the ensuing labors of the else weary day.

On the site of Cole's Block formerly stood Union Hall, the cradle of several of the local churches, and the gathering-point for the village entertainments of many years ago, when our now decrepit fathers were active and earnest young men, full of hope and life.

At the end of this miniature forum of commerce stands the venerable Nonantum House, one of the landmarks of old-time Newton, looking very forlorn in contrast with the fresher modern life about it, having long ago passed into pathetic semi-ruinousness, and looking venerable enough to have been a hostel for the crusaders of Richard Cœur de Lion. The land hereabouts was at a very early date owned by Richard Dummer, grandfather of William Dummer, Governor of Massachusetts and founder of the famous old Dummer Academy, in Newbury. He sold it to William Clements, Jr., from whom it passed to Daniel Bacon, in 1669. In the year 1799, after his return from Europe, General William Hull acquired the place, and built a brick residence, which he occupied for several years, while engaged in the practice of law, and in the small diplomacy of the Massachusetts Legislature.

In 1805 he left it, and entered upon his unfortunate Governorship of Michigan. After General Hull's time the house was used as a boarding-school for young ladies, under the care of the celebrated Susanna Rawson, who opened her establishment here in the year 1803, and remained for several years. This was the first female seminary in the United States, and within its walls many daughters of the most distinguished families received their education, not only in the commoner matters of school-lore, but also in those ornamental branches which the sagacity of teachers has always ranked as "extras." Among the charming maidens who then lighted up the dull little rural hamlet with their bright eyes were the daughters of Governor Claiborne, of South Carolina, a bevy of West-Indian beauties, and many other fair patricians from the outlands. The stately Madame Rawson found more value in caring for the manners of her pupils than in giving them scholastic instruction, believing that America had more need of cultivated ladies than petticoated pundits. Her own career was as romantic as a chapter from the old English novelists. The daughter of a retired lieutenant of the British navy, who settled at Hull, Massachusetts, she saw the fierce forays and fighting of the beginning of the Revolution, and won a great (but ephemeral) fame as author of the thrilling novels, "Charlotte Temple," "Rebecca," "The Inquisitor," and "Victoria," and also the popular songs, "America, Commerce, and Freedom," and "When Rising from Ocean." Her father, Lieutenant Haswell, was banished from Massachusetts in 1778, and went to England, where Susanna married William Rawson, son of George III.'s armorer, and himself a trumpeter in the Royal Horse Guards. In later years he used to play the trumpet for the Boston Handel and Haydn Society, with such effect, especially in the magnificent air from the "Messiah," "The trumpet shall sound, and the dead shall be raised," that one might almost see the graves opening, and the dust quickening into life. Mrs. Rawson's first book was a two-volume novel, "Victoria," "calculated to improve the morals of the female sex, by impressing them with a just sense of the merits of filial piety." It was published under the patronage of the famous Duchess of Devonshire, whose beauty was so resplendent that an Irish laborer averred, "I could light my pipe at her eyes." By this great lady Mrs. Rawson was introduced to the Prince of Wales (afterwards George IV.). The novel of "Charlotte Temple" met with a sale of over 25,000 copies in a very short time.

While at Newton, she published "Miscellaneous Poems by Susanna Rawson, Preceptress of the Ladies' Academy, Newton, Mass.," a volume of 227 pages, with 245 subscribers, whose names, in the quaint old way, were printed in the book. Many other works of fancy or of learning, aggregating thousands of printed pages, were produced by this wonderful woman, while distracted also by the care of her sixty maidens. Her adopted daugh-

HOTEL HUNNEWELL.— SETH K. HARWOOD, PROPRIETOR.
Washington Street, Brighton Hill, Newton.

ter, and assistant and successor in the charge of the school, was the beautiful Miss Frances Maria Mills, a descendant of Christopher Kilby, the agent of the Colony of Massachusetts at the Court of Great Britain, and herself the mother of Mrs. Georgiana Hall, the author, and (by a second marriage) of Richard S. Spofford, the Essex-County statesman. This notable lady of the old school died at Newburyport, late in the year 1887.

About the year 1837, John Richardson enlarged the old mansion by the addition of wings, and opened a hotel, which was for a long time a favorite summer-resort of Bostonians, who came in such numbers that it was found necessary to colonize them among the neighboring farmers. The great summer resting-places among the White Mountains, and the Massachusetts islands, and along the Eastern coast, were then unknown and almost inaccessible; and the gentry of Boston found here plenty of country air and quiet, in the midst of a region of charming scenery and good roads. For a long period the hotel was kept by Mr. Marshall, and had a wide celebrity among the adjacent towns. In front of it, swinging from a lofty arm, hung a gayly painted signboard bearing a peacock on both sides; and the Peacock Tavern had a vogue limited only by its capacity for accommodation. In later years, the house bore the name of the Tontine. For some time, also, the tavern was run by bluff old John Davis, a member of the Ancient and Honorable Artillery Company and the National Lancers, and lieutenant of Lafayette's escort. From about 1850, for over fifteen years, the tavern was kept by Abel Harrington, and won and retained a goodly renown for its comfort and cheer. But after the Secession War the old inn lost its prestige; for Newton was fast filling up with houses, and the more attractive places of summer plaisance arose farther afield.

Nonantum Street runs away on the east to the pleasant old riverside estate once occupied by W. S. Tuckerman, celebrated for his transactions as treasurer of the Eastern Railroad. It became in later days the home of Prentiss Hobbs, and is now inhabited by the family of the late William Parsons, a wealthy Surinam and East-India merchant, and afterwards a leader in the manufacturing development of Massachusetts. Farther out on the same street is the estate of Francis J. Parker, colonel of the 32d Massachusetts Infantry in the Secession War, and now a prominent cotton manufacturer of Boston. The house was built about the year 1837, by Mr. Ellis, who has long since joined the great silent majority.

On Nonantum Street was the home of Henry Lemon, a deep and earnest scholar, and one of the foremost Egyptologists of America, who devoted the last thirty years of his life to study and to the propagation of anti-slavery opinions. He was closely associated with Garrison, Phillips, and other leaders in this cause, and in his rich library frequently entertained Charles Sumner and General B. F. Butler. He divided his time between

RESIDENCE OF FRED A. HOUDLETTE,
Washington Street, near Waverley Avenue, Newton.

the study of antiquarian problems and a series of acrimonious law-suits against the town and city, and finally voluntarily took his departure for the Unknown Land, where he perhaps hoped that there would be no lawyers. Mrs. Lemon was a daughter of Francis D. Mallet, of Bordeaux, who came to America on Lafayette's staff, and remained after the Revolution, and founded the first conservatory of music in the United States, in connection with Carl Graupner, an excellent German musician.

In the northeastern corner of the city rises the long plateau of Brighton Hill, or Hunnewell Hill, a part of which is within the corporate limits of Boston, in its outlying *faubourg* of Brighton; while near its eastern base is Oak Square, the terminus of the Brighton and Boston horse-car line. As it rises the long slope of Brighton Hill, on the Newton side, Washington Street keeps the width and smoothness and hardness of an imperial highway, and is lined on either side with pleasant estates, well detached from each other and retired from the road. Around this beautiful highland was one of the centres of the settlement of Newton, the Capitoline Hill of this little Rome. Here the English immigrants of the seventeenth century rested in their westward march, overlooking the Indian-haunted wilderness beyond, until a new wave from the uneasy sea of Englishry flooded past them up the valley. It is not certain who built the first houses in Newton. They were up along the Charles River, near the Brighton line; and in 1639 one of them was purchased from Miles Ives of Watertown by John Jackson, the first permanent settler of Newton. This sturdy pioneer, then in his thirty-seventh year, came from the parish of Stepney, in London, with a good estate, and became a freeman of the town and a deacon of the church, to which he gave an acre of land (now in the old cemetery on Centre Street). The cellar of his house still remains, and the decrepit pear-trees that he planted. There were five other settlers who came in with Jackson, and settled near him; but one by one they moved away, in search of fairer fields in the fast opening domains of the colony. His house stood on the site where Edwin Smallwood built a new mansion about the year 1850; and some of the pear-trees planted at that ancient date survived for over two centuries, being the oldest trees of their kind in New England. One of these outlived the terrible storm of 1869, and for years afterwards bore small and luscious fruit every year. The site of the Smallwood place is now occupied by the Fred A. Houdlette mansion, a very picturesque house, nearly opposite the Hotel Hunnewell, with a noble old elm close in front of it.

One of the sons of John Jackson, the founder of Newton, became a gallant soldier in the Indian wars, and was slain in the battle at Medfield, when King Philip rode into that town at the head of three hundred Narragansett warriors, and massacred many of its citizens. Another son was Abraham, a thrifty farmer, who married Elizabeth Bisco, and was grandfather of Ephraim Williams, the founder of Williams College. Captain John Jackson, the son of Abraham, became the richest man in town, thanks to the estate that

RESIDENCE OF COL. ALBERT A. POPE, Washington Street, opposite Waverley Avenue, Newton.

Deacon John brought from England, augmented by Abraham's wisdom and the added domain of the Bisco family; and so he contentedly paid the largest tax in Newton, and sat in the highest seat in the meeting-house, and was ministered unto by his own obsequious slaves. Furthermore, he built a great house (which stood until 1833), and lived luxuriously, to the no small amazement of his Puritan neighbors. In the next generation the estate, already nearly shattered by the worthy Captain's generous ways, was distributed to other lords; and the only surviving descendants of Deacon John now dwell in distant places.

Old Deacon John Jackson, the pioneer, found great gratification when his brother Edward closed up his nail-shop in Whitechapel, London, and came out to the Massachusetts Colony, where he bought the Governor-Bradstreet farm of five hundred acres, extending from the crest of Brighton Hill over almost to West Newton. The first possessor of this estate was Thomas Mayhew, of Watertown; and for some years the new-comer dwelt in the farm-house that he bought with the land. Afterwards he built a new and larger mansion to the eastward, on the hill near his brother John's, where he abode in peace for many years. There was a hall of considerable size attached to this house, but not from any idea of feudal grandeur, since it is surmised that its chief use was for holding religious meetings. Jackson was a magistrate and large landholder, for seventeen years Deputy to the General Court, a surveyor of land, husband to the widow of Chelsea's first minister, ancestor of sixty grandchildren, and a slave-holder withal, leaving at his death two male slaves. This notable personage was thus characterized in "The Wonder-working Providence of Sion's Saviour in New England": "He could not endure to see the truth of Christ trampled under foot by the erroneous party."

The homestead descended to the son of the pioneer, Deacon Edward Jackson, a prominent and useful town-functionary in general, whose grandson, Captain Samuel, pulled down the old mansion, and built a greater one, where he lived in much content, rejoicing in a good store of Madeira and Port, until at last the once noble estate was ruined, and he became a partial pensioner on the town. The Jackson mansion subsequently passed into the possession of Jonathan Hunnewell, Esq. One of Deacon Edward's grandsons became a famous Commodore in the British navy; and his son Edward was a Harvard graduate, and minister at Woburn, at whose ordination the parish provided the following evangelical concomitants: 600 meals, £1 worth of pipes, $6\frac{1}{2}$ barrels of cider, 25 gallons of wine, 4 gallons of rum, and 2 gallons of brandy.

Edward Jackson should be held in honorable remembrance, for forty-four of his descendants were enrolled in the Continental Army, and did noble service for their country. Later, in the great dispersion from New England, they passed out into all parts of the Union. There are several groups of them in Vermont and Maine, others in Georgia, and still others in the remoter Rocky-Mountain provinces of the great Republic.

The dignified colonial house on the left-hand side of Washington Street, with its grand air of old-time stateliness, fifty years ago was the home-building of the Hunnewell farm, which in those days held the distinction of being the finest rural estate (or "show farm") in the vicinity of Boston. Grand avenues of trees followed its main lines; and its driveways led down through alleys of pine-trees to and along the banks of the bright river. Here Harriet Hosmer used to come on botanizing excursions, while yet a school-girl in Watertown; and many another famous individual of those days found pleasure in rambling under the pines which stretched along the bluff.

Just beyond the whilom Hunnewell domain is "The Hunnewell," a villa enlarged by later additions and surrounded by lawns, flower-banks, and trees. "The Hunnewell" was bought some ten years ago by Seth K. Harwood, for nine years connected with the Commonwealth Hotel of Boston, and also Hotel Wellesley of Wellesley, one of the largest summer houses in New England. "The Hunnewell" is a favorite hotel for Bostonians and others during the summer, and its accommodations are always unequal to the demand. Mr. Harwood, besides being the proprietor of the admirably conducted "Hunnewell," devotes considerable of his time to public matters, having served on the Board of Aldermen, etc.

In this locality are the beautiful estates or residences of Col. Albert A. Pope, whose name is indelibly associated with the bicycle; James W. French; Ephraim S. Hamblen; William P. Wentworth, the architect; Charles J. Bailey; Henry C. Hardon, the school-teacher; Samuel P. Whittemore; and Mrs. Nellie V. Walker, the publisher of exquisite souvenirs.

Nearly opposite the Hotel Hunnewell is the pretty modern mansion of Charles W. Hall, beside which Waverley Avenue diverges down the glen, by the reclaimed site of the old Smallwood factory. Above the hotel are groups of pretty modern villas, in well-kept grounds, and with the pleasant-sounding Copley and Grasmere Streets diverging along the plateau, toward the river. Here are the homes of Henry B. Wells, Charles E. Whitmore, George Allen, James A. Sawtell, E. W. Pope, and other Boston merchants, Dr. James W. Bartlett, the late Henry Claflin, and others.

From the summit of the hill a great panorama of cities is outspread, including Cambridge, Somerville, Waltham, Arlington, Belmont, Watertown, and sections of Boston's western wards. On the other side, across a deep valley, rises the high wooded ridge of Nonantum Hill, apparently still in the embrace of the wilderness. On the top of the hill is a low stone post, marked "N" and "B," the boundary between Newton and Boston.

Centre Street stretches away from the historic Nonantum corner into Watertown, where it is prolonged as Galen Street, a broad and umbrageous avenue, lined with pleasant cottages, and traversed by tintinnabulating horse-cars.

At the corner of Carleton Street is the home of the Rev. Dr. Absalom B. Earle, who has labored successfully as an evangelist in thirty-seven States of the Union, although since 1856 his home has been in Newton. Not far distant is the house of James H. Earle, the publisher of religious and evangelical books. Near the corner of Galen and Boyd Streets lives the Rev. E. A. Manning, the *Sagamore* of the Boston *Journal*, and longtime Secretary of the New-England Conference. Just across the Watertown line, on Galen Street, stands the old Seger house, a long, low, gambrel-roofed structure of great antiquity, largely remodelled in later times. Here the maidens of the family used to make delicate lace, when the century was young, and Napoleon yet remained in his noxious glory. High up on the left, on a tree-covered knoll, rises the ancient mansion of the Morses, sometime lords of this region, but now departed. Nearly opposite was the birthplace of Anne Whitney, the sculptor; and in sight, across the river, stood the birthplace and early home of Harriet G. Hosmer, one of the most illustrious of American sculptors, now for many years a resident of Rome. Her noble works adorn English manorial halls and Italian churches and American parks. Here, also, is the old Coffin house, built in 1762 by one of the fathers of the hamlet, as a home for himself and his children's children. At the corner of Galen and Williams Streets stands the house of the Perry family, for some years the home of William Stevens Perry, Bishop of Iowa. At this point Galen Street enters the singular quadrilateral section of Watertown called "the Morse Field," which has been cut out of Newton at this point, and is tenaciously held by the former town, like a *tête-du-pont* in an enemy's country. In 1635, when Boston and Watertown ceded great tracts of their territory to Cambridge, Watertown carefully reserved to herself 75 acres on the south side of the Charles, being a strip 200 rods long and 60 rods wide, to protect her fishing interests, which then and for 200 years afterwards were valuable and highly prized. In 1679, when New Cambridge was set off from Cambridge, Watertown strenuously clung to these Wear Lands; and again in 1705, and in subsequent readjustments of the line, she has gained ground each time, until now there is an irregular tract of 150 acres belonging to Watertown south of the Charles River. It is valued at a million dollars, and has 600 inhabitants. Half a century has passed since the alewives ceased to come up here to delight the fishermen; and during that period Newton has made several unsuccessful attempts to annex the Wear Lands, which seem to belong to her geographically and socially, as well as by considerations of municipal public works, drainage, etc. But the Watertown influence in the General Court is in this matter as powerful as it was a quarter of a millennium ago; and time waits for some Napoleonic mayor to order out the Claflin Guards, and rectify the boundaries into what Lord Beaconsfield would have called "a natural frontier."

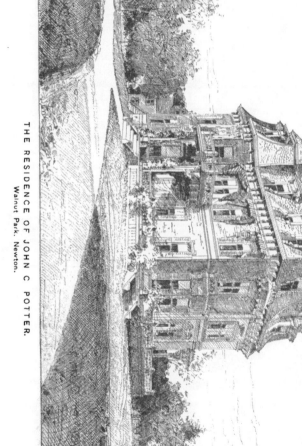

THE RESIDENCE OF JOHN C. POTTER.
Walnut Park, Newton.

The fisheries in the Charles were so important and valuable, for nearly two centuries, that the town annually elected Fish-Reeves, to see that the laws on the subject were enforced. Away back in 1632, the Watertowners built a wear in the Charles, "where they took great store of Shads." The people up the valley as far as Medfield and Sherborn resented all attempts to prevent the yearly migration of fish up the silvery stream, and fought against them in the General Court, which nevertheless passed an act authorizing the lower river-towns to regulate their own fisheries. In 1805 the General Court gave Newton the exclusive right of taking fish in the Charles River, within the limits of the town, and regulated the times for catching shad and alewives. Up to within a half-century, the town of Newton annually sold at auction the right to take shad and alewives, and thus realized considerable sums of money. But the multiplication of bridges and dams, from Prison Point in Charlestown up through Cambridge and Watertown, has interposed a series of barriers beyond which the wary "shads" will not venture; and so the fishing interest of Newton has become valueless, except as a source of pastime to juvenile Izaak Waltons.

Near the bridge still remains the venerable mansion that was known a hundred years ago as the Coolidge Tavern, having been kept as a public house by Nathaniel Coolidge from 1764 to 1770, and afterwards by his widow, being known as "The Sign of Mr. Wilkes near Nonantum Bridge." In 1775 it was appointed as a rendezvous by the Committee of Safety, in case of an alarm; and in 1789 it became the lodging-place of President George Washington, who spoke disparagingly of its frugal accommodations. Opposite is the old house in one of whose chambers Paul Revere engraved his plates, and struck off the colony notes, by order of the Provincial Congress. General Henry Knox, Harry Jackson, and other officers were quartered here during the siege of Boston.

Just across the bridge, in Watertown, stood the house into which Benjamin Edes removed his types and presses from beleaguered Boston in 1775. Here the valiant old patriot carried on the official printing for the Provincial Congress, what time the thunder of British artillery for months re-echoed up the valley. At Luke Robinson's, General Joseph Warren passed the last night of his life, riding gallantly forth the next morning to his fate at the battle of Bunker Hill.

Just across in Watertown dwelt Francis Knapp, a graduate of St. John's College, Oxford, and son of a British naval captain, who spent the final years of his life here, in the quiet pursuits of a scholar. His music and his poems were published, in quaint little colonial tomes, in which he praised the Charles River's mirror-like surface, wherein

> "From nei'bring hills the stately horse espies
> Himself a feeding, and himself envies."

RESIDENCE OF DARIUS R. EMERSON.
Jewett and Waban Streets, Newton.

In our prosier modern days, there are several small industries located in this neighborhood. In Water Street are the works of the American Magnesium Company, producing ingots, spirals, powder, and ribbon magnesium, and colored lights for signalling; and also the Warren Soap Manufacturing Company. On Maple Street are the works of the Newton Machine Company, making the Ballou lathes and other machinery for the Howard and Waltham Watch Companies, and for mills throughout the world.

Westward from Galen Street extend acres on acres of dwellings, each set in its bit of greenery of lawns and shrubs, with little parks here and there, and the comfortable surroundings of New-England village life. This vicinity was once the ecclesiastical quarter of Newton, with the Unitarian, Episcopal, and Baptist churches, all of which have moved away to larger temples. The Baptist church, at the corner of Hovey and Washington Streets, was secularized and carried off in 1886. It was on this site that the workmen discovered an ancient Indian cemetery, with coins, arrowheads, and other relics, side by side with the dry skeletons of their former owners. The old Channing Church has been utilized for the armory of the Claflin Guard (Company C, 5th Massachusetts Militia), with handsome interior decorations in terra-cotta, sage-green, and white satin, and the armorial bearings of the United States, Massachusetts, and Newton. Here are the rooms for the officers and non-coms., the rifle-range, gun-racks, lockers, and other paraphernalia of a first-class armory. The Claflin Guard was organized in the year 1870, and assigned to duty as Company L of the 1st Massachusetts Militia. Its most arduous campaign was after the Great Fire in Boston, in 1872, when it was detailed (W. B. Sears being its captain) for two weeks to aid in guarding property in the afflicted city. One of its treasures is a magnificent American flag, presented by ladies, with an address by Governor Claflin. It was organized with Isaac F. Kingsbury as captain; Fred. P. Barnes, first lieutenant; Frank G. Park, second lieutenant.

On Hovey Street stands the Rebecca-Pomeroy Home for Orphan Girls, a noble local charity, founded about fifteen years ago, after the closing of the Girls' Asylum at Newton Centre, and installed in the old Episcopal rectory. Children are received here between the ages of five and eleven, and kept until they are able to support themselves. This charity is a memorial of Miss Rebecca R. Pomeroy, distinguished as a nurse in the Secession War, and author of "Echoes from the Hospital and White House." She died in 1884, and her obsequies were conducted at the Eliot Church, under the flag whose heroes she had so tenderly cared for.

Jewett Street is a pleasant street of quiet homes, leading northward to the locality so famous for its deep glacial markings, now nearly obliterated by the cutting down of the hill and its ledges. At the corner of Waban Street is the fine estate of Darius R. Emerson, and near Washington Street is the home of Alderman J. Edward Hollis.

The fine estate of John C. Potter is near the Washington street end of Walnut Park. The residence is one of the most imposing in Newton, and the grounds are delightfully laid out.

Waban Park is notable as the locality where land in Newton was first sold by the foot. It was laid out and offered for sale in 1844, by William Jackson, one of the founders of the modern village. In this region is the home of the late Seth Adams, formerly one of the rich residents of the city. After amply providing for his family, and for various Massachusetts charities, he left, in 1872, the bulk of his fortune for the foundation of the Adams Nervine Asylum, for the alleviation of nervous diseases by diet, good air, gymnastics, hot and cold baths, and the movement cure, with special

John T. Langford's Residence, Walnut Park, Newton.

attention to genial associations and religious exercises. In 1877, the institution received its incorporation, having an endowment of about $600,000.

The house at the corner of Waban Park and Jewett Street was the birthplace (in 1854) of Clara Louise Burnham, one of the most delightful of American novelists, and the author of "Young Maids and Old," "Next Door," "A Sane Lunatic," and other pleasant and popular books of recent dates, whose field is the close and loving delineation of New-England character. Mrs. Burnham's father was Dr. George F. Root, the eminent musical composer (of Root & Cady, the Chicago music-publishers), who also dwelt for years in this beautiful locality. Dr. Root's musical compositions have had the most profound effect on America, and have moved to high enthusiasm thousands of men. Among these thrilling melodies were "The Battle-Cry of Freedom," "Tramp, Tramp, Tramp, the Boys are Marching," and "Just before the Battle, Mother." Dr. Root has endeared himself to every Christian by his exquisite hymns and anthems.

Near the great Roman-Catholic Church of Our Lady Help of Christians, at the point where Washington Street crosses Cold-Spring Brook, stood the cradle of modern civilization in Newton, and the ancient homes of the powerful Jackson clan, Edward and Sebas and Michael, and many another,— a martial family, furnishing many good officers and soldiers for the Provincial and Continental armies. The great and venerable old house, now near to its eightieth year, rises above gardens of velvet roses and old-fashioned flowers, opposite the place where Bellevue Street descends from the lovely terraces of Mount Ida, and enters Washington Street. In one corner of the garden stands an enormous acacia-tree, perhaps the largest in New England. Inside the house, now occupied by Jacksons of the eighth generation, are many interesting relics of the earlier centuries, quaint old furniture and pictures, including an interesting portrait of Admiral Sir Isaac Coffin, presented by him to the Rev. Dr. Homer, of Newton. In the garden still blooms the famous "Grandmother rose," brought here over eighty years ago by the young bride (born Sarah Winchester) of Major Timothy Jackson. The old Mayhew house was built here before 1638, by one of the nameless and forgotten pioneers of Newton, and remained until 1708, much of the time being used as Edward Jackson's home. It stood between General Michael Jackson's house and the brook, and its cellar-hole was visible as late as the year 1850. This appears to have been the first house built in Newton, the germ from which all the splendid civilization of the modern city may date its origin. Edward Jackson was a great personage in his day, and used to accompany the Apostle Eliot on his evangelical missions, to write down the questions of the Indians and Mr. Eliot's answers. On his death he bequeathed an estate of 400 acres to Harvard College. Edward Jackson's grandson, Jonathan, became one of the wealthiest merchants and manufacturers of Boston; and his son, Edward (also a Boston merchant), married the fair Dorothy Quincy, the grandmother of Oliver Wendell Holmes. Sebas Jackson, a son born to the first Edward on the voyage from London, inherited his two-story house, 18 by 22 feet in size, with 150 acres of land, and two gilded silver spoons. The house was built in 1670, and enlarged in 1690, and stood until 1809. Here dwelt Sebas's son, Joseph, a bold litigant and amateur lawyer, clothier, and farmer, celebrated for his great hives of bees, from whose stores he supplied his pastor and neighbors, besides making some of it into a peculiarly heady metheglin. From Joseph the estate passed down to Timothy, a gallant officer in the old French war; and from

Timothy to his son Timothy, who in the year 1809 razed the house to the ground, and erected on its site the mansion that is still standing. This worthy gentleman had great occasion to enjoy the peaceful charms of home, for his early life had been full of strange adventure and vicissitude. Before he had reached his twentieth year, he had fought the British on several well-contested fields, and was captured on a privateer (after being grievously wounded) by the frigate "Perseus," and kept six months on a prison-ship at New York. Thence he was sent to London, and put on a Spanish-built guard-ship; cruised to Lisbon on the "Experiment"; sailed to the West

Jackson Estate, Washington Street, near Walnut Park, Newton.

Indies on Lord Howe's flag-ship; escaped at Antigua; sailed to North Carolina in a pilot-boat; was again captured and taken to New York; escaped, and journeyed two days toward the American lines; was recaptured by the Hessians, and spent another six months in a horrible prison; was exchanged after the battle of Monmouth; and finally, after years of involuntary wanderings, reached his old home again, and settled down, right contentedly, to till the soil of Massachusetts. Such a wide-wandering Ulysses found great favor among the quiet home-bodies of the valley, who made him schoolmaster, deputy-sheriff, selectman, brigade-major, etc., until he was as full of honors and duties as the supercilious Pooh-Bah himself.

Near his home, across the Cold-Spring Brook, was the abode of Michael Jackson, a minute-man, who, called from the ranks to the command of the Newton company, at dawn on the day of Lexington, marched his men at quick time to Watertown, where he said to the hesitating officers of the Middlesex regiment: "If you mean to oppose the march of the British troops, leave forthwith, and take up your march for Lexington. I intend that my company shall take the shortest route to get a shot at the British." His men soon came in contact with Lord Percy's reserve, and were scattered by their firm discipline and steady fire, but rallied in the woods, and hung, relentless, on the enemy's rear, until the unhappy redcoats reached the boats at Lechmere's Point. At Bunker Hill, a few weeks later, in the thick of the fight, he slew a British officer, in a hand-to-hand encounter, and received a musket-ball in his own body. A year later, he was desperately wounded in the thigh, in the engagement at Montressor's Island, New York; and afterwards became colonel of the Eighth Massachusetts Regiment of the Continental Line, which rank he held until the close of the war. When this noble old warrior's soul went onward to Walhalla, in 1801, Generals Knox, Jackson, and Brooks, Colonel Ward, Doctor Eustis, and Joseph Blake were his pall-bearers, while Cheney's battalion of infantry formed the escort, and the artillery company fired minute-guns.

William Jackson, the son of old Major Timothy Jackson, was born here in 1783, and lived until 1865, a long, happy, and useful life, in which he had earnestly fought Freemasonry, negro slavery, and the traffic in liquor, in the General Court and the National Congress, as well as in the rural councils of his native town. For the first eight years of its existence, he was President of the American Missionary Society; for eight years also a leader in the Liberty Party; and then in the Free-Soil Party. As early as the year 1826, he began to lecture on the subject of railroads, advocating them fearlessly in the face of a torrent of guffaws, and in time becoming a prominent leader in railroad construction in New England. The development of Newton as a place of residence was largely due to his efforts, in securing comfortable transit and laying out large districts in streets and parks. His brother, Francis, won an enduring fame as the historian of Newton, having published (in 1854) an accurate and valuable history of the town. Another scion of this family was Frederick Jackson, who brought home two bitter wounds from the Secession War, and settled to rest as Superintendent of the Newton Free Library. In 1887 he died, at St. Paul, where he had become engaged in large commercial undertakings.

Turning backward toward the central square of the village, the amateur geographer may ramble pleasantly among the scenes south of the Albany

ROSEDALE, THE RESIDENCE OF JOHN C. CHAFFIN.
Vernon Street, between Washington and Eldredge Streets, Newton.

track. Near the Newton railway station, appropriately secluded from the street, is the Free-Library building, the home of one of the most popular institutions of the city. It had its origin as far back as the year 1848, when twenty-six gentlemen of the village formed the Newton Book Club, subsequently incorporated as the Newton Library Association, and in 1851 opened to all paying for the privilege of taking out books. In 1865 the Association began to plan for a free public library, to meet the literary wants of the fast-rising village. In 1866 Messrs. George H. Jones, John C. Chaffin, Isaac T. Burr, and ten others bought the present site of the Free Library, to hold in trust for the erection of a library building. A year and a half later, the Hon. J. Wiley Edmands gave $15,000 for the foundation of a library here, followed by a subscription of $18,353 from other gentlemen, and subsequently by $5,000 from John C. Chaffin, Esq., and a second general subscription of above $10,000. The building was erected in 1868-70, of rough-faced stone from Newton Centre, trimmed with Hallowell cut stone. The Board of Managers elected in 1869 included Messrs. Jones, Chaffin, Burr, Edmands, George W. Bacon, J. S. Farlow, A. B. Underwood, Joel H. Hills, George S. Bullens, George S. Harwood, and A. I. Benyon.

The Newton Free Library was organized in September, 1869, and received the property of its parent, the Newton Library Association; and in 1875 the stockholders transferred the entire estate to the city of Newton. The amount subscribed by citizens to the foundation of this great agency of civilization was $65,000. The location of the building is central, contiguous to the post-office, the railway station, and the two newspaper-offices, and on Centre Street, the ancient main thoroughfare of the town. Back of an emerald expanse of lawn rise the stone walls that shelter the library, covered thickly with ivy in its season, and presenting an aspect as nearly venerable as is consistent with a public building in a wide-awake New-England city. Inside, the library divides into two sections, the downstairs reading-room, and Chaffin Hall, sacred to multitudinous newspapers and magazines, and the upstairs library, or Edmands Hall, with its 25,000 books, its attentive and attractive guardians, and its large portraits of gentlemen instrumental in the foundation,— J. Wiley Edmands and others. Among the treasures of this institution are several large and costly series of foreign photographs, illustrating the great cathedrals of England, and other interesting objects in the Old World. On the right of the entrance is the Farlow Reference Room, handsomely fitted up in cherry, and containing long tables and other conveniences for study, together with a large reference-library. Here also is a copy of Raphael's "Transfiguration," made in the inspiring presence of the original picture, in the Palace of the Vatican. Back of Edmands Hall opens Jones Hall, with its monitor roof overarching the long book-stacks. The librarian's room and the work-room (for the

FARLOW PARK. VIEW OF THE LAKE, THE BRIDGE, AND GRACE CHURCH.
Eldredge, Vernon, and Church Streets, Newton.

deliveries to the various Newton agencies) are also on this floor. The remarkable success of the Newton Library is largely due to the genius of the first librarian, Miss Hannah P. James, who had it in charge from its foundation until 1887. There are upwards of 25,000 books here, and the annual circulation for home use reaches nearly 100,000. The total agency distribution in 1886 was 48,076 volumes, divided as follows: Newtonville, 11,394; Newton Centre, 10,482; Auburndale, 6,873; Newton Highlands, 6,616; West Newton, 4,752; Newton Upper Falls, 4,476; Newton Lower Falls, 2,743; Nonantum, 356. The library is open from 10 to 12 in the morning, and from 2 to 8 in the afternoon; and the reading-rooms are open from 9 to 12, and from 1 to 9. Its superintendent for many years until 1888 was the Rev. Dr. Bradford Kinney Peirce, a Methodist clergyman, but for the past forty years engaged mainly in authorship and philanthropy; for some time a State senator; chaplain of the reform schools at Lancaster, Massachusetts, and Randall's Island, New York; and for nearly two decades editor of *Zion's Herald*. The present librarian is Miss E. P. Thurston.

Among the projectors and benefactors of the library were George H. Jones, who established a fund for the purchase of books on mechanics and kindred topics; David B. Jewett, who gave $5,000 (and his widow also gave $5,000); Hon. John S. Farlow, who has given many thousand dollars; John C. Chaffin, a liberal and active benefactor; Charles A. Read, who bestowed a large fund for the purchase of books; Isaac T. Burr, George W. Bacon, George S. Bullens, George S. Harwood, A. B. Underwood, and several other gentlemen. The village of Newton Centre gave its library of 1,400 volumes to this institution; and the village library at Newton Lower Falls was also added to it by donation.

Around the corner on Vernon Street adjoining Farlow Park is "Rosedale," the residence of John C. Chaffin, in whose honor Chaffin Hall in the Free Library has been named. And across the street is Dr. L. R. Stone's residence.

A few rods distant from the Free Library, eastward on Vernon Street, opens the celebrated Farlow Park, in ancient times a wretched and unsightly bog, but in 1883-85, by the munificence of John S. Farlow, and liberal municipal grants, converted into a handsome urban pleasure-ground, with trees and shrubbery, flowers and lawns, a pretty pond, and a pretentious rustic bridge, and other beauties of Nature improved by art. One of its most attractive features is in the contiguity of three of the finest churches in Newton, "Channing," "Grace," and "Eliot," whose picturesque stone walls and spires are seen to noble effect across these expanses of greenery, and also the pleasantly situated Underwood Primary School. On Baldwin Street, between Farlow Park and Elmwood Street, is Gorham D. Gilham's residence, where Queen Kapiolani was entertained in 1887.

Grace Church is a beautiful stone structure, in the most pleasing form of Gothic architecture, with a noble stone spire. The first services of what subsequently became "The Parish of Grace Church, Newton," were held in the house of Mr. Stephen Perry, on Galen Street, just over the Newton line, in Watertown. A parish was organized, Sept. 27, 1855. On account of some previous informalities, it was newly organized, March 24, 1856. On the 20th of May, 1856, services were begun in Union Hall, Newton (where Cole's Block now stands). The hall was

GRACE (PROTESTANT EPISCOPAL) CHURCH, NEWTON.
Eldredge Street, corner of Church Street.

neatly fitted up for the purpose, and was often well filled with attentive congregations. Here confirmations were administered, and one person was ordained Deacon. The new Deacon, W. S. Perry, then very active in the affairs of the young organization, has been advanced from one position to another of honor and usefulness in the Church, until now he is a Bishop. The services, held first in Stephen Perry's house and then in Union Hall, were frequently conducted by the Rev. T. F. Fales, of Waltham. Occasionally other clergymen were engaged. When the parish was organized, a call was extended to Mr. Fales to become its Rector; but he declined, and recommended that the Rev. John Singleton Copley Greene, his assistant, be invited to the position. Mr. Greene became the Rector, Jan. 1, 1856, and served until Oct. 1, 1864. He was a man of the most sincere personal piety, and of a very benevolent spirit. Being possessed of means, he gave freely of his wealth for the Church's welfare. One of his gifts to the parish was the rectory, on Hovey Street, now occupied by the Pomeroy Orphanage. Jan. 1, 1857, land at the corner of Washington and Hovey Streets was bought by the parish, and a wooden chapel was erected. At a later date, the chapel received an addition by the construction of a Sunday-school building in the rear. This was another of Mr. Greene's gifts. After laboring for eight years, Mr. Greene resigned the rectorship, and removed to Longwood, where he subsequently died, never having accepted charge of any other parish than Grace Church. It was his first and only parish, and most nobly did he labor for its welfare. He was succeeded, Nov. 1, 1864, by the Rev. Peter Henry Steenstra, D.D., who remained until July 1, 1869, when he accepted a call to a professorship in the Episcopal Theological School at Cambridge. The third Rector was the Rev. Henry Christian Mayer, who came Aug. 8, 1870, and stayed until May 26, 1872. During his rectorship began the movement for securing a new church, the chapel having become overcrowded. Owing to the nearness of the railroad to the Washington-Street lot, it was resolved to move to another neighborhood, and so a purchase was made of land at the corner of Church and Eldredge Streets. May 26, 1872, Mr. Mayer resigned. He was succeeded, July 1, 1872, by the Rev. Joseph Sherburne Jenckes, Jr., LL.D. Sept. 4, 1872, the corner-stone of the present beautiful building was laid; and on Advent Sunday of 1873 worship was held in it for the first time. Mr. Jenckes remained Rector until Sept. 2, 1874, when he resigned. His successor was the Rev. George Wolfe Shinn, D.D., who entered upon his duties Jan. 3, 1875, and still remains in charge. On the 14th of July, 1884, ground was broken for a chapel and parish-house on the north side of, and connected with, the church; and the first service in the new chapel was an early celebration of the Holy Communion, on Christmas morning of 1884.

The parish has grown from a small beginning to considerable strength, and now rates as one of the most prominent Episcopal congregations in Massachusetts. Its contributions to religious and benevolent objects are generous, and its own parochial societies are carried on with vigor. The seats in the church are always free at night to every one, and strangers are

CHANNING (UNITARIAN) CHURCH, NEWTON.
Vernon, Eldredge and Park Streets.

welcomed at all times. Services are held regularly the year around on Sundays, at 10.45 A.M. and 7.30 P.M.; and the Holy Communion is celebrated every Lord's Day and on all the great Festivals. On other Festival Days services are held at 4.30 P.M. During Lent there is a daily service. From Advent to Easter, Friday-night services are held in the chapel.

The present church cost $105,000, after plans by A. R. Esty. The chime of bells was presented by Mrs. Elizabeth Trull Eldredge, in 1873, and includes 9 bells, the largest weighing 2,140 pounds, and the smallest 295 pounds. They are remarkable for their purity and sweetness of tone. The walls are of conglomerate stone, laid in rubble pattern; and the clere-story is upheld by columns of polished Belgian marble, with sandstone bases and capitals. The chancel-arch rises from pillars of Lisbon marble; and the altar and font are of Nova-Scotia stone. The ceiling is open to the ridge-pole; and there are several brilliant memorial windows. The church seats 700 people.

The parish-house, contiguous to the church, was built by Architect William P. Wentworth, at a cost of about $14,000. It is similar to the church in its style and material, and with it forms a broad and rambling pile of masonry, reminding one of the old parish-churches of England, with their connected buildings for religious and charitable uses. In the parish-house are found the assembly and Bible-class rooms, reading-room, and other offices, besides a beautiful little chapel. The church, having got clear of debt, was consecrated in the spring of 1888.

Not far from Grace Church, on the same side of Farlow Park, is the beautiful pile of stone buildings occupied by the Channing Church, surrounded by wide and well-kept lawns, and crowned by a graceful stone spire. The Channing Church was organized Sept. 2, 1851. Previous to that time, the few Unitarian families in what was then called Newton Corner had attended the services at the First-Parish Church of Watertown. Until 1856 the new religious society held its services in Union Hall. But on Feb. 28, 1856, it dedicated a small wooden church, which had been erected by means of the generosity of twelve gentlemen of the parish, on Washington Street, near the railway station. Ten years later, however, this had been outgrown, and was no longer fitted to the needs of the increasing church. In consequence, the old building was enlarged one-third, and greatly improved. This was occupied until 1882, when the new church, situated on Vernon and Eldredge and Park Streets, was dedicated. It is built of brown-stone from Indian Orchard, Massachusetts, and trimmed with Ohio sandstone. It is well placed, standing altogether apart from surrounding buildings, and almost facing Farlow Park. The interior is tasteful and quiet in decoration, and is adorned with memorial windows to Rev. Dr. William Ellery Channing, and also to Dr. Henry F. Bigelow and Deacon Bailey, who were

among the earliest members of the church, and most deeply interested in
its foundation. Other windows are memorials of Rev. Dr. George W. Hosmer and Rev. Joseph C. Smith, former pastors of the church, and to
Deacon Bender and Miss Noyes. The main audience-room of the church
will seat over seven hundred persons, and is exceedingly well adapted both
for seeing and hearing. There is not a poor seat in the church. The
arrangements of the whole structure have been wisely devised with special
reference to the needs of a modern church. It contains a beautiful Sunday-
school room, an infant-class room, church-parlor, dining-room, kitchen, and
so on. The total cost was about $110,000, of which nearly the whole has

Underwood Primary School, Vernon, corner Eldredge Street, Newton.

been already paid. The architect was Mr. George F. Meacham of Newton,
who built the South Congregational Church, in Boston, and the new Eliot
Church of Newton. Since its organization, the Channing Church has had
five ministers. Rev. Joseph C. Smith was the first, from 1852 to 1857, when,
owing to illness, he resigned, and soon afterwards died, in the Sandwich
Islands. The second minister was the Rev. Edward J. Young, D.D., who
served the church from 1857 to 1869, when he retired to accept a professorship in the Divinity School of Harvard University. The third minister
was the Rev. Eli Fay, D.D., whose pastorate extended from May 4, 1870, to
March, 1873. Dr. George W. Hosmer, who had just retired from the presi-

dency of Antioch College, Ohio, became pastor in November, 1873, and remained so until, on account of increasing years, it seemed best to him to retire, Oct. 1, 1879. Since this last date, the Rev. Francis B. Hornbrooke has been the pastor. The parish comprises at present upward of two hundred families

On one side of Farlow Park, where the old Muzzey farm once spread its green acres, was for many years the home of the late General Adin B. Underwood, who rose from a captaincy in the famous 2d Massachusetts Infantry to a brevet major-generalship, and received an almost deadly wound in

George Strong's Residence, Vernon Street, corner of Waverley Avenue.

the storming of Lookout Mountain. For many years after the war he was Surveyor of Customs, at Boston.

Eastward of Farlow Park, several lines of quiet and embowered streets climb the gentle slopes toward Nonantum Hill; and on these streets may be seen many of those homes for which all the villages of Newton are so famous. On Vernon Street, just east of the park, is the fine estate of Mrs. Susan C. Rawson, beyond which are the homes of ex-Mayor William P. Ellison and George Strong, the boot and shoe manufacturer.

On Vernon Street, also, is the Misses Allen's School for Girls and Young Ladies, founded and conducted by Julia G. and Hannah Allen, with a corps of well-known instructors, under Miss S. Alice Ranlett as principal. The school was established in 1888, to meet the wishes of many parents for a school where careful attention is paid, not only to the intellectual development of pupils, but also to their physical and religious training. The aim is to train up girls with healthy bodies, sound minds, and refined manners. The facilities can hardly be excelled. The boarding pupils enjoy a well kept home in a charming situation. Preparation is made here for all universities and colleges.

The Misses Allen's School, Vernon Street, between Park Street and Waverley Avenue.

Elmwood Street received its name from Mr. George W. Hall, in 1856, because it was lined with noble elm-trees, fifty or sixty feet high. It runs eastward from the railroad station to Park Street. On it is the residence of the Rev. Francis B. Hornbrooke, pastor of the Channing Church.

Taking it by and large, Centre Street, which runs from the Nonantum House through Newton and Newton Centre, a distance of two miles, is the most interesting thoroughfare in the city, passing numerous country-seats.

colonial and modern, and several interesting historical localities, and giving views over many leagues of lovely New-England scenery. Centre Street leads from the railway station and the Free Library, near the park and all the church edifices, around Mount Ida into the open country diversified with historic estates.

One of the most imposing public buildings in the city is the new meeting-house on the corner of Centre and Church Streets. Eliot Church took its name from a missionary, not from a denomination. For many years it was the only church in this village, and it has always worked in peace with all true Christians and with other churches which have grown up around it. It is indebted to its founders for this combination of loyalty to the Congregational faith and polity with a catholic and progressive spirit. About half of them belonged to the Jackson, Bacon, Woodward, Trowbridge, and Cobb families. They held prayer-meetings for missions, for temperance, and "for the slave"; built a meeting-house from foundation to spire in four months; and placed under its corner-stone a prophecy of William Jackson which has recently been found and read with awe: that before its seal should be broken the sin of slavery would be removed from the land by awful judgments of God! They formed a volunteer choir which has been sustained with enthusiasm ever since, and praised the Lord with their own voices, with violin, flute, post-horn, and Deacon Woodward's bass-viol. And they gave an impetus to education, reform, and all the refining influences of the gospel, which still pervades the whole community.

The church has had five ministers: William S. Leavitt (1845-53), Lyman Cutler (1854-died 1855), Joshua W. Wellman (1856-73), Samuel M. Freeland (1875-78), and Wolcott Calkins since 1880. The vigorous organization and spirit of the church, and its natural increase from the growth of the place, have left them free to give their whole strength to the ingathering and training of Christian families in this city of homes. They are provided with a valuable library of reference, increased by liberal annual contributions. The healthful growth of the church is seen from its roll: 37 members at its organization July 1, 1845, 173 in 1855, 455 in 1865, 724 in 1875, and 1,093 in 1885; removals deducted, the membership in 1889 numbers 529. Contributions for church expenses and benevolence have advanced from $382.31 in 1845 to $18,404.31 in 1888; and for new buildings and furniture, from $7,790.69 in 1845, and $50,900.00 in 1860, to about $175,000.00 in 1887-89.

The meeting-house of 1860 was burned Jan. 16, 1887. The new edifice has been recently completed and dedicated free of debt. It is a Romanesque building of granite and brownstone, designed by George F. Meacham. The auditorium is an amphitheatre, rising gradually on all sides for a congregation of 1,100. Brackets are left for three galleries with 700 additional sittings, if they are needed in the future. There is a very ornate bell-

ELIOT CONGREGATIONAL CHURCH AT NEWTON.
Centre Street, corner Church Street.

tower, and pretty rose-windows; and the spacious interior is overarched by heavy beams, which rest on carved stone corbels. There are also polished granite columns, with carved capitals, rich memorial windows, loggias, and other attractive interior decorations; and the comfort of the various elements of the society is assured by chapels, class-rooms, parlors, choir-room, and a well-fitted study for the pastor. On the tower is an illuminated clock.

Near the Eliot Church was the home of Richard Park, which, after resisting the storms of a century and a half, was pulled down in the year 1800. During this period it was owned successively by Deacon Ebenezer Stone, shoemaker; John Jackson, tanner; Stephen Parker, tanner; Nathaniel Parker, yeoman; Harbuttle Dorr; Philip Norcross, shoemaker; and Captain Joseph Fuller, butcher.

On the corner opposite the church is the home of Doctor J. F. Frisbie, the founder and for many years the head of the Newton Natural-History Club, whose summer field-days and winter meetings have been productive of many interesting monographs. The society was organized Oct. 28, 1879, and incorporated Feb. 26, 1883. It has upwards of a hundred members, and keeps its collections of minerals, birds, and other curiosities in the Newton Free Library, although it has hopes of in time possessing a building.

Not far away from the Eliot Church, on Church Street, to the westward, stands the new meeting-house of the Baptist Church, an interesting and attractive edifice of brown-stone, designed by H. H. Richardson, the greatest of American architects, in that massive South-of-France Romanesque architecture of which he was so complete a master. It reminds one of a suggestion of Trinity Church, in Boston, with its ponderous stone tower rising from the intersection of nave and transepts, and its handsome triple doorways, in noble Roman arches. The ground-floor contains the lecture-room, parlor, class-rooms, kitchen, and dining-rooms; and overhead is the church proper, with the baptistery in its apse, surrounded by a stone curbing. Small as it is, and simple in its forms, it stands as a type of the noble architecture with which Richardson was enriching our country when Death summoned him, too soon, to that land which is all a church of thanksgiving. As Phillips Brooks said: "He loved a broad, unbroken stretch of wall. And yet out of this simplicity could burst a sumptuousness of design or decoration all the more captivating and overwhelming for the simplicity out of which it sprung." The Baptist religious society dates from 1859, and worshipped for some years in Middlesex Hall and Union Hall; after which it occupied the meeting-house, built for its use, at the corner of Washington and Hovey Streets. The pastors have been the Rev. Gilbert Robbins (1860–61), Rev. Jeremiah Chaplin (1862–63), Rev. J. Tucker, Jr. (1865–70), Rev. Thomas S. Samson (1873–80), Rev. H. F. Titus (1880–88), and Rev. J. P. McCullough. The membership of the church is 270.

THE NEWTON BAPTIST CHURCH.
Church Street, west of Centre, Newton.

On Church Street was the birthplace of the Hon. John Davis, born in 1851, and a graduate of Heidelberg, Berlin, and Paris, and latterly a distinguished lawyer, and Assistant-Secretary of State, and now Associate-Justice of the United-States Court of Claims. This brilliant young statesman is a grandson of "Honest John Davis," Governor of Massachusetts in 1833-35 and 1840-41, and United-States senator in 1835-41 and 1845-53.

A little farther out on Centre Street is the modest gray church of the Methodists. The society worshipping in this place was founded in 1863, and passed its first years in Union Hall, the cradle of so many churches of Newton. The present edifice dates from 1867. The church has 138 members; and the Sunday-school has 135. Among its pastors were the Rev. J. C. Cromack, Rev. C. S. Rogers, Rev. S. F. Jones, Rev. A. A. Wright, Rev. Fred. Wood, Rev. W. E. Huntington, Rev. S. Jackson, Rev. W. S. Studley (1880-81), Rev. J. B. Gould (1882-83), Rev. J. M. Leonard (1884-85), and Rev. Fayette Nichols (1886-89).

The Wesleyan Home, on Wesley Street, near the church, is an institution founded for the care of the children of missionaries, and the orphans of Methodists and others, being supported by contributions from the Methodist churches of New England. The building was given by the Hon. Alden Speare, the furnishings by Mrs. Charles W. Peirce, and an endowment of $20,000 by the Hon. Jacob Sleeper. The Rev. Dr. Bradford K. Peirce is president.

Mount Ida is the bold hill which rises from the plain not far from the Newton station, and is covered with handsome houses and estates. In the year 1816, the entire hill was bought by John Fiske at a valuation of $3,300; and in 1850 it was held at $10,000. At the close of the Civil War, the ridge was purchased by Langdon Coffin, who bestowed upon it the name of "Mount Ida," and laid it out for habitations. There were then but three houses on it; and now the valuation of the real estate exceeds half a million dollars. The hill-top is traversed by the broad, firm roadway of Bellevue Street, from which one gains admirable and extensive views of the valley-towns on the north,— Cambridge, Watertown, and Waltham,— the long and shaggy ridge of Prospect Hill, the blue highlands of Essex, the spires and towers of Boston, the shining waters of Massachusetts Bay, the many villages of Newton, and the far-away azure crests of Wachusett, Monadnock, and other inland mountain-peaks. Let us remember — as we look out hence over those populous western towns, and remember that behind them lie Worcester and Springfield, and Chicago and St. Louis, and Denver and San Francisco — that the old surveyors who were sent out to fix the limits of the Massachusetts colony planted their outermost stakes at Woburn and Weston, reporting that in their opinion the Puritan State would never grow beyond those limits.

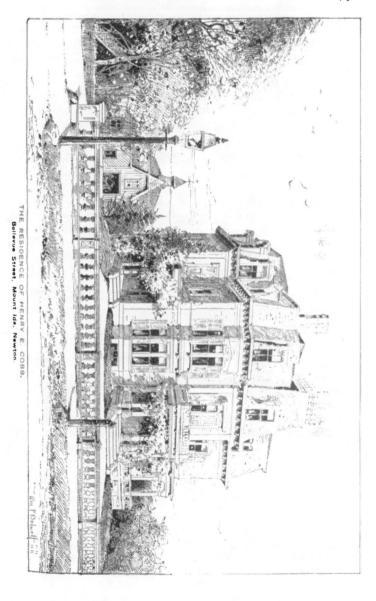

THE RESIDENCE OF HENRY E. COBB,
Bellevue Street, Mount Ida, Newton.

One of the finest estates on the ridge pertains to Henry E. Cobb, the Boston banker. Near by is the far-viewing house built by the late Job Turner, and now the property and home of Charles E. Riley. Nearer Centre Street is the parsonage of the Rev. Dr. Wolcott Calkins, pastor of the Eliot Church, and author of "Keystones of Faith," and other valuable works; and farther down, fronting on Centre Street, is the imposing new brick mansion erected by the late Mr. Bayley (of Potter, White & Bayley), and now owned and occupied by Cyrus J. Anderson (of Lawrence & Co.). On Bellevue Street lives John Becker, the inventor of the "World Typewriter," already in such extensive use. On the western slope of the hill is the home

Edmund W. Converse, Jun., Residence, Fairmount Avenue, Mount Ida.

of J. Eliot Trowbridge, the composer of the oratorio of "Emanuel," which has been rendered successfully by a picked chorus of two hundred voices, and a group of soloists. On the north slope of Mount Ida, on Newtonville Avenue, is the home of the Hon. John C. Park, for over half a century prominent in Boston affairs as lawyer and statesman, and commander of the Boston Light Infantry in the halcyon days of that famous company, when the New-England Guards and the City Guards were its only rivals.

In his monograph on "Glacial Moraines," Dr. J. F. Frisbie says: "Mount Ida is a typical specimen of a lenticular hill,— elliptical in shape, steep

THE RESIDENCE OF CHARLES E. RILEY
Bellevue Street, Mount Ida, Newton.

sides, gently rounded top, and always a beautiful picture in the landscape." The lenticular hills of which this is so perfect a type were the ground moraines of the great glacial age,— the sandy and rocky deck-loads of the continental ice-sheet, deposited on the melting of the glaciers.

A little way beyond Mount Ida, on the right of Centre Street, is the beautiful and spacious domain of E. W. Converse, a wealthy Boston merchant, with its half-hidden Italian mansion, and park-like grounds extending to Cabot Street. On the site of this house the early colonists erected a strong defensive block-house, with a stone base and a loopholed superstructure of logs. To this impregnable fortress they planned to retreat, if ever the hostile Indians should invade their precincts, as they had done at Sudbury and Medway and so many others of the Bay towns. How often, amid the alarms of those perilous days, the Puritan yeomanry assembled in their stronghold, with their wives and children, to await, with dry powder and divine faith, the onslaught of the heathen hosts! But the red warriors of the forest avoided this bulwark; and after many years, when they had been pressed beyond the Connecticut and the Hudson, and into the unknown West, the old tower fell into decay, and disappeared. Isaac Lombard early recognized the beauty of the location, and erected the present mansion, and adorned the grounds, at a cost of $60,000. In 1866 it passed into the possession of the Converse family. Towards the end of the time in which the old garrison-house remained, as a monument of the heroic days of old, it was the home of Enoch Baldwin, whose sons became eminent Boston financiers, the younger Enoch being President of the Shoe and Leather Bank, and Aaron, President of the Washington Bank.

The fine old white house nearly opposite the Converse estate is the home of the venerable George Hyde, of the sixth generation that has occupied this same site. The founders of the Hyde family were Deacon Samuel Hyde and his wife Temperance, who settled here in 1640, having then just arrived from London, whence also his brother Jonathan came, seven years later. These two gentlemen bought 240 acres, of the Danforth and Sparhawk estates, which they held in common until 1662, and then divided it. Since then, the name of Hyde has been widely diffused over Newton, and many of the members of the family have been prominent in the councils of the town and city.

The Shannon estate occupies the west side of Centre Street for a long distance, beginning at Cabot Street. This fine old house was built in 1798, by Joseph Blake, of Boston, and early in the century it bore the name of the Sargent place. Nearly fifty years ago, it passed into the Shannon family, being acquired by Oliver N. Shannon, son of a lieutenant in the United-States Army, who died at Sackett's Harbor during the War of 1812. From that time until her death, in 1887, it was the home of Miss Mary

RESIDENCE OF JOHN BECKER.
Bellevue Street, Mount Ida, Newton.

Clarke Shannon, a noble and philanthropic woman, conspicuous in all good deeds and lovely charities. As was written of her by Edna D. Cheney: "Mary Shannon was of the rarest and noblest type of women. Majestic in person, with a countenance of noble beauty, full of glowing health and life, she at once impressed all who saw her, in woods or garden, in her large hat, with staff in hand, as a goddess of nature. She was Diana in the woods,— close ally and friend of trees and flowers and streams, and every animal and living thing. She knew their secrets, and met their wants from sympathy. She loved even the brown earth; and, when she took it in her hands and rubbed it, she felt in it the potency and promise of all the beauty and use that would come out of it. 'I have known the love of God in human beings and nature,' she said. Humanity in every form was dear to her." The estate is now occupied by Miss Mary Shannon, a niece of the lady aforementioned.

The estates along this part of Centre Street (the old Dedham path), including the Shannon and Edmands and other places and the Claflin place at Newtonville, belonged to the 500 acres granted in 1634 by the General Court to Lieutenant-Governor Dudley, who sold it to Thomas Mayhew, from whom it was conveyed to Simon Bradstreet.

This domain was afterwards owned by Edward Jackson, one of the pioneers of Newton; and when his daughter Sarah married the Rev. Nehemiah Hobart, the bridegroom received thirty acres of good land here, as a part of her dowry. Hobart was the son of the Rev. Peter Hobart, a graduate of English Cambridge, who settled at Hingham, and sent five sons through Harvard College, four of whom became ministers. From one of these descended John Henry Hobart, Bishop of New York from 1816 to 1830. Nehemiah became the second minister of Newton, and had six daughters, upon four of whom he settled this estate, and the house that he had built upon it. The Latin inscription on his tomb signifies that "In this tomb are deposited the remains of the Rev. and very learned teacher of divinity, Nehemiah Hobart, an estimable fellow of Harvard College, a highly faithful and watchful Pastor of the church of Newtown, for forty years. His singular gravity, humility, piety, and learning, rendered him the object of deep veneration, and ardent esteem, to men of science and religion." Hobart's pastorate lasted from 1674 to 1712, through the terrible period of King Philip's War. The house built by this gentle scholar in 1678 passed in 1715 into the possession of the next of the village pastors, the Rev. John Cotton, the great-grandson of the celebrated divine of the same name, once rector of St. Botolph's Church, in the Lincolnshire Boston, and in compliment to whom the capital of Massachusetts received its now well-honored name. Coming to Newton in 1714, when but twenty-one years old, and four years out of Harvard College,

RESIDENCE OF EDMUND W. CONVERSE.
Centre Street, corner of Cabot Street, Newton.

it is recorded that "so high was the respect cherished for the virtues and accomplishments of this youth that the Town in general went in procession, and met and gave him a joyful welcome, upon his first entrance into it." The life that passed on this quiet little estate among the graceful hills that hemmed the Dedham road is thus epitomized in the quaint and stately epitaph that rests over his grave: "Here lies the mortal part of the Rev. and truly venerable JOHN COTTON, lately the very faithful, prudent and skilful pastor of the church of Newton. He was eminent for the faculty of praying and preaching; was respected for his piety, and held in high and universal esteem for his pure and attractive virtues. His loss is especially deplored by his flock, to whom, even dead, he ceases not to preach. Fame shall spread his enduring name more loudly, extensively, and permanently than the most durable marble." He left three sons, all graduates of Harvard,— John, a physician, Nathaniel, a minister, and Samuel, who lived until 1819. The late Commodore Hastings, of Medford, was a great-grandson of the Newton dominie. The old house was burned to the ground in 1720, and a new one arose quickly on the same site. The next occupant of the estate (1765-1793) was the courtly and accomplished Charles Pelham, originally of Medford, an Episcopalian and patriot (in those days a rare combination), who opened an academy in the old house, where he fitted students for Harvard College, most of his pupils coming from Boston and the sea-coast towns.

In the year 1854, the estate passed into the hands of John Cabot, after whose time the house, grown old and uncomely, was moved away. Hither came young Theodore Parker, many and many an evening, while he was teaching school in the adjacent hamlet of Watertown, to see the fair daughter of the house, Lydia D. Cabot, whom he afterwards made his wife, and who stood as a tower of strength and beauty for the great philanthropist to stay himself by, during his lifetime of trial and adversity. These are the resolutions that Theodore Parker wrote in his journal on his wedding day: —

1. Never, except for the best of causes, to oppose my wife's will.
2. To discharge all duties for her sake, freely.
3. Never to scold.
4. Never to look cross at her.
5. Never to weary her with commands.
6. To promote her piety.
7. To bear her burdens.
8. To overlook her foibles.
9. To love, cherish and forever defend her.
10. To remember her always, most affectionately, in my prayers.

Thus, God willing, we shall be blessed.

THE MARY SHANNON ESTATE.
Centre Street, Newton.

Many a happy day did the great theologian spend in the depths of the Cabot Woods, in the western part of the estate, with no companions but the wise and frolicsome squirrels. On the Brackett estate, also, amid the rude and quiet forest, were two flat rocks, which with great pains Parker converted into primitive seats, where he ruminated deeply on the great problems of the life that now is and the life that is to come. The great tree north of the Shannon house, now broken, and protected by sheets of metal, once overarched the Cabot mansion; and at its foot Theodore spent many an hour, poring over his books.

The Cabot Woods may be approached from Cabot Street by going south on the first road turning off after leaving Centre Street, and passing beyond the gravel-pits. The road runs through a beautiful and entirely uninhabited land of hills and pastures and groves, with the forest rising nobly on the east. This road, one of the most interesting and least known, comes out on Mill Street, not far from Bullough's Pond, in Newton.

On the south side of the Shannon place, sheltered from the street by a high wall of masonry, is an old-fashioned garden of an acre or more in area, filled with box-hedges, hollyhocks, sweet-williams, marigolds and other favorite flowers of the olden time.

At the crest of the hill, on the west side of Centre Street, is the fine old colonial mansion now occupied by Mrs. Julia F. Francis. It is a dignified and stately white house, surrounded by spacious and ornamental grounds, with noble trees and brilliant masses of flowers and shrubbery. Early in the present century this estate belonged to Nathaniel Tucker, the leader of the choir in the First Church, and one of the best singers in St. David's Musical Society. From this melodious gentleman it passed to Thomas Edmands, of the Boston book-selling firm of Lincoln & Edmands, who spent the later years of his life here. The house stands near the site of the ancient parsonage of the Rev. John Eliot, Jr., who, at his death in 1668, bequeathed the estate (which included the twenty acres of the southern corner of the Mayhew farm), to his son John, after whose death it was sold (in 1733) by order of the General Court, to get money to carry the younger John Eliot through Yale College. The little domain, lying between Ensign John Spring's land on the south, and the Rev. John Cotton's on the west and north, was purchased by Henry Gibbs, Esq., for £415. Three years later Mr. Gibbs sold it to the Rev. John Cotton, whose heirs transferred it to Charles Pelham, in 1765.

A little way off Centre Street, on Sargent Street, is the handsome modern house of J. Howard Nichols, an old-time merchant in the Chinese treaty-ports, and now treasurer of the Dwight Manufacturing Company. On the adjoining estate stands the magnificent home of E. C. Fitch, the president of the American Waltham Watch Company.

RESIDENCE OF J. HOWARD NICHOLS.
Sargent Street, between Centre and Park Streets, Newton.

The grand colonial dwelling owned and occupied by Francis A. Brooks, with the practical exterior approved of by the best of the founders of our country, stands superbly at the corner of Centre and Sargent Streets.

Beginning near the crest of the hill, beyond Cabot and Sargent Streets, on the east side of Centre Street, beyond the handsome stone house of Mrs. Prescott, and running down to the old cemetery, is the noble and beautiful domain of the Edmands family, with its velvety lawns, tall old forest trees, and bright waters. This was the home of the Hon. John Wiley Edmands, who came to Newton in 1847, and died in 1877. He was born in 1810, the same year as Gardner Colby; and at the age of twenty entered the firm of Amos & Abbott Lawrence, from which he retired, rich, in 1843. In 1864 he became Treasurer of the vast Pacific Mills, and retained that position until his death, extending the operations of the corporation until it employed 5,000 persons; its stock stood at the highest point ever reached by that of any American stock company; and its goods were known and sought all over the world. In 1852 he was elected to Congress. In his later years, he depleted his fortune by putting in the best part of a million dollars, at different times, to hold up a firm of East-India merchants, in which his family had an interest. In the eulogy pronounced after his death, the Hon. Alden Speare said: "Should I say that Boston, the metropolis of New England, had lost one of its largest-minded and most honored merchants, that the largest manufacturing establishment, not only in Massachusetts, but of the world, had lost its controlling mind, and our nation had lost one whose counsels for many years have been sought after in shaping its legislation, I should then come short of the measure of the influence of the life and labors of the Hon. J. Wiley Edmands."

Opposite the old cemetery is the great Gardner-Colby estate, a yellow Italian villa on high ground, with venerable trees bordering its emerald lawns, and brilliant red masses of coleus gleaming from the old-fashioned house-gardens. This home is now occupied by the widow of Gardner Colby, who came to Newton in the year 1846. His story, in its main elements, is a familiar one in the annals of New-England life. A poor boy, son of a Maine shipbuilder who was ruined by the War of 1812, he was brought up to Boston by his widowed mother, and became an errand-boy in a grocery store; next a dry-goods clerk; then opened a dry-goods store, with five hundred dollars borrowed from his mother's slender purse; and at last became a dry-goods importer, on Kilby Street, where, in the brisk years between 1837 and 1848, he amassed a fortune, and retired from business, being then under forty years old. But two years later he and J. Wiley Edmands acquired practical control of the mills at Dedham, and Mr. Colby was for thirteen years their selling agent, in Boston. Once more he laid aside the burdens of business, and for seven years lived the tranquil and

THE RESIDENCE OF MRS. CHARLES B. PRESCOTT.
Centre Street, near Cabot, Newton.

preservative life of a country gentleman; but in 1870 the fascination of active endeavor allured him from this seclusion, and he became President of the Wisconsin Central Railroad, then being built through the savage region of 340 miles that lies between Menasha and Ashland, on Lake Superior. When this good Baptist gentleman was summoned to the white army of angels, his public bequests amounted to nearly half a million dollars, half of which went to the three great Baptist institutions of New England, Colby University, Brown University, and the Newton Theological Institution.

Near the Gardner-Colby place was the ancient home of Lieutenant John Spring, who came to America in 1634, and settled here among the earliest comers, building the first mill in town (on Smelt Brook), and filling many offices of grave dignity in the little forest republic. He was selectman, representative, lieutenant of the train-band, sealer of weights and measures, pound-keeper, tithing-man, and sweeper of the meeting-house. The homestead by Mill Lane descended to his son, Ensign John, and his grandson, Samuel, and his grandson, Samuel, Jr., who moved away into central Massachusetts, when the house, after 140 years of the Springs, passed into other hands. From this family came Samuel Spring, chaplain of Arnold's expedition to Canada, and Gardiner Spring, for over half a century pastor of the Brick Church, in New York.

Near the old cemetery was the site of the first of the many churches of the town. It was away back in the pastorate of "Matchless Mitchell," the successor of the saintly Shepard, that the people of Newton began their agitation for secession from the church at Cambridge, and were met with a firm and decided negative. In 1660 they went so far forward as to build their first church, and thereupon were freed from the Cambridge church-rates. Four years later, the church was formally and officially organized, and John Eliot, Jr., the son of the great Apostle to the Indians, received ordination, there being present in the plain little colonial meeting-house John Eliot and Richard Mather and the Elders and messengers of the churches of Roxbury and Dorchester. Here also gathered the Jacksons, and Hydes, and Prentices, and Kenricks, and Hammonds, and other chief families of this region, the membership including forty men, and an equal number of women. After the death of the eloquent and popular Eliot, in 1668, the little church fell into such dissension that the county court at Cambridge admonished it severely (in 1670), saying: "Understanding (to our great grief) that there are divisions among you, about calling and settling a minister, which thing is scandalous to our profession, and a hindrance to our edification, we, therefore, think it our duty to signify unto you our earnest desires and prayers, for your union and agreement, entreating you to put on the spirit of meekness, humility, and self-denial, and to submit to

RESIDENCE OF EZRA C. FITCH.
Sargent Street, between Centre and Park Streets, Newton.

one another, in the fear of God, and either to agree this matter among yourselves, or attend such means as God hath appointed in such cases, for the issue thereof, and acquaint us therewith, otherwise we shall take ourselves in duty bound, to use such other means, according to God, as may be expedient for a further inquiry into your case, and for the healing the breaches in your Zion." To this Elder Wiswall made answer, still in the old ecclesiastical language of decorum and stateliness: "May it please you, yours of April 5th, 1670, I received, and after serious perusal and consideration, did communicate it unto the Church; but with grief and shame may we say, we had no comfortable return to make." After a few years came the Rev. Nehemiah Hobart, who, for his services during forty years in healing these unhappy dissensions, was called "the repairer of breaches." This bringer of peace was allowed the salary of £70 a year, one-third of which should have been in money; but the payments were not fully made, and the pastor often remitted parts of his over-due stipend (meagre though it was). In 1698 the old church was abandoned, and for many years served (probably) as an armory for the local train-band, and for other civic purposes.

Opposite the old burying-ground in 1696–98 the townsmen built a new meeting-house, to replace the contiguous one founded in Eliot's day. It stood close to the Gardner-Colby house, on land probably given by John Spring, and which reverted to him when the site was abandoned. The west side of the new temple was set apart for the boys; and the east and north side pews were for women and children, "but they shall not be sold to strangers." In the house of God, distinctions of family were not recognized, and the people were seated according to age and sex. In 1721 Waltham bought the old meeting-house, and moved it into her own demesne.

The church was indeed not destined to rest for long in its new shrine, for as early as the year 1705 the Wards and other families began to agitate the parish with demands that the meeting-house should be removed. Their complaint stated that "the neerest of us are fore miles and a half, and we cante attend the publick worship in Newtown without great difikulty to us and our families, espeshely in the winter season." For many years this contest was waged, while the townspeople tried by diplomacy and argument to quiet their southern brethren. The subsequent history of the mother-church of Newton is found in the chapter on Newton Centre.

There is a tradition of buried treasure here, which has called out the efforts of many a hopeful searching party, working diligently with spades and picks, by moonlight or sunlight, but always to no purpose. Three young men of the Prentice family were supposed to have concealed a large quantity of valuables here, in the troublous days of the Revolution, near the brook north of the burying-ground. After that, they went off to the wars, and never returned.

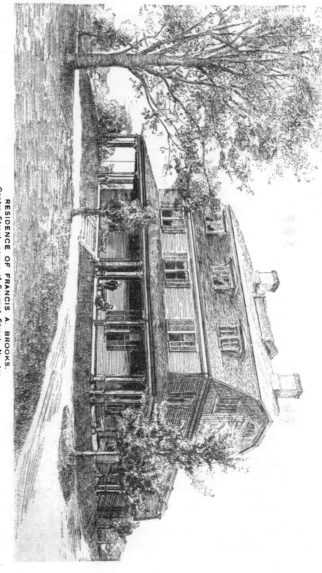

RESIDENCE OF FRANCIS A. BROOKS.
Centre Street, corner of Sargent Street, Newton.

At the corner of Centre Street and Cotton Street (the ancient *Rural Lane*) is the old cemetery,* where, amid the most peaceful surroundings of field and forest, the venerable founders of the city sleep. This domain was ceded to the town by the Jackson family, Deacon John Jackson giving one acre in 1660 for a meeting-house and burying-ground, and his son Abraham giving another acre (in 1701) for a school-house, burying-ground, and training-field. It had been a part of Deacon Jackson's twenty-acre share of the common lands of Cambridge, divided by lot to him, in 1662, and named *Chestnut Hill*. John Jackson, of the fourth generation, endeavored to reclaim the land from the town, in 1755, on the ground that no deeds had been given of it; but the actual possession had been so long vested in the people that the young man was beaten, and recovered but half an acre. In the year 1765 the burying-ground was fenced in, and thenceforward for more than a generation it served as a convenient pasture-ground for the sexton's cows, whereby many of the ancient tombstones were broken and disfigured.

The rites of sepulture were performed in those early days with great simplicity, and no less decorum. From the Town Records these items show the public provisions made for mortuary honors: —

"March 19, 1759.— VOTED, to provide a Cotton Velvet Pall to be used at funerals.

"May 11, 1763.— VOTED, to let the Velvet Pall to the inhabitants of other towns, and that those persons that shall hire said Velvet Pall shall pay half a dollar every time it is used.

"May 13, 1799.— The town was authorized to purchase two hearses for the use of the town, when in their opinion the money can with convenience be spared out of the Town Treasury."

Here was buried the Rev. John Eliot, Jr., with his wife Sarah, the daughter of Captain Thomas Willett, first mayor of New York. On Eliot's tablet is an inscription, of which this is a part: —

"Learned, pious and beloved by English and Indians. 'My dying counsel is, secure an interest in the Lord Jesus Christ, and this will carry you to the world's end.' As a preacher, lively, accomplished, zealous and accurate. He ripened fast for heaven." The Eliot monument is near the middle of the old cemetery. The Rev. John Eliot was the son of the great Apostle to the Indians, who taught him in the language of the aborigines, and made him an assistant missioner. He was settled as first pastor of Newton in 1658, when but twenty-two years old, and remained there until his death, ten years later, after preaching also to the unfortunate Indians at Ponkapag and Natick. He had the then rare accomplishment of a wide scientific knowledge, besides great proficiency in the Greek and Roman classics; and was pen-painted as a comely, cheerful, and ruddy-faced man, full of attrac-

---

* See illustrations, page 21.

THE J. WILEY EDMANDS ESTATE, THE RESIDENCE OF A. LAWRENCE EDMANDS.
Centre Street, near Sargent Street, Newton.

tiveness, and quick of apprehension. Two marble monuments of similar form, on a little green mound, mark the last resting-places of the two venerable clergymen who labored side by side for nearly half a century,— the Rev. Jonathan Homer, D.D., pastor of the First Congregational Church, and the Rev. Joseph Grafton, pastor of the First Baptist Church. Their memorials were erected by their grateful parishioners. Hobart, Cotton, and Merriam, ancient pastors of the First Church, now rest here; and with them is the Rev. Mr. Cutler, of the Eliot Church.

Here may be found also the graves of Edward Jackson, the companion of the Apostle Eliot in his missionary wanderings among the Indians; Dr. John Cotton, the son of the pastor, and Madame Mary, his mother; Francis Jackson, author of the History of Newton; Francis Skinner; the Hon. William Jackson; General Michael Jackson, of the old 8th Massachusetts Continental Regiment; Colonel M. Jackson; Major Timothy Jackson; Lieutenant Ephraim Jackson, of the 10th Massachusetts Continentals; Dr. John King, and many other men, once of high local distinction.

The tomb of General William Hull is marked by a sandstone tablet on pillars, and a weeping willow from Napoleon's grave at St. Helena.

Here rests the gallant old General, and his negro, Tillow, who was the last slave owned in Newton. And here also are the remains of Judge Abraham Fuller, and his daughter, Mrs. General Hull; and Captain Abraham Hull, who was killed in the battle of Bridgewater, in Upper Canada, in 1814.

Judge Abraham Fuller refused to be buried on his farm, saying: " I never was bought nor sold when alive, and I won't be sold after I die "— for which reason his remains were laid away in the family tomb at Newton Centre. Nine years later, the body was in perfect preservation, turned into a wood-like hardness, and of a dark color; and so many scientific persons and other curious visitors came to see this marvel, for a term of years, that the family was obliged to close the tomb with a marble door. Twenty-five years later, it was found necessary to get a new coffin, the old one having mouldered away, while still that marvellous figure remained intact.

The tablet over the remains of John Kenrick contains this brave sentence: " Early impressed with the unlawfulness, impiety and inhumanity of Slavery, and its peculiar incompatibility with republican government, he strove long and unassisted to awaken his countrymen on the subject; he wrote often and persuasively for the press; he republished gratuitously the writings of others; and if there had been 'ten' like him in these States, the stain of slavery would not have darkened another Star in the North-American Constellation." This powerful epitaph was composed by David Lee Child.

Near the east side are twenty-two mossy tablets of slate over the graves of the Wards; and near Centre Street is a long line of Jackson graves.

METHODIST EPISCOPAL CHURCH OF NEWTON.
Centre Street, corner of Wesley.

Elsewhere rest the Woodwards, the Hydes, the Kenricks, and their comrades of the ancient immigration.

In 1852 a number of the descendants of the first settlers erected here, on the site of the ancient church, a marble monument, bearing simple memorial inscriptions to the first Minister and Ruling Elder, and the donors of the land, and the names of the earliest colonists, with the dates of their settlement, and of their deaths, and their ages, as shown on this page.

The inscriptions on three sides of the monument are as follows: —

FIRST SETTLERS OF NEWTON.
Times of their Settlement and Deaths, with their Ages.

Name	Settled	Died	Age
John Jackson,	1639	1674	
Samuel Hyde,	1640	1650	79
Edward Jackson,	1643	1684	79
John Fuller,	1644	1698	87
John Parker,	1650	1686	71
Richard Park,	1647	1665	
Jonathan Hyde,	1647	1711	85
Thomas Prentice,	1649	1710	89
Vincent Druce,	1650	1678	
Thomas Hammond,	1650	1675	
John Ward,	1650	1708	82
Thomas Wiswall,	1654	1683	
Thomas Prentice, 2d.,	1650		
James Prentice,	1650	1710	81
John Kenrick,	1658	1686	82
Isaac Williams,	1661	1708	69
Abraham Williams,	1662	1712	84
James Trowbridge,	1664	1717	81
John Spring,	1664	1717	87
John Eliot,	1664	1668	33

Names on First Settlers' Monument.

"Thomas Wiswall, ordained ruling elder July 20, 1664. His son Enoch of Dorchester Died Nov. 28, 1706, æt. 73. Rev. Ichabod, minister of Duxbury, 30 yrs, Agent of Plymouth Colony in England, 1690. Died July 23. 1700, æt. 63. Capt. Noah, of Newton, an officer in the expedition against Canada, killed in battle with the French and Indians July 6, 1690, æt. 50, leaving a son Thomas. Ebenezer of Newton died June 21, 1691, æt. 45."

"Rev. John Eliot, Jr., first Pastor of the first Church, ordained July 20, 1664. His widow married Edmond Quincy, of Brain. Died in 1700. His only Daughter married John Bowles, Esq., of Roxbury, and died, May 23, 1687. His only son, John, settled in Windsor, Connecticut, where he died in 1733, leaving a son John, a student in Yale College."

"Dea. John Jackson gave one acre of land for this Burial Place and first Church which was erected upon this spot in 1660. Abraham Jackson, son of Dea. John, gave one acre, which two acres form the old part of this cemetery. Edward Jackson gave 20 acres for the Parsonage in 1660 and 31 acres for the Ministerial Wood Lot in 1681. His widow, Elizabeth, died Sept. 1809, æt. 92."

Nonantum Hill.

KENRICK PARK.— THE APOSTLE ELIOT.— THE FIRST PROTESTANT MISSION IN THE WORLD.— A REVOLUTIONARY HERO.— ONE OF CROMWELL'S RIDERS.— THE FIRST UNITARIAN OF NEW ENGLAND.

Little over half a mile from the centre of Newton village, as the roads run, is the beautiful eminence of Nonantum Hill, covered by fields and orchards and trees, very much as in the old Indian days, when Charles was King of England. On the one side opens the ravine towards Brighton Hill, and on the other is the deep defile toward Waban Hill, with two bright lakelets in its eastern opening, beneath the gray stone walls of the diocesan

The Brackett House, on Waverley Avenue. Built in 1792 by Col. Joseph Ward.

seminary for Roman Catholic clergy. From the crest of the ridge, 230 feet high, one gains a bird's-eye view of the surrounding suburbs, Charlestown and Cambridge, Somerville and Brighton, Waltham and Watertown, the wide-winding river, the distant blue sea, and far away in the west and northwest the dreamy outlines of noble mountains, Wachusett and Monadnock and their mighty brethren of the wilderness.

The northerly slope of Nonantum Hill was included in the estate of John Jackson, the pioneer, one of whose descendants married Dr. Edward Durant's only daughter, and died. This part of the estate passed to his widow (on the death of her son); and she afterwards married Reuben Moore.

Their daughter became the wife of James Ricker, of the well-known Maine family of that name; and for many years the Ricker farm, on this site, was one of the best-known regions of Newton. The daughter of this family married Edwin W. Gay (of the old Boston stationery house of Aaron R. Gay & Co.), who lives on a part of the ancestral domain on Waverley Avenue, at the head of Church Street.

Waverley Avenue runs through a large part of the old Ricker farm. At the corner of Tremont Street is the estate occupied for some years past by Professor Carlyle Petersilea, whose fame as a musician extends throughout the land. This imposing residence stands directly at the head of Vernon Street.

Edwin W. Gay's Residence, Waverley Avenue and Church Street.

At the corner of Waverley Avenue and Arlington Street is the fine large estate of George S. Bullens, President of the National Revere Bank. Around on Arlington Street are a number of beautiful homes, including those of Samuel L. Powers, Esq., attorney at law; James C. Elms, Vice-president of the National Shoe and Leather Bank; the late Hon. William S. Gardner, judge of the Supreme Court of Massachusetts; Marcellus P. Springer (Springer Brothers, the great cloak manufacturers); Samuel A. D. Shepard, president of the Massachusetts Pharmaceutical Association, etc.

Just off of Arlington Street, on Belmont Street, is the quiet home of Moses King, the publisher of a long list of valuable guide-books, particu-

RESIDENCE OF PROFESSOR CARLYLE PETERSILEA.
Waverley Avenue, corner of Tremont Street, Newton.

larly his series of "King's Handbooks," one of which is this "Handbook of Newton." On this street is also the home of William Carver Bates.

Not far from Waverley Avenue, at the corner of Durant and Pembroke Streets, is the residence of ex-Alderman David W. Farquhar, one of the delegates to the Chicago Convention of 1888, which nominated Benjamin Harrison for President.

All around this substantially built-up section may be seen the homes of well-to-do and well-known people.

In the year 1860 Nonantum Hill had only the Ricker farmhouse on its massive western shoulders, and land was worth hardly $500 an acre, where now it would command thirty times that sum. The greater part of it was covered with scrub oak, through which the wintry winds whistled mournfully. Farther to the eastward, on the ridge, Messrs. Haven and Wiggin, of Boston, erected two houses, in 1807, on a domain of seventy acres bought from General William Hull. These fine old mansions belong to Mr. Dexter D. Bowman, who dwells in one of them; and nearer the Farlow estate, on the west, is the house and domain of John J. Haley, of the Haley Manufacturing Company. Later, William Kenrick built a mansion on the Newton (or western) slope of the hill, and surrounded it with attractive grounds, embellished with rare trees which he imported from Europe. Kenrick's nurseries and farm of sixty-seven acres here included the finest collection in America of fruit and ornamental trees; and the results of his experiments in grafting, transplanting, etc., were recorded in his work, entitled "The New American Orchardist." The house was subsequently moved away, to Woodland Vale; and its site is now occupied by the beautiful mansion of the Hon. John S. Farlow, near Waverley Avenue, overlooking the great valley to the westward. Besides the most notable variety of trees and shrubbery in the country, the Farlow estate has large conservatories, farmlands, and gardens, stretching well up along the hill. Mr. Farlow is a millionaire, with great holdings in railroad securities. His benefactions to the city of Newton include the beautiful Farlow Park, the mortuary chapel at the cemetery, large sums to the Free Library, and other notable gifts.

Opposite this estate is the pleasant home of the Hon. George C. Lord, the President of the Boston & Maine Railroad, the largest system of railways in New England.

Kenrick Park, a little way to the westward, was laid out in 1845 by Alexander Wadsworth, for William Kenrick, and then bore the name of Woodland Vale. Forty house-lots were sold here at auction, on a pleasant June day of 1845, Colonel Marshall P. Wilder, Elias Hasket Derby, and other gentlemen of Boston standing for references. It is now a beautiful oval reservation, thickly covered with ancient oaks, beeches and chestnut-trees, and surrounded by pleasant country-houses. Here is the home of Nathan

RESIDENCE OF SAMUEL LEE POWERS.
Arlington Street, near Waverley Avenue, Newton.

P. Coburn, of William Claflin, Coburn & Co., the great Boston leather and boot and shoe house; and the estate of Isaac T. Burr, one of Newton's most highly esteemed and most public-spirited citizens, President of the Bank of North America, director of the Atchison road. Just beyond Kenrick Park, on Park Street, are the residences of Andrew S. March; Wallace D. Lovell, of the banking house of Potter Lovell Company; T. Edgar White, a Boston manufacturer; and ex-Alderman Warren P. Tyler.

At the corner of Franklin Street, fronting on Kenrick Park, is the charming vine-covered stone cottage home of Elestus M. Springer, the well-known cloak manufacturer.

Moses King's Residence, Belmont Street, near Arlington Street, Newton.

On Franklin Street are the beautiful homes of Levi B. Gay, publisher of the "Banker and Tradesman"; Thomas Weston, the lawyer; Charles E. Billings, the millionaire importer of drugs; Charles M. Gay, for many years engaged in the publishing business in Boston, and until within a few years one of the publishers of *Littell's Living Age;* Charles H. Buswell, a Boston merchant; and Dr. Henry M. Field, Professor of Therapeutics and Materia Medica in Dartmouth College.

Just beyond Kenrick Street, which descends the deep vale between Nonantum Hill and Waban Hill, stands the venerable colonial mansion of the Kenricks, with its odd little Gothic summer-house. Inside may be seen Colonel Ward's secretary, a quaint piano made in London in 1785,

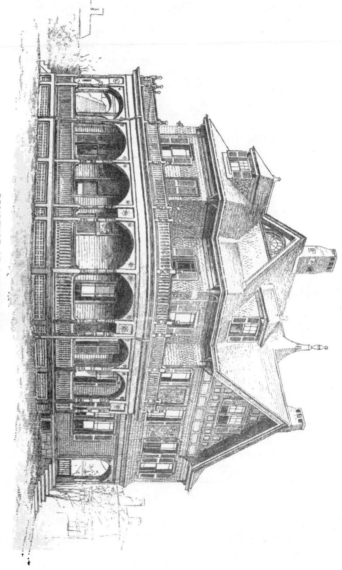

RESIDENCE OF DAVID W. FARQUHAR.
Pembroke and Durant Streets, Newton.

ancient portraits of General Hull and Dr. Freeman, and other mementos of the remote past, which elsewhere would be rare curiosities, but here are but appropriate adjuncts of the heavy wooden cornices and wainscots and massive uncovered beams of the venerable mansion. The estate is famous for its noble magnolia trees, which bring forth thousands of fragrant blossoms every May, filling the glen with a rich exotic perfume. Nearly opposite the house are several of the finest purple beeches in New England. Here, in the quiet old days of 1732, came Captain Edward Durant, a rich Bostonian, and established a country-seat, which descended to his son Edward, one of the foremost patriots of Newton, who delighted in twisting the British lion's tail with speeches and resolutions, as a Delegate to the Provincial Congress. His son, Dr. Edward Durant, went to sea during the Revolution, as a privateer, and disappeared from sight and

Kenrick House, Waverley Avenue, Newton

memory. The house was sold by the Durants to John A. Kenrick in the year 1775, and is still occupied by his posterity. This worthy family is descended from John Kenrick, who was born under the gray skies of Old England, in the year 1605, and came to Boston about thirty years later, and to Newton in 1688, where he acquired a farm of 280 broad and tangled acres. His great-great-grand-daughter was the mother of President Franklin Pierce. Another descendant was John Kenrick, President of the New-England Anti-Slavery Society, and founder of the benevolent Kenrick Fund. His orotund epitaph we may read in the old cemetery on Centre Street. Away back in the year 1817, when Wendell Phillips and William Lloyd Garrison were school-boys, and John Brown was a lad tanning hides in Ohio, John Kenrick published his fiery and impassioned little book, "Horrors of Slavery," with its preface dated "Newton."

RESIDENCE OF THE HON. JOHN S. FARLOW.
Waverley Avenue, Newton.

The first large nursery in New England was established here in 1790 by John Kenrick, who raised a great number of peach-trees from the stones, and afterwards cultivated apple, cherry and other fruit-trees. In 1797, he made a nursery of ornamental trees, including two acres of Lombardy poplars, then a highly esteemed tree. It is generally supposed that the Lombardy poplars of New England all took their origin in Newton. Mr. Kenrick admitted his eldest son, William, into partnership, and in 1833 bequeathed the business to him. William Kenrick in 1836 issued his first catalogue of trees, etc., claiming then to have thirty acres under cultivation, with half a million trees and shrubs. He had imported largely from the London Horticultural Society, from Dr. Van Mons of Louvain, and other European cultivators; and had enriched his glowing collections of flowers with specimens transplanted from Canada, Virginia and Ohio. He sold more fruit-trees than any other nursery-man in New England; and also, during the silk-culture period, raised hundreds of thousands of *Morus multicaulis* trees. William Kenrick was the author of "The New American Orchardist," a rich and exhaustive work of over four hundred pages; and also of "The American Silk-Grower's Guide."

His brother, John A. Kenrick, had his famous Nonantum Dale Nursery, away back in the early fifties, as is shown by the Annual Catalogues still preserved, and bearing on their covers a rude picture of the Israelitish spies returning from Canaan with huge bunches of grapes. This work of horticultural literature asserts that Nonantum Dale was the first Public Nursery in Massachusetts; and that it was "half a mile from the Worcester Railroad depot at Newton Corner, from whence there is a conveyance to Boston regularly six times a day." John conducted the business here after William's death (in 1860), until his own demise, in 1870.

Near Kenrick Street is the home of Charles B. Lancaster, a wealthy shoe-manufacturer of Boston, and the architect of his own great fortune.

Monument Street leads down from Waverley Avenue into the narrow and sheltered glen between Nonantum Hill and Waban Hill, and to the memorial which stands on the site of the first Protestant mission-station in the world. It bears this inscription, carved in the rock: —

HERE AT NONANTUM, OCT. 28, 1646, IN WABAN'S WIGWAM
NEAR THIS SPOT JOHN ELIOT BEGAN TO PREACH THE GOSPEL TO
THE INDIANS. HERE HE FOUNDED THE FIRST CHRISTIAN
COMMUNITY OF INDIANS WITHIN THE ENGLISH COLONIES.

WABAN.   SHEPARD.   GOOKIN.   HEATH

Thus the site of Waban's wigwam, near the cool spring of living waters, has been marked by a handsome stone terrace, with a stone balustrade, and tablets bearing the names of the first missionaries to this place. Here, in

KING'S HANDBOOK OF NEWTON.

RESIDENCE OF NATHAN P. COBURN.
Kenrick Park, Newton.

the language of the old Puritan chroniclers, "The alabaster box of precious ointment was first broken in the dark and gloomy habitations of the unclean." A fund has long been accumulating for the erection here of a statue of the ancient Puritan missionary, on the scene of his earliest triumphs. President Eliot, of Harvard University, is one of the later descendants of this noble missionary family, whose American record of quarter of a millennium is full of honor and distinction.

Waban was a Concord Indian, who advanced himself in the world by marrying Tasunsquaw, the eldest daughter of Tahattawan, sachem of Concord; and a little after the year 1630 he moved to Nonantum. Waban's wife and his son, Weegrammomenet, were attentive listeners during the preaching of the Christian teachers, and extended many pleasant services to their white brethren. The name Nonantum was given by the Apostle Eliot, when the Christian Indians asked him to christen their new town, near Waban's wigwam. He therefore selected a name from their own language "which signifies, in English, REJOICING, because they, hearing the word and seeking to know God, the English did rejoice at it, which pleased them much; and therefore that is to be the name of their town."

Here stood the wigwams of the Indians, whose hunting-grounds in happier days covered all this part of the valley of the Charles. They were a clan of the once great Massachusee tribe, and acknowledged the chieftainship of the wise and magnanimous Waban. The first settlers of Cambridge covenanted with this sachem to allow six-score head of dry cattle to graze on his meadows, he to be responsible for their safety, and to receive in return £8, to be paid mainly in Indian corn, after Michaelmas.

When John Eliot had acquired the Indian language, he made his first missionary tour (in 1646) to the home of this clan, accompanied by three other gentlemen and Christians. They were met on the way by Waban and two of his braves, Wampas and Piambouhou, who conducted them to a wigwam in which many of his tribesmen had gathered to listen to the new doctrine of the pale-faces. In a sermon of an hour's duration, the Apostle set forth the principles of Christianity, beginning with their own conceptions of natural theology; then explaining the Ten Commandments, unfolding the beautiful history of Christ's incarnation, life, suffering, and resurrection, the sorrows of Hell, the joys of Heaven, the infinite greatness of God, the absolute need of repentance and purity. Occasionally Eliot found himself at a loss for a phrase in the Indian language; and then he called to his aid Nesutan, a Long-Island Indian who had been captured by the English in war, and held as a prisoner in Dorchester, where the Apostle had taught him many things. Eliot bore witness, with much pleasure and amazement, to the facts that "none of the Indians slept in sermon, or

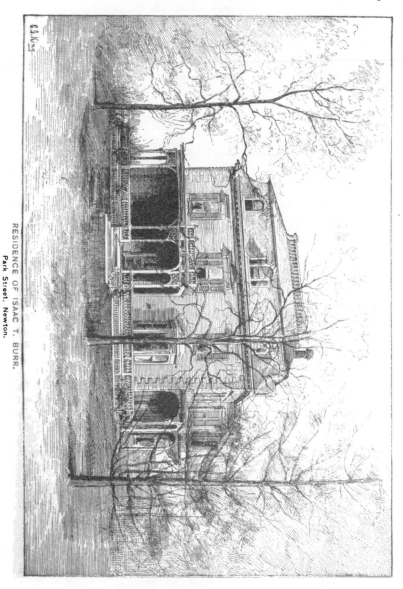

RESIDENCE OF ISAAC T. BURR.
Park Street, Newton.

derided God's messenger." After the discourse was over, the Indians propounded six questions to their visitors: —

" How could they learn to know Jesus Christ?"
" Does God understand Indian prayers?"
" Were the English ever so ignorant as the Indians?"
" What is the image of God, which, in the second commandment, is forbidden to be worshipped?"
" If the father be bad, and the child good, will God be offended with the child for the father's sake?"
" If all the world had once been drowned, how came it now to be so full of people?"

In such wise passed the first Protestant sermon in a heathen tongue, the first effort of a Protestant mission in heathendom. The solemn evangelist could not resist the opportunity of a cunning play upon words, for he chose as a text the words of Ezekiel: " Prophesy, son of man, and say to the wind, Thus saith the Lord God, Come from the four winds, O breath, and breathe upon these slain, that they may live." As the name of the chief, Waban, meant " The Wind," the text was interpreted, " Prophesy, son of man, and say unto *Waban*," etc.; so that the address appeared to have an interesting personal bearing, which gave great content to the red sachem. Many of the gravely listening audience signified their understanding of the discourse; and some hours were spent thereafter in questions and answers, in which the Indians strove to clear up doubtful and half-understood points. Subsequently, the native powahs, or priests, started a hostile movement against this rising tide of Christianity; but Eliot boldly and solemnly faced them, and brought their wiles to naught. Soon afterward, these children of the forest led their boys and girls in, and begged the Englishmen to instruct them also in the way of life. But even in that early day the sanctified teacher enunciated the idea (now every year becoming more evident) that " The Indians must be civilized, as well as Christianized." To this end he secured from the General Court permission for them to dwell on the high land at Nonantum, and furnished them with spades and mattocks, wherewith in a short time they erected a compact village of bark wigwams, each with several apartments, and surrounded with ditches and stone walls. They also constructed a commodious church, in which their visiting teachers might expound the mysteries of revealed religion. They had orchards and corn-fields, and were taught carpentry and other trades, the women learning to spin and braid baskets and make brooms. In the springtime and summer the Indian villagers sold berries and fish to their white neighbors, and thus accumulated some small funds. Here, for the first time, the aborigines of North America were made regularly amenable to English civil laws, replacing their old barbaric code with a milder and more equitable system of government.

RESIDENCE OF ELESTUS M. SPRINGER.
Park Street, corner Church Street, Kenrick Park, Newton.

At times Waban exhorted his people to follow the sweet teachings of Christianity; and another chief, wrapped in a robe of marten-skins, arose and said to Eliot: "My heart laughs for joy on seeing myself before thee; we have all of us heard the word which thou hast sent us. Come with us to the forests; come to our homes by the great river; there shall we plant the Tree of Life of which thou speakest, and our warriors shall rest beneath its leaves; and thou shalt tell us of that land where there is no storm nor death, and where the sun is always bright."

> "In a grave silence, yet with earnest eye,
> The ancient warrior of the waste stands by,
> Bending, in thoughtfulness, his proud gray head,
> And leaning on his bow."

The Indian villagers punished Sabbath-breaking and wife-beating and theft with a stringent hand. They were impatient at contention; and when one of their number found an Englishman and his wife bickering, he left the house, saying, "I will not abide here, for God does not dwell in this house, but Hobomok (the Devil)." One of them killed a cow, and sold it to the grave and unwitting officials of Harvard College for a moose, but was admonished by his brethren in meeting, and compelled to confess his fault. This was the same comical fellow who arose in one of the meetings, and cried out, "Who made sack, Mr. Eliot, who made sack?" whereat he was strenuously reprimanded by his red neighbors.

At some of the meetings, divers of the magnates of the colony presented themselves as helpers. Hither came Dunster, the President of Harvard College; Shepard, the saintly pastor of Cambridge; Allen, of Dedham; Wilson, of Boston; and other learned divines. Wampas and Totherswamp and Piambouhou and other Christian Indians, and their wives, met them, and sought anew their counsel and guidance, in all simplicity and sincerity. Waban broke out with the impassioned prayer: "Take away, Lord, my stony heart. Wash, Lord, my soul. Lord, lead me, when I die, to Heaven." When Wampas came to his death-bed, he said: "God doth give us three mercies in this world. First is health and strength; second, food and clothes; third, sickness and death. And when we have had our share in the two first, why should we not be willing to take our part in the third? For myself, I am ready." And his last words were, "O Lord, give me Jesus Christ!"

Yet there were many problems to disturb them, and the English missionaries were rounded up with such questions as these: —

"If a man be *almost* a good man, and die, whither goes his soul?"

"When the soul goes to Heaven, what doth it say when it comes there?"

"Since we see not God with our eyes, if a man dream that he see God, doth his soul then see him?"

RESIDENCE OF CHARLES M. GAY.
Franklin Street, corner Eldredge, Newton.

" If a man should be enclosed in iron a foot thick, and thrown into fire, what would become of his soul ? Could the soul come forth, or not ? "

" Why did not God give all men good hearts, that they might be good? And why did not God kill the Devil, that made all men so bad, God having all power ? "

The Lord's Prayer, as used in the Massachusee language, reads thus : —

Nooshun kesukgut guttianatamunach kooweswonk.
Peyanmooutch kukketassootamooork, kuttenaulamook ne vi, nach ohkeit neanckesukgut.
Wummectmongash asckesukokish assamamneane yeuyeu kesukok.
Kah ahquoantanaiinnean nummatcheseongash neane matcheuchukqueagig nutahquonlamounrononog.
Ahque sagkompagunaiinnean eu gutchhuaouganit, webe pohquohwussinean wutch matchitut ; newutche kutahtaurm kelassecoonk, kah menuhke·suonk, kah sohsumoonk mickeme.

In later years, Piambouhou of Nonantum became ruling elder of the native church at Hassanamesit; and, when dying, he admonished his people to "make strong their praying to God." Waban, in his old age, warned the colonists of King Philip's coming forays, and was among the sorrowful bands of Indians confined on Deer Island. He died about the year 1680, his farewell to this strange world being in these words: " I give my soul to Thee, O my Redeemer, Jesus Christ. Pardon all my sins, and deliver me from Hell. Help me against death, and then I am willing to die. And when I die, O help me and relieve me ! "

There was much strong opposition to Eliot's preaching, among the chiefs and powahs of the tribes, who, foreseeing the loss of their personal power, made fearful threats against him. But he told them: " I am about the work of the great God, and he is with me, so that I fear not all the sachems of the country. I will go on, and do you touch me, if you dare ! " The deep interest of this apostolic man in his red-skinned catechumens was partly due to the fact that he considered them to be descended from the ancient Hebrews; and, in support of this theory, he published a learned and ingenious little book.

The holy tasks of teaching and catechising went on at Nonantum for five years, until 1651, when the Indians here all moved to the new colony of Christian natives at Natick. The subsequent history of the praying Indians was one of declension and disaster. Their church was organized in 1660, and in 1670 had fifty communicants; but these had become reduced to ten in 1698, and eighteen years later the church was broken up. The tribe numbered several hundred in 1660, but sank away to 166 in 1749, 37 in 1763, and 20 in 1797. In 1826 it was extinct. The influence and mem-

RESIDENCE OF CHARLES H. BUSWELL.
Franklin Street, Newton.

ory of their first Christian leaders and converts having passed away, they became dissolute and idle, and sold their neglected lands to English comers, and so grew more and more dispirited, and faded slowly away, until they became extinct.

Two great visible results sprang from Eliot's labors in this obscure tribe. The first was the erection of several large communities of Christian Indians, including 4,000 souls, whose firm and heroic alliance prevented the New-England settlements from being blotted out a few years later, when King Philip led his confederated nations of aborigines against the feeble colony, and was met on nearly every battle-field by the fearless Indian converts, standing side by side with the English train-bands. The second was the extensive preaching of the Gospel to the natives of Ceylon and Java, which was begun by the Dutch colonists in those remote regions as soon as they heard of Eliot's success here. As another result, Cromwell's Parliament passed an act (in 1649) beginning: "Whereas the Commons of England, assembled in Parliament, have received certain intelligence from divers godly ministers and others in New England, that divers of the heathen natives, through the pious care of some godly English, who preach the Gospel unto them in their own Indian language, not only from barbarous have become civil, but many of them forsake their accustomed charms and sorceries and other satanic delusions, do now call upon the name of the Lord, and give great testimony to the power of God." It has been stated that out of this movement sprang the Society for Promoting Christian Knowledge and the Society for the Propagation of the Gospel in Foreign Parts, two vast and powerful associations, whose missionary and philanthropic enterprises have affected almost every nation.

When art becomes a part of the life of New England, there may rise up an inspired painter, to make a noble historical picture of this scene,— the devoted men of God, in their quaint Puritan garb, the children of the forest gathered around them, scarred old veterans of the Tarratine and Mohawk wars, wizened crones in deer-skin robes, fair Minnehahas of the East, and undraped little red cherubs, lovelier than Titian's North-Italian babies or Murillo's children of Valencia; on one side, the great spring of limpid water, hard by the clustered wigwams; on the other, the ancient forests of Nonantum Hill; and, over all, the dreamy splendor of Indian summer in New England.

As the author of "Nonantum and Natick" says: "Pilgrimages are made to spots far less interesting. Besides the great natural beauty of these highlands, from which may be seen river, woods, spires, roads, dwellings, colleges, gardens, and the distant capital, and the sea, the associations connected with the place lend it a peculiar charm. . . . As long as the crooked Charles flows winding to the sea, and autumn suns shine down upon Nonan-

RESIDENCE OF DR. HENRY M. FIELD.
Franklin Street, Newton.

tum, and wheresoever the Gospel is preached, shall not this, that this man Eliot hath done, be told for a memorial of him?"

> " Somewhere, we know not when:
> 'Twas after Eliot taught the red-faced men,—
> The Indian dwellers on Nonantum Hill,
> Round which the blessed memories linger still."

We turn away from these memories of a vanished nation, to trace the footsteps of those who replaced them, and who have, in their turn, long since passed away into the land which to us is so silent. Farther out on the beautiful curving line of Waverley Avenue is the old Skinner Farm, with its charming views of the western environs of Boston, Cambridge, the Back-Bay churches, and Boston Light, over the long flanks of Corey Hill, and the nearer wooded slope of Waban Hill. The estate was acquired in 1845 by the well-known Francis Skinner, of Boston, and has recently been occupied by the handsome modern residences of Messrs. George S. Harwood, William H. Emery, Charles E. Johnson, Nathan P. Cutler, George A. Hull, George E. Hatch, and Otis Norcross Howland.

Back of this group of modern palaces stands the fine old white house of Frederick W. Sargent, with four white and black chimneys and a notable entrance-hall, lined with columns. This place was built in 1805, on an estate of eighty acres bought from Obadiah Curtis, by his grandson, Dr. Samuel Clarke, the father of James Freeman Clarke and step-son of Dr. James Freeman. After some years of absence, Dr. Clarke returned to Newton in 1811, and practised medicine here, living in the old Obadiah-Curtis house, and riding his professional rounds through Watertown and Brighton and Brookline. At a later date, Mr. Curtis repurchased the place, and gave it to his daughter, Martha, the wife of Dr. Freeman and grandmother of James Freeman Clarke. The courtly old rector of King's Chapel made it his country-house for twenty-five years, entertaining many distinguished guests from all parts of the world. Dr. Freeman was a scholar of Priestley and Belsham, and an intimate friend of Hazlitt. It became a matter of course, then, that his adhesion to orthodoxy gave way; and, when the Bishop refused to ordain him, he received induction from the wardens of King's Chapel, in 1787. There he remained for nearly forty years, assisted, in the later decades, by Samuel Cary and F. W. P. Greenwood. Dr. Freeman prepared for the use of his people a liturgy based upon that of the Anglican Church. In 1826 he gave up his city parish and retired to Newton, where he tranquilly awaited Death for nine years, and at last welcomed his coming. He was the first man who preached Unitarianism, under that name, in America. Of his own life here, the saintly Dr. Clarke said: "I consider myself fortunate in having been brought up in the country. Until I was ten years old, I lived in Newton, having been adopted by my grandfather, James Freeman.

RESIDENCE OF T. EDGAR WHITE.
Park Street, Newton.

My father and mother, my sister, and four brothers lived near by, in the same town; and my grandfather Hull also lived in Newton, so that as a boy I had three homes in the place. My grandfather Freeman's house was on high ground, and from its windows the eye ranged east, over valleys and hills, as far as the ocean; and, with one sweep, we saw a part of Boston, all Charlestown, Cambridge, Watertown, on to the hills of Weston. As I lay in my bed at night, I could see Boston Light through a little gap in the Brighton woods. There were only farms and woods around us, and I grew up enjoying all country pleasures, — learning to ride, swim, skate, and rambling about the fields, exploring the region for ponds and brooks, where a few speckled trout were still to be found. I am grateful that my mind was thus early fed on nature."

Amid his theological and philanthropic labors, Dr. Freeman solaced his summer days with pleasant experiments in horticulture and fancy farming. The first tomatoes in Massachusetts were raised here, in 1830, from seed that Dr. Freeman brought from Baltimore. The people did not understand how to eat them, and began very inauspiciously by frying them, while still very green and hard. The good doctor objected earnestly to the usual custom of supplying farm-hands with rum, and induced his Jonathans and Jehosaphats to forego their drams by paying them a dollar a month extra.

In this vicinity, in a humble cottage on Waverley Avenue, Roger Sherman was born, in 1721. He learned his father's trade of cordwainer, besides many other things of greater moment, that enabled him to make a notable name for himself in his adopted state of Connecticut, where he became deacon, judge, Representative, signer of the Declaration of Independence, and Senator of the United States. We have it on the authority of Thomas Jefferson that "he never said a foolish thing in his life." Among his descendants are Senator Wm. M. Evarts of New York and Senator George F. Hoar of Massachusetts.

Nearly opposite this group of costly modern houses (across Waverley Avenue) stands the ancient and deserted mansion of Colonel Joseph Ward, with its colonnaded portico, and long carriage-sheds in the rear. There is an extensive view from its ruinous piazzas, including the State House, Bunker-Hill Monument, and bits of the blue sea in the far east. Joseph Ward, the son of a Newton farmer, was born in 1737, and became a prominent educator in the old Bay Province. He opened an English Grammar School in Boston, next to the Treasury Office, where, according to the advertisement in the Boston *Gazette*, he taught " Reading, Writing, Arithmetic, English Grammar, Logic, Composition, Polite Letter Writing, on business, friendship, etc. Price, fifteen shillings per quarter." He enjoyed an intimacy with Adams, Otis, Hancock, and other patriots, and wrote many brilliant political papers for the Provincial journals. On the out-

RESIDENCE OF WALLACE D. LOVELL.
Park Street, Newton.

break of war, he became aide-de-camp (the first aide-de-camp ever appointed in an American army), and secretary to General Artemas Ward, and served at Bunker Hill. In 1777 the Continental Congress appointed him Commissary-General of Musters; and a year later the British incarcerated him in one of their strongholds, where he wrote his celebrated poem, "The American Prisoner," closing with these lines: —

> "Each future sun sees WASHINGTON,
> In peace and triumph ride,—
> Each brilliant star shines from afar,
> Propitious o'er his head.
>
> "On Fame's bright wing fresh laurels spring,
> And round the hero shine;
> While angels write with sunbeams bright,
> His deeds in verse divine!"

When he left the service, in 1780, Washington wrote to him: "You have my thanks for your constant attention to the business of your department, the manner of its execution, and your ready and pointed compliance with all my orders, and, I cannot help adding, on this occasion, for the zeal you have discovered, at all times and under all circumstances, to promote the good of the service in general, and the great objects of our cause."

In later years Colonel Ward opened a land-office and brokerage business in Boston, with Nathaniel Prime as his clerk and a member of his family. In 1792 he retired from business, and erected this spacious mansion, which he named "Chestnut Hill," overlooking Boston and its environs; and here the gray veteran hoped to enjoy the tranquil life of a country gentleman, during his declining years. But Destiny proved unkind to the weary sexagenary. He lost his fortune within ten years by the dishonest legislation of Georgia and Mississippi, and by indorsements; and was compelled to sell his estate to Charles Coolidge, son of Joseph Coolidge, a wealthy Boston merchant, and move to Boston. After Mr. Coolidge's death, in the year 1810, the estate was bought by Charles Brackett, to whose descendants it still pertains.

A little way beyond the ancient Ward place, on the same side of Waverley Avenue, and at the corner of Cotton Street, extends the rich modern estate of Mrs. Mary T. Goddard. Next south, at the corner of Ward Street and Waverley Avenue, was the house of Thomas Harbach (who came to Newton in 1805) still standing, after 120 years, and owned by the Harbach family, who dwell in the next house to the eastward, on the same side of Ward Street. The older house has high wainscots, uncovered beams in the living rooms, and other delightful evidences of antiquity. It was built about the year 1760, by Captain John Clark, on the old lot of Captain John Prentice. Opposite the Harbach place

RESIDENCE OF GEORGE S. HARWOOD,
Ivanhoe Street, Nonantum Hill, Newton.

once stood Captain Hammond's house, in which, as far back as the year 1825, the sessions of the Newton Theological Institution were begun. Until 1809 a public school-house stood near the Harbach house, on this fair rural demesne. One day a mischievous lad climbed up on the roof and lowered a fishing-line and hook down the chimney, and another waggish confederate managed to slip the hook into old Master Hovey's wig, which flew away up the chimney, to the vast amazement of the pedagogue.

On the Harbach site dwelt for half a century, from 1663, the valiant old trooper, Captain Thomas Prentice, who had been one of Cromwell's iron soldiers against King Charles, and who, in later years, commanded a company of Massachusetts cavalry in the war against King Philip, and raided gallantly throughout the doomed Narragansett country. When Sudbury was assailed by the savages, and well-nigh overpowered, it was Prentice who galloped into the burning town with a band of his rough-riding troopers, and rescued the beleaguered garrison. But after the war was over the Indians turned to him as their best friend, and he kept one of the Nipmuck sachems and a band of warriors at his house for a long time. The tribes at Natick, Ponkapoag, Wamesic, and other places petitioned the General Court (in 1691) to make him their ruler. Prentice and his dragoons composed the escort sent to lead Sir Edmund Andros a prisoner into Boston, after that hot-headed cavalier had well-nigh escaped from Massachusetts. The old captain's courage was so great that he seemed to know no fear. One day a huge bear made a foray into his domain, during haying time, and fiercely attacked one of the farm-hands. The trembling yokel kept his assailant at bay with a pitchfork, until Prentice ran up with an axe, and despatched the shaggy intruder. Until the very last, the old trooper remained in the saddle, riding through the wild Newton glens; and at the age of 89 this Prince Rupert of the colonies met his death by a fall from a horse; and the company of troopers followed his remains to the grave. His son was a member of the company, with carbine and pistols and cutlass; and his grandson, Captain Thomas Prentice, inherited the old estate, where he held slaves, and cherished the sword. It was on his grave that this quaint verse was written: —

> " He that's here interr'd needs no versifying,
> a vertuos life will keep ye name from dying,
> he'll live, though poets cease the'r scrib'ling rime,
> when y't this stone shall mouldred be by time."

Back of the Harbach place is the old mansion of Obadiah Curtis, a valiant patriot of the Revolutionary era, and a member of the famous Boston Tea-Party. He was so detested by the Royalists that on the outbreak of hostilities he feared to remain here, within a half-hour's gallop of the British light cavalry, and took refuge in Providence until the siege of

RESIDENCE OF CHARLES E. JOHNSON.
Ivanhoe Street, Nonantum Hill, Newton.

Boston was over. He died in 1811, and was buried in the old cemetery on Centre Street.

In this same region of heroes dwelt Ebenezer Brown, a minute-man in the company commanded by President John Adams's brother; sergeant in Bailey's 2d Massachusetts Regiment; shot through the body by Burgoyne's yagers; an ensign in Vose's 1st Massachusetts; a veteran of Lafayette's Virginia campaigns; and then for sixty years a citizen of this fair and breezy upland.

Another of Newton's warriors was Nathaniel Seger, who fought at Bunker Hill; helped build Fort Montgomery on the Hudson; served through the Canadian campaigns, the Saratoga battles, and the Rhode-Island campaign of 1778; and was led a captive by the Indians from Bethel, Maine, to Canada, in 1781, together with two other Newton-born pilgrims, Lieutenant Jonathan Clark and Benjamin Clark.

Turning abruptly from this era of hauberks and morions and spontoons to the practical comforts of to-day, let us notice that one of the most interesting features of the Cochituate Aqueduct is the great tunnel on the Harbach estate, east of Waverley Avenue, cut through 2,410 feet of intensely hard porphyritic rock. The work was furthered by two shafts, 84 feet deep, sunk from the surface of the ground to the bottom of the tunnel.

Not far from the region which we have now reached in our ramble, the gray spires of Newton Centre may be seen on one side, and on the other side rises the reservoir on high Waban Hill. All around stretch peaceful farm-lands, running along the fair plateau, and fringed with lines of ancient trees.

Newtonville.

HULL'S CROSSING.— OLD-TIME SCHOLARS.— THE VILLAGE SQUARE. THE NEWTON CLUB.— WASHINGTON PARK.— THE HIGH SCHOOL.— THE CLAFLIN ESTATE.— GEN. WILLIAM HULL.— SLAVERY IN NEWTON.— BULLOUGH'S POND.— THE NEWTON CEMETERY. HEROES OF THE LAST AMERICAN WAR.

As one rambles westward from Newton, past the Jackson estate and the tall Church of Our Lady, in a mile or two he enters another quiet and cleanly village, known as Newtonville, which may be interpreted as the

General Hull's House, Walnut Street, Newtonville. Now the Newton Club.

City of the Town that is New. And a few of the things that the friendly explorer may find here we shall set down, briefly, and in order. It is a place of about 2,500 inhabitants, covering the plain between the Cheesecake Brook and Cold-Spring Brook, along the line of the rushing and thundering Albany Railroad. It has four comfortable little churches, a dozen or more of shops, and several score of pleasant and quiet homes, strewn fortuitously about in a region of trees and lawns and rural streets. It is generally believed that a large amount of capital from this village is invested in Western mines, which may give a certain romantic glamour to the place, as including among its appanages Led-Horse Claims and Coyote Cañons and Calamity Lodes far away among the dark Rockies. There was a time, too, when there was a First National Bank here; but this financial institution came to grief, a score or more years ago, and sank away in the Lethe of insolvency.

The ville is much younger than most of its sister-villages, as was shown by Dr. S. F. Smith, when he wrote his biography of Father Grafton, and spoke of "the villages of Newton Corner, Newton Centre, West Newton, and the Upper and Lower Falls, and the incipient settlements of Auburndale and Newtonville." Indeed, it was not until the year 1842 that John Bullough erected at the railway crossing a small building for the storage of grain and meal, ground at his mill, up where old Ensign Spring founded the colonial grist-mill; and the infrequent passengers who wished to take the cars here were admonished to shake the little station-flag, as a signal for the engineers to stop. The locality was then known as "Hull's Crossing," from its contiguity to the home of General William Hull, and the intersection of the old county highway by the then new Worcester Railroad. The seclusion and quietness of the little hamlet attracted to it men of studious tastes, who to some extent moulded its future destinies. Here dwelt Joseph William Jenks, one of the editors of the "Comprehensive Commentary on the Bible," graduate of the Royal School of Languages at Paris, founder of the first agricultural paper in Ohio, life-member of the American Oriental Society, etc. He was chaplain of the war-ship "Concord," under Commodore Perry, before the foundation of the Naval Academy at Annapolis; and taught the science of mathematics to many bright midshipmen, including three who afterwards became Rear-Admirals,— Alden, Almy, and Rogers. He was an extraordinary linguist, with a practical knowledge of thirty languages, so that he might have found himself more at home in Naples or Nijni-Novgorod than in this quiet Yankee glen.

Another dweller here for some years was F. J. Campbell, some time conspicuous in the Perkins Institution for the Blind, and later the founder and President of the Royal Normal College and Academy of Music for the Blind, at London.

Another was Charles Barnard, famous and praiseworthy as the founder of the evening-schools of Boston, which he established at first in the Warren-Street Chapel.

With a few such citizens as these, and land held at a low rate, and easy

RESIDENCE OF EX-GOVERNOR WILLIAM CLAFLIN.
Walnut Street, near Cabot Street, Newtonville.

transit to and from Boston, Newtonville advanced heartily, in houses and population, and was strong enough to wage a hot war with its venerable neighbor, West Newton, for the possession of the Town Hall, and to secure the High School as a token of its local spirit.

Close to the station, on the north, opens the quiet and eventless public square of the village, — an irregular open space, containing a small flag-staff and watering-trough, and surrounded by the emporiums of local commerce, — the markets and other shops, the apothecaries, the Post-office, and the hall of the Nonantum Cycling Club. It is all very neat, comfortable, and commonplace, but fortunately there is not much of it; and, beyond, the half-rural streets fare away in every direction over the plain. On one side of the *plaza* is the office of the real-estate agent, by whose aid people are inducted into "suburban residences" hereabouts; and opposite, amid the wooden Gothic glories of Central Block, the undertaker has his rooms, and stands ready to conduct others to the portals of a city that is fairer than Newtonville. On another side are the railway gates, which appear to be forever shutting downward, or opening into the air, to the accompaniment of a rataplan by the warning gongs. Down the street to the eastward stands the wooden building occupied by the Central Congregational Church, a late-comer into the ecclesiastical life of the village. It began in a series of local prayer-meetings, in the year 1867; and a year later took possession of the chapel, which the Methodist brethren had abandoned in favor of their finer temple of brick. The pastors of this growing flock have been: the Rev. Joseph B. Clark, from 1868 to 1872; the Rev. James R. Danforth, in 1873 and 1874; the Rev. E. Frank Howe, from 1876 to 1882; the Rev. Frank W. Gunsaulus, 1883 to 1885; and the Rev. Pleasant Hunter, Jr., who was installed in 1886. More than once the church has had to be enlarged, to accommodate the rising tide of modern Puritans, fleeing from the mild provincial babel of Boston to this serene rural vicinage. The church has more than 300 members, with a still larger number in the Sunday-school.

Farther eastward on the same street, and close to the old haunts of the great Jackson family, gauntly rises the tall and lonely-looking Church of Our Lady Help of Christians, built in 1873–75, by a newly-formed society of Roman Catholic worshippers. The Rev. Michael Dolan is the priest in charge of this parish. To the west of the church stands the large brick house of the priests. In 1803 there was not a house on the south side of Washington Street, between Newton Corner and West Newton. At that time, Colonel William Trowbridge built the old house near the corner of Crafts Street, and thus began the development of the village.

On Brooks Avenue was for a time the home of one of our most famous Irish-American poets, James Jeffrey Roche, for years the mirth-provoking secretary of the Papyrus Club. He is widely known by his inimitable poem, "The V-A-S-E," and other similar *jeux d'esprits;* and to more serious thinkers by his strong and ringing poems on Ireland, and about earnest religious themes. His muse found the surroundings of Newtonville too sensible for *persiflage*, and too happy for tragic legend, or else these dull pages might have been lightened up with many a welcome flame of wit and wonder. The dwelling occupied by Mr. Brooks, on Brooks Avenue, dates from the year 1680, and used to be known as the Sturtevant house.

The people of Newtonville are much given to society rituals, for here are the headquarters of Charles-Ward Post (No. 62) of the Grand Army of the Republic, meeting fortnightly; the Goddard Literary Union, meeting also fortnightly; the Every-Saturday Club, with 40 members; the Newton High-

Swedenborgian Church, Highland Avenue, Newtonville.

School Lyceum; the Newton Philatelic Society; the Newtonville Woman's Guild; the Nonantum Cycling Club; the Young Men's Literary and Debating Society; the Dalhousie and Fraternity Lodges of Masons, chartered respectively in 1861 and 1875, and meeting in Masonic Hall; the Gethsemane Commandery of Knights Templar; the Union Masonic Relief Association; the Eliot Lodge of Knights of Honor, etc.

The Charles-Ward Post 62, G. A. R., was organized July 21, 1868, with 10 charter members and a total membership of 70. The first meeting took place in Middlesex Hall, Newton; and Captain William B. Fowle became the first commander. His successors were General J. Cushing Edmands and General A. B. Underwood, in 1869; Charles P. Clark and Captain

W. W. Carruth, in 1870; Captain Geo. F. Brackett, in 1871 and 1872; Major F. D. Graves, in 1872; Lieutenant Hosea Hyde, in 1873 and 1874; Wm. C. Emerson and D. A. Conant, in 1875 and 1876; Thomas Pickthall, in 1877; Captain W. W. Carruth, in 1878; Lieutenant H. W. Downs, from 1879 to 1883; W. A. Wetherbee, from 1883 to 1886; W. H. Park, Jr., in 1886; Austin T. Sylvester, in 1887 and 1888; and Rodney M. Lucas, in 1888. The post numbers 129 men; and during its 20 years of existence it has disbursed in charities nearly $20,000.

The new Linwood Park, between Walnut Street, Crafts Street, and Linwood Avenue, was founded by the contribution of $2,000 by citizens in the vicinity, with a handsome donation by W. J. Towne, and a subsidy of $1,000 from the city. It will be one of the ornaments of Newton, when all its decorations are complete.

The most conspicuous object in Newtonville, as one lands at the railway station, amid its pleasant gardens, is the tall church of the Methodists, making a brave show over the green lawns, with its honest, round-arched architecture, and its massive brick tower and public clock. It was begun before the War, by a Baptist society, which events forced to abandon the work part-finished. In later days this comfortable structure belonged to the Newtonville Lyceum; and then it passed into the possession of an evanescent society of Unitarians. Meanwhile, the little Methodist class that had begun its devotional meetings in the panic year of 1857 had waxed strong and hopeful, and built for itself the chapel now occupied by the Central Congregational Church. This also was outgrown in a brief period; and in the year 1863 the society bought their present church, and entered upon its prosperous possession.

The pastors have been the Rev. G. W. Mansfield (1860-61), the Rev. Z. A. Mudge (1862), the Rev. Henry Baker (1863-64), the Rev. George Prentice (1865-66), the Rev. Wm. M. Ayres (1867), the Rev. C. L. Eastman (1868-69), the Rev. John D. King (1870), the Rev. J. S. Wheedon (1871), the Rev. Frederick Woods (1872-74), the Rev. John Smith (1875), the Rev. Wm. L. Lockwood (1876), the Rev. L. R. Thayer (1877), the Rev. Elias Hodge (1878), the Rev. T. W. Bishop (1879-81), the Rev. Daniel Dorchester, Jr. (1882-83), and the Rev. Raymond F. Holway (1884-86).

Opposite, at the corner of Walnut and Austin Streets, is the old General-Hull house, moved here in 1846 from the site of ex-Governor Claflin's residence. For some years the house was occupied by the famous private school of Mrs. Weir. It then became the home of Mrs. John L. Roberts, a leader in the literary and social circles of the village; and many a notable reception and parlor lecture took place within its hospitable walls. In 1886 the mansion was bought by the Newton Associates, who erected on this adjacent land a brick block, for shops and offices. In the summer of 1887 the old house became the home of the Newton Club, then just organized, and now the swell social organization of the city, affording at its receptions the pleasant neutral ground where all ward rivalries and political dissensions are forgotten.

Entering the club-house from a broad piazza, one finds himself in a large square hall, with its old-fashioned stairway. To the right is the spacious parlor. It is brilliantly lighted by a handsome chandelier, in the shape of candelabra of cut glass and gilt. Upon the walls are a number of fine engravings, etchings, and photographs. A Chickering upright grand piano, near which stands a handsome piano lamp, is a noticeable piece of furniture. Across the hallway is the library, with its fireplace, broad oak tables, and comfortable arm-chairs. Adjoining the library and opening into the hall is the dining-room. On the second floor is the secretary's office. Over the parlor is the billiard room, and a larger room for social purposes. There are several of these apartments, one of which is brightened by a bay-window, and is used for cards. One of the prettiest rooms is the pool-room. In addition there are bath-rooms, kitchens, and pantries. Ample accommodations for horses and vehicles are provided in stables in the rear.

Just beyond the club-house on Walnut Street, between Highland Avenue and Austin Street, the magnificent residence of Austin R. Mitchell attracts universal attention. It is one of Samuel J. Brown's best architectural efforts, being a very interesting free treatment of old Colonial forms of building.

Not far distant, on Highland Avenue, stands the meeting-house of the New-Church Society, which originated in a series of parlor-meetings, established about the year 1850, and after 1857 held in various halls, under the preaching of John Worcester. The little chapel now occupied received its dedication in 1869, when a society was formed, which has since doubled in membership and has about seventy communicants. In 1886 a handsome stone building was erected, back of the chapel, for social and parochial purposes.

John Worcester, the first minister of the New Church Society in Newton, lives on Highland Avenue, not far from the church. On the same thoroughfare, are the homes of Stephen A. Schoff, the celebrated engraver and etcher, Henry H. Carter, the stationer, Dr. Edward A. Whiston, Ellis W. Redpath, Francis A. Dewson, and other well-known gentlemen. Here, too, is the charming cottage known as the "Heathcote," the home of Daniel C. Heath, the publisher, and his wife, Mary Knox Heath, the author of many standard school-books, such as "Mrs. Knox's Grammars," etc.

On Otis Street is the pretty residence of Charles Curtis, the sewing-silk merchant. Farther up the hill, on Alpine Street, near Mt. Vernon Street, is the home of Francis A. Waterhouse, for a number of years principal of the Newton High School and now head master of the Boston English High School.

Murray Street runs out from Newtonville through a short belt of pretty modern homes, across Highland Avenue, and past the cricket-ground and the old factory under the ridge. The steep slopes of West-Newton Hill crowd along the west; and presently the street fades into a rough, winding, and picturesque country lane, running between rows of wild shrubbery, and ascending the pass between West-Newton Hill and the heights about Bullough's Pond, with pleasant rolling grass-lands, ancient orchards, and august bits of tall forest, forming a charming park-like country. As it approaches its end, a line of bold and picturesque crags appears on the right, commanding from their summits a pretty view over the villages and hills to the southward. In the old days these bastions of Nature's masonry were called "Tom's Rocks," from some now forgotten legend of the redoubtable Tom Bullough, the predaceous Rob Roy Macgregor of Newton.

The wooded plateau beyond is traversed by quiet forest-paths, amid whose solitudes one can ramble for hours, sometimes coming out on old and overgrown roads, now for a time usurped by sweet-fern and scrub-oak. It was this bit of delicious wilderness to which the name of "Sylvan Heights" was given, some years ago, when optimistic land-owners hoped to renew here the beauties of Auburndale and Chestnut Hill.

Alongside the spacious Claflin School, back on Walnut Street, diverges the little park, or boulevard, laid out by Dustin Lancey, in 1865, and extending almost to the clear waters of Cold-Spring Brook. This is the long-drawn Washington Park, a green ellipse a sixth of a mile long and sixty feet wide, bordered on both sides by pretty houses, each in its little greenery of home domain.

The whole is watched over by a small but handsome stone church in Elizabethan Gothic architecture, appertaining to the Universalist denomination. The society dates from 1870, and has 60 members and a congregation of 200, the pastors having been the Rev. J. Coleman Adams (1872–80), the Rev. C. Ellwood Nash (1881–84), and the Rev. Rufus A. White. The church was dedicated in 1873, having cost $20,000. The society fell heir to the silver communion-service which had once belonged to the First Universalist Church of Boston, and afterwards to the Newton and Watertown Universalist Society, organized in 1827 and dissolved about forty years later. In this historic service is a silver cup that was brought from England by the Rev. John Murray, the founder of Universalism in America. The Hon. J. Wesley Kimball, for some years past the mayor of Newton, and who declined to be re-elected in 1888, dwells on Washington Park. A little way from the end of Washington Park, about the corner of Harvard Street and Newtonville Avenue, is the great mansion, with its conservatory

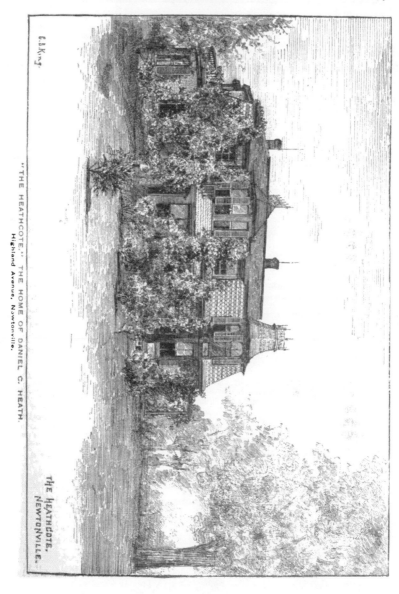

"THE HEATHCOTE," THE HOME OF DANIEL C. HEATH. Highland Avenue, Newtonville.

and gardens, of Fayette Shaw, of the famous leather-tanning firm of F. Shaw & Brothers. On Cabot Street, close to Walnut Street, is the home of the Hon. John W. Dickinson, the Secretary of the State Board of Education.

Less than half a mile from the railway station, on Walnut Street rises the Newton High School, a spacious and commodious structure, whose increasing wants were met by a noble enlargement in the year 1886. Here, also, are kept the valuable collections in natural history, made by S. R. Urbino, affording many objects of interest for the study of the pupils. Pleasant lawns extend around the buildings; and during school-hours the walls are lined with tall bicycles, on which the boys come to the scene of their studies. The High School was established in 1859, after ten years of arguments, pro and con, and immediately sprang into full and successful operation, so that it has had to be enlarged several times, and has graduated hundreds of students. Its collections of casts and other objects to assist in art education are unexcelled in the State, and afford exceptional facilities for the arousing of interest in sculpture, architecture, and the kindred arts. The situation of the school, on the broad and quiet Walnut Street, close to the park-like Claflin domain, is peculiarly advantageous; and, every morning of the educational year the lads and lasses of Newton are seen wending their way hither by scores, those from the remoter villages coming in barges or by the railway trains.

An interesting feature of the high-school curriculum is the military drill, in which the lads are carefully instructed, being formed into a well-disciplined, armed, and uniformed battalion. B. P. Shillaber says : —

"The Newton High School has a wide reputation for excellence of quality as regards scholarship, and its classes are composed of the most wide-awake boys and girls that ever a community produced. They are awake for all expedients for fun or profit outside the curriculum, and carry their school-teaching beyond the limit of school requirements,— extending to class-parties, concerts, dramatic exhibitions, a school paper, all of which tend to keep the school fire burning out of school; and, lastly, the entire school has formed into a parliamentary society, which will do great good and is worthy of imitation, for the discussion of great questions on local or general topics. A regular parliament is chosen from the entire school (not recognizing the feminine right to speak, however), from the chancellor to the lowest secretary, before which the subjects are brought for argument, which is conducted, pro and con, with great vigor; and then it is submitted to the vote of the entire school for its judgment. If the ministry is sustained, it retains its position; if the reverse is the fact, they resign the government and a new ministry is chosen, according to the English mode. The greatest interest is thus secured, and 'full benches' is the order. The parliament incites to study guiding rules, precedents, history, creates confidence and readiness to meet the requirements of keen debate, and affords practical instruction for the duties of active life. It is a capital educator in its way."

The school system of Newton has grown nobly, from the day, in 1699, when the first little school-house, 16 x 14 feet in size, was built, and John

Staples became teacher, holding his scholastic sessions four days in each week, for a stipend of two shillings a day. The parents of that time were obliged to pay threepence a week for each child learning to read, and fourpence for each student of the higher mysteries of writing and ciphering. How vast has been the change, from those little huts to the great school houses of Newton to-day, in which upwards of 3,000 students are found in attendance! In the World's Exposition at Vienna, Newton received a Diploma of Merit for its school system; and equal honors were awarded it at the Paris Exposition.

Charles Curtis's Residence, Otis Street, Newtonville.

Just beyond the High School begins Brooklawn, the great estate of ex-Governor Claflin, with its broad sweeps of greensward and meadows, and groups of noble trees, and the mansion fairly sequestered from the road, beyond the limpid ponds of Cold-Spring Brook. In this princely home Harriet Beecher Stowe, John Greenleaf Whittier, James Freeman Clarke, President Hayes, Chief-Justice Chase, and other notables have been welcome guests; and the old-time chieftains of the Free-Soil party have held their deliberations, what time their cause seemed hopeless. Its present lord, William Claflin, was born in an old Milford farmhouse, away back in 1818, and received his education at the Milford Academy and in a year's study at Brown University. His convictions compelled him to advocate Abolitionism and abstinence, and he fought the fight so well in behalf of these reforms that Hopkinton kept him in the General Court from 1848 to 1852. Three years later, he moved to the Hull estate, in Newtonville, and was chosen to the State Senate, of which he became President in 1861.

Then for three years he held the office of Lieutenant-Governor, in good time receiving his promotion to the governorship of Massachusetts, which he administered from 1869 to 1871. Five years later, he went into the Congress of the United States, where he served the interests of his people and his principles with noteworthy fidelity and efficiency.

This Claflin estate should be called the "Farm of the Governors," since no fewer than four of its owners have borne that title of dignity and responsibility. The first recorded owner was Thomas Mayhew, an old Southampton merchant, who lived for some years at Watertown, and then secured from the Earl of Stirling a grant of the Island of Martha's Vineyard, of which he held the governorship for forty years. The prince-evangelist of the Massachusetts islands had no use for his farm up in the valley of the Charles, although it was a fair domain of five hundred acres, stretching from Brighton Hill nearly to West Newton; and so he sold it, in 1638, for a trifling matter of six cows. The purchaser was Simon Bradstreet, a scholar of old Emanuel College and sometime steward of the Countess of Warwick's estates, who afterwards held the governorship of Massachusetts for ten years, before and after the despotic reign of Sir Edmund Andros. In 1646 he sold his Newton lands to Edward Jackson for £140; and, since the market value of a cow in those days was about £9, he made a neat profit of nearly 200 per cent. Subsequently this part of the estate passed into the possession of General William Hull, for many years Governor of Michigan Territory; and in 1854 (after Mrs. Hull's death) it was acquired by William Claflin, whose services as Governor of the Commonwealth of Massachusetts are still fresh in memory. The scene savors more of Old England than of New England, in its perfect finish and repose, its park-like cultivation, and the evident antiquity of its civilization. In ancient times it was the home of the Fuller family, one of the most powerful of the local clans, which was founded by John Fuller, one of the first emigrants from England, who acquired a great estate of a thousand acres, and lived near Cheesecake Brook. His son was Captain Joseph Fuller, who received as his wife's dowry, from her father, Edward Jackson, twenty acres of land, to which two hundred more were added by his father, making a broad and dignified domain, on which he erected his home, about the year 1680. Captain Joseph Fuller held the command of the Newton Troop of Horse, and in 1735 gave to them a training-field, which was discontinued half a century later, and reverted to Judge Fuller. The old cavalry captain

THE UNIVERSALIST CHURCH.
Washington Park, near Walnut Street, Newtonville.

was quick with his weapons of war; and until 1830 there hung in the mansion a pair of branching horns, whose original owner, a fine tall buck, was shot by him, from the doorway of his farmhouse. He had been the recipient of town-bounties for slaying wolves, in the adjacent Trosach-like forests; and many a gallant deer thereabouts fell before the shot from his trusty flintlock. The estate descended from Captain Joseph to his son, Joseph, and his grandson, Abraham, one of the chief men of the county, and a descendant, also, of Abraham Jackson, whose father was the first settler of Newton. Judge Fuller was a man of great size, with a voice that was often heard from Newtonville to Angier's Corner, and even to Watertown. In his full-bottomed powdered wig and queue, and green homespun coat with broad gold buttons, and lace-bordered and hugely ruffled shirt, he presented a noble appearance in the eyes of his frugal neighbors, and won their easy suffrages for high offices in the community. It was he who changed the name of the town from Newtown to NEWTON, of his own motion; and, since he held the town-clerkship for many years, he was enabled to make the new title official.

This ancient house was erected in 1776, as an addition to the farmhouse that was nearly a century old. General Hull built the front addition in 1814, having won the estate by the easy process of marrying Sarah, Judge Fuller's daughter; and solaced his leisure hours by adding six rooms to the mansion.

The old house was removed in 1846 from its place on the present site of Governor Claflin's house to the vicinity of the railway station. It is now occupied by the Newton Club.

It was on this estate that General Hull passed the sad declining years of his life, after he had been tried by court-martial for treason and cowardice, and sentenced to death on the latter charge. His offence had been the surrender of Detroit and its garrison to the British General Brock, while he held the positions of commander of the North-western army and Governor of Michigan. Cut off by a British fleet on the lakes and hordes of hostile Indians in the Ohio forests, with less than a thousand effective men in his garrison, and suffering under a fierce bombardment, he deemed it wisest to avert useless bloodshed, and save the infant settlements from the tomahawk, by capitulating to the united Anglo-Indian-Canadian forces, released to be concentrated upon him by General Dearborn's armistice on the Eastern frontiers. The colossal disaster in the North-west enraged the whole country, and the Government made General Hull its scapegoat. The soldier who had led the charge at Stony Point, and fought in the foremost files at Monmouth and White Plains, was adjudged worthy of death for cowardice by a tribunal of politico-military officers, and retired in disgrace to his rural home, to await the executioner. Here he lived a sweet and tranquil

FAIRLAWN: THE RESIDENCE OF AUSTIN R. MITCHELL, NEWTONVILLE.
Walnut Street, Between Highland Avenue and Austin Street.

SAMUEL J. BROWN, ARCHITECT.

life, full of simple hospitality and charity, with his table always ready for unbidden guests, a bevy of whom (of humble rank) were always present in the servants' hall. Among the gentry who often visited the old hero were Lucius Manlius Sargent, William Sullivan, David Henshaw, Nathaniel Greene, Gorham Parsons, and Marshall Spring.

Hull's father died in 1775; and the young patriot declined his share of the paternal estate, saying: "I want only my sword and my uniform." With these knightly belongings, he journeyed to Washington's camp at Cam-

Newton High School, Walnut Street, Newtonville.

bridge, and followed the fortunes of the great Virginian until the close of the war. He defeated the Hessian Yagers at White Plains; was promoted by Washington for heroism at the battle of Trenton; fought in St. Clair's Ticonderoga campaign, with Arnold at Fort Stanwix, with Gates at Saratoga; beat up the British quarters at Morrisania; and relieved Lafayette in Virginia. The 4th United-States Infantry, the chief command surrendered at Detroit, was enlisted in New England in 1808, and after its release from captivity in Canada the regiment went into barracks at

Charlestown, in 1812. In this beautiful spot, where the graceful elms overshadow the fair lawn, and the streamlet ripples through the broad domain, passed the declining years of the old officer of the Revolution, the friend of Washington and Lafayette. Many a story he used to tell of his service with the old 8th Massachusetts Infantry, at White Plains, the retreat from Lake George, the relief of Fort Stanwix, the surrender of Burgoyne, the dreary camps at Valley Forge, the battle of Monmouth, the storming of Stony Point, the long march against Shays's army, the desperate scenes of the French Revolution.

Mrs. Hull had Dr. Homer's portrait painted, in his dignified cap and bands; and manifested her love to the church, in strange wise, by sending it a Genoa velvet pall, to be used at funerals. Her life had been full of picturesque incident, for she used to accompany her gallant husband on his campaigns, and was in at the finish at Saratoga, where she helped to assuage the grief of Lady Acland, the Baroness Riedesel, and other patrician attendants of Burgoyne's shattered army. She had also given to her country a beloved son, Captain Hull, of the United-States Infantry, who was killed in one of the battles in Upper Canada.

Whatever the officials at Washington may have thought of the old General, here he was the grand seigneur of the countryside; and his easy hospitality found a worthy helper in the gracious manner of Madame Hull, and was often assisted by Dr. Homer, the pastor of the First Parish. Here too were the seven agreeable daughters of the family, and many were the merrymakings, when old Tillow, the General's devoted negro, fidddled away half the night for the dances in the hall. There were two or three score slaves held in Newton, early in the last century, when the names of Phyllis, and Pompey, and Dimbo, and Dinah, and Quartus were familiar to the people of the scattered farms. These negro slaves were probably introduced here from Barbadoes, which then enjoyed a large trade with Massachusetts, several of whose families (including one or two from Newton) had migrated to that far-away West-Indian island. Besides a vessel which brought in fifty negro captives from Madagascar, in 1678, there were but half a dozen slave-ships that came to Boston. Chief-Justice Sewall, the Quakers, and other gentle and pious men fought against the traffic; and the local Abolitionist movement began in 1766, and went forward gradually and steadily until 1783, when the Supreme Court declared that no master had a right to beat or imprison his slaves. In 1788 the slave-trade was abolished by law, and the institution, which had here always been patriarchal in its character, rather than despotic, passed away forever.

James Freeman Clarke, by an unhappy accident, was not a native of Newton, but of a New-Hampshire town where his parents (both of them Newton people) were temporarily sojourning. At the age of two months he was brought back to Newton, where he dwelt until his college-life began. He wrote: "There is scarcely an acre of the town I did not ramble over during my boyhood, or was not familiar with. My grandfather Freeman's place, and that of my grandfather Hull, always seemed to me the most charming homes in the world; and I make an annual pilgrimage to Newton to refresh my memory of the familiar places. Here (I say) lived Mr. Bracket; here Mr. Ward, or Hyde, or Trowbridge, or Harbach; this was 'Rural Cave'; here lived the good old minister, my uncle Homer; and here in Baptist Pond, we once set sail, my brothers and I, in a fragile bark made by our-

Samuel J. Brown's Residence, Walnut Street, near Bullough's Pond.

selves, to catch perch. This was the house of the Lorings, of the Tuckers, the Cabots; and in 'Cold Spring' we caught our first trout."

James Freeman Clarke's mother used to be a great admirer of the pastoral scenery where the greatest New-England cemetery now is, and she called the locality, in the days of her girlhood, "Sweet Auburn." This pretty name, which Chief-Justice Bigelow says she first applied to the place, gained such sure foothold that when the cemetery was established, the Massachusetts Horticultural Society retained for it Miss Hull's title, dignifying it by changing the first word into "Mount."

Nearly opposite the Claflin estate opens the ancient domain of the Trowbridges. The last Englishman of that ilk dwelt at Taunton, in Somersetshire, where he founded a still-existing charity for poor widows. His son was a Barbadoes merchant, whose son, Deacon James Trowbridge, moved to Newton in 1664; bought Deputy-Governor Danforth's estate; and became a magnate of the little plantation. His wife was Margaret, the daughter of Major-General Humphrey Atherton, Captain of the Ancient and Honorable Artillery Company in the year 1650. His son William was lieutenant, deacon, miller, and slaveholder; and his grandson, Edmund, became the foremost jurist of his generation in New England, Attorney-General and Chief-Justice under the Crown, and a confirmed Royalist. The State authorities offered him a safe-conduct, to go to England; but he preferred to remain here, saying: " I am not afraid of my countrymen." He retired to Byfield, a little hamlet of Essex North, where he taught the elements of law to Theophilus Parsons, afterwards one of our most eminent jurists.

On Trowbridge Avenue, near Walnut Street, is the home of Henry C. Hayden, whose volume of sweet and pathetic domestic poems was published in 1887.

A little way beyond the Claflin estate, Walnut Street enters the beautiful region around Bullough's Pond, and so passes on, by the great Newton Cemetery, to Newton Centre. Bullough's Pond is near the geographical centre of Newton, rather less than a mile from the Newtonville station, or from Newton Highlands, or Newton Centre, being somewhat nearer the first named, by the lovely avenue of Walnut Street. It is a deep basin of pure spring-water, nearly half a mile long; and Walnut Street divides it into two parts. The glen is surrounded by hills of singular beauty, covered with tall forests, and rising gracefully on either side, so that, as the poet historian of Newton says, it resembles "a sapphire gem set round with emeralds." A few years ago, an attempt was made to convert these lovely glens and dales and highlands into a public park, for the enjoyment of the city; but the great attendant cost militated against the scheme, and it was allowed to fall into abeyance. This Central Park was to have included 174 acres of land, then valued at $87,000; and in the hot debates which preceded the adverse settlement of the question (in 1883), Messrs. Farlow and Pulsifer championed the cause of the park, while Farquhar, Bacon, and other tribunes of the people vigorously opposed it. Since that time, much of the land has been acquired by George W. Morse and Austin R. Mitchell, who have opened magnificent avenues across it, and have even schemed to render it more accessible by building a horse-railroad from Newtonville square to Newton Highlands. On the high ridge west of and overlooking the pond a line of handsome houses was erected, in 1887. An attempt has been made to change the ancient name of Bullough's Pond to "Pearl Lake."

NEWTONVILLE SQUARE AND THE METHODIST CHURCH.
Junction of Walnut and Washington Streets.

The pond commemorates John Bullough, an old-time miller, whose estate extended along the west side.

Early in the present century, the wild places of the woods in this locality were the haunt of another Bullough, the terror of the town, a desperado and ne'er-do-well, who stole General Hull's horses, and spent much of his time in the State Prison. It was the son of this hapless village convict who redeemed the clouded fortunes of the family by becoming an honest miller, in the old mill on Walnut Street. Tom Bullough, the bandit, was a merry and waggish fellow, withal, and one of the first of the Socialists, averring that he never *stole* things, but merely converted the superfluity of rich men's goods to the use of the poor, of whom he was chief. One day he made a foray on one of the neighboring farms, and began to measure off with his cane a piece of new homespun cloth, then drying on the grass. The housewife demanded to know his purpose; and he rejoined: "I'm measuring off enough for two shirts." To which she made answer: "Tom Bullough, if you take any of that, you will answer for it at the Judgment Day." And lightly tossing all of it on his shoulder, he replied: "Well, then I'll take the whole piece," and so retired to his den among the rocks by the pond. Dreadful stories were told of this outcast and the "lewd fellows of the baser sort" whom he used to gather around him here; and the Puritan mothers of the adjacent valleys used to frighten their refractory children with the grim name of Tom Bullough.

At the outlet of the pond, Ensign John Spring erected his mill, before George Washington was born; and in 1737 the town's surveyors of highways "Voted, to stake out the way that leads from Dedham road to Ensign Spring's mill, called Mill lane." This was the first grist-mill in Newton, and among its part-owners were the Parks, Williamses, Wards, and Trowbridges. Before the dams were built, sea-fish ascended the little stream to the pond; and its name of Smelt Brook was derived from the schools of smelt that used to run up its limpid course. In the lowlands south of the pond are deposits of bog-iron ore, which used to be sent in large quantities to the forges at Easton, early in the present century.

On a dreamy day of Indian summer, one can hardly choose a lovelier rambling-ground than these voiceless solitudes about Bullough's Pond, amid the scarlet glories of the barberries and sumachs, the vivid gold of the witch hazel, the pyrola's pale green, the wild cherry's orange and crimson, the oak's sprays of fiery glow, the deep-green of the bittersweet, the sombre shadows of the evergreens. The metallic blue of the lakelet is overhung with a glamour of haze; troops of fearless squirrels scamper over the falling leaves; and the sound of the woodsmen's axes comes far, faint, and dull on the sweet and languid air. In the old days game abounded in these forests, then much more extensive, and in fact hardly broken by the infrequent clearings of the settlers. Bears were shot from the door-yards of the farms; and the town treasury paid out many a pound sterling for wolf-scalps. In 1717 and in 1741 the town appointed Deer Reeves, to prevent the wanton extermination of its deer. Bounties were paid by the selectmen for the killing of blackbirds, woodpeckers, and jay-birds; and a goodly fine was imposed upon all dogs "that shall be taken damage feasant."

. .On Walnut Street, at the corner nearest the dam, is the pretty cottage home of Samuel J. Brown, the well-known architect, whose many specimens of exquisite domestic architecture are to be found in the numerous suburbs of Boston.

Farther out on Walnut Street is the beautiful Gothic gateway of the Newton Cemetery, surmounted by the emblem of our salvation, and half-hidden under masses of climbing vines. *Et in Arcadia Ego* is inscribed on a pictured tomb in one of Poussin's loveliest landscapes; and even so in this Arcadian town continually came the Reaper, Death, so that it became needful to find broader accommodations for his myriad victims. There was a broad tract of shady groves and graceful hills nearly in the centre of the great ellipse of villages; and in the year 1855 this domain was secured by the Newton Cemetery Association, and set apart for a quiet and beautiful city of the dead. On a blue-skied day of June, two years later, the cemetery received its consecration. Frederic Dan Huntington (since Bishop of Central New York) delivered the address; and the Rev. Dr. Samuel F. Smith, the Poet Laureate of Newton, contributed a hymn, beginning: —

> "Deep, 'mid these dim and silent shades,
> The slumbering dead shall lie,
> Tranquil, as evening fades
> Along the western sky.
>
> "The whispering winds shall linger here,
> To lull their deep repose;
> Like music on the dewy air,
> Like nightfall on the rose."

During the first twenty-three years, the cost of the cemetery was $90,000; and 3,102 interments took place in that period. Nearly 100 acres are consecrated to the repose of the departed bodies, amid the fairest scenes of nature. The Bigelow Mortuary Chapel stands well within the grounds. It was presented to the cemetery by John S. Farlow, and is a pure Gothic building, of heavy stone masonry, with high terra-cotta dado, and open timber roof. Back of the pulpit are fine tablets of Tennessee marble, the central one bearing this inscription: —

"To commemorate the virtues and unselfish labors of Dr. Henry F. Bigelow, who died at Newton, Mass., January 21, 1866, this chapel was erected by one who esteemed him, and who cherished his memory as that of a kind friend, a true Christian and public benefactor."

In front of the pulpit is a raised bier, which can be lowered by machinery to the room below, whence its sad burden may be taken to the grave. One entire side of the chapel opens by three Gothic arches into the great conservatory, which is 35 x 54 feet in area, with rockeries and fountains and a surrounding walk lined with tropical plants.

One of the lots in the cemetery pertains to the American Baptist Missionary Union, whose veteran heroes, returning to the home-land after long conflict for Christ in heathenesse, are buried here, when called to their final joy. The first occupant of this sacred ground was the Rev. Benjamin C. Thomas, who died in 1869, after twenty years of consecrated labors in Burmah.

Among those who rest in the cemetery are Dr. Henry F. Bigelow, who was for fifteen years Chairman of the School Committee, and had a prominent part in laying out and adorning the Cemetery; the Rev. Joseph Smith, some time pastor of the Channing Church; Dr. Hitchcock, Dean of the Harvard Dental School; and the Rev. E. Frank Howe, long time pastor of the Central Church at Newtonville.

Near the chapel rises the monument * to the men from this town who gave their lives for America during the great civil conflict. The dedicatory oration was by the Rev. Dr. Hackett, of the Newton Theological Institution. The monument is a shaft of Quincy granite, 28 feet high, bearing the inscription: IN MEMORIAM PERPETUAM. PRO PATRIA MORTUI SUNT; and near it is an entablature containing the names of 59 Newton soldiers who gave up their lives in the sacred cause of the Union of States. Of the 106,330 men sent by Massachusetts into the National army, Newton contributed more than her share; and of the 12,534 who died in the service, her loss was not the least. It was wisely resolved that the monument to the dead heroes of Newton should be erected by the free subscriptions of the people; and to that end 1,200 citizens of the town gave one dollar each, and 1,100 school-children gave a dime each. The Newton Soldiers' Monument was the first one erected in New England, and received its dedication on the 23d of July, 1864, on that sad day when the armies were at truce before Atlanta, burying their dead on the field of honor. And in Dr. Smith's requiem hymn occurred these prophetic lines: —

> "Round this fair shaft let summer leave
> Its fragrant airs, at morn and even,
> And golden clouds in sunlight weave
> Pathways of glory into heaven.
>
> "Again the flag of Peace shall float
> O'er all the land, from sea to sea;
> O'er all the land shall swell the note
> Of Freedom's final Jubilee."

* See illustration on page 27.

Before this perpetual memorial of the patriotism of her children, let us pause, and glance at the military history of Newton in the Secession War. On the 19th of April a town-meeting was called, to consult about raising funds for the families of volunteers, and for the purchase of warlike equipments. $20,000 was appropriated for the latter of these purposes, and the faith of the town was pledged for the families, and this resolve also passed: "And if any should perish in said service, the town will tenderly care for their remains, and furnish them with a suitable burial." A year later, $50,000 more was appropriated; and in 1864 the town set apart $58,000. The quota assigned to Newton during the war was 1,067 men, and she actu-

Newton Cemetery Gateway, Walnut Street, Newtonville.

ally furnished 1,129 soldiers, besides 41 sailors in the navy, many volunteers in other States, and officers and soldiers who went out for short enlistments. 323 men enlisted for three years. The Newton contingent included two Generals (Underwood and Edmands) and 36 other commissioned officers. They were in 30 Massachusetts regiments, and fought on 75 fields of battle. There were more than a score of Newton men in the 1st Massachusetts Infantry, one of the best three-years regiments of the Army of the Potomac, whose firm-fronted files traversed the hostile plains of Virginia, from Bull Run and Williamsburg to Chancellorsville and Spottsylvania, with a memorable side-trip to Gettysburg. Two-score more of Newton soldiers marched with the gallant 16th Massachusetts Infantry, in the Peninsula and Northern Virginia and Pennsylvania campaigns, and seven of them died on the field. It was this regiment that General Hooker credited with saving the army, at the battle of Glendale. Another score were enrolled under the colors of the 24th Massachusetts Infantry, in the long and weary campaigns among the Carolinas, and the hunting of Lee about Petersburg. The 32d Massachusetts Infantry had 8 officers and 89 men from Newton, and lost 26 of these. Wherever there were heroic deeds to do, at Malvern Hill, Manassas, Antietam, Fredericksburg, Chancellorsville, Gettysburg, the Wilderness, Petersburg, the old Fort-Warren Regiment was thrown to the burning front, and Company K, the Newton command, stood among the steadiest on the color-line. The regiment lost at Gettysburg 81 men, out of 229 taken into action; at Laurel Hill, 96, out of 260; at Dabney's Mills, 74; and out of 2,286 men enlisted, it brought back but 1,087. When the 32d was advancing in line of battle, under a scathing artillery-fire on the 9th of April, 1865, a flag of truce was seen approaching its iron ranks, bearing General Lee's request for a cessation of hostilities, which was followed within two days by the surrender of the Confederate army. This regiment, and its brigade, in solemn and impressive silence, received the arms of the heroic but overmastered Southern infantry, on the day of surrender.

The 33d Massachusetts Infantry was commanded by a Newtonian, General Adin B. Underwood, who received a hideous wound at the battle of Lookout Mountain. To one who condoled with him at the apparent approach of death, he said: "Chaplain, this is what I came for. I thought it all over before I enlisted. I have expected and am prepared for such a result; and, if the salvation of my country calls for the sacrifice of my life, I am ready to render it." The 33d fought in the front of the battles at Fredericksburg, Chancellorsville, and Gettysburg, and on Sherman's wonderful march through Georgia. The 44th Massachusetts Infantry had 5 officers (including Colonel Francis L. Lee) and 112 soldiers from Newton, including Company B and parts of other companies. Their campaigning was amid the lowlands of North Carolina, and among its episodes were the engagements of Whitehall and Kinston, and the heroic defence of Little Washington. The 45th, with 27 Newtonians, distinguished itself in the North-Carolina wars, suffering severe losses at Kinston and Whitehall, and winning the admiration of the army.

In the 1st Massachusetts Cavalry there were 27 Newton troopers, who gave a good account of themselves at Antietam and Gettysburg and the Wilderness, and up in Aldie, and wherever else that hard-riding command drew its flashing sabres. Another group of our townsmen served in the 2d Massachusetts Cavalry, under the gallant Lowell. Nine more served in the 3d Massachusetts Cavalry, that flower of discipline and valor, whose marches exceeded 15,000 miles, and whose rolls bore the names of 30

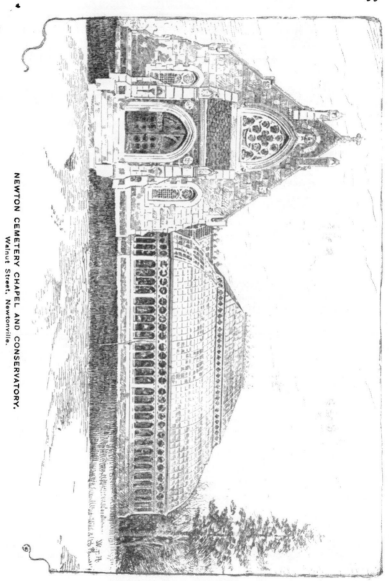

NEWTON CEMETERY CHAPEL AND CONSERVATORY.
Walnut Street, Newtonville.

engagements. Nine more Newton cavaliers rode with the 4th Massachusetts Cavalry, who were hammered into such stern and formidable veterans that they formed a worthy section of Sheridan's matchless corps, and stood full in the path of Lee's whole army until his checked retreat sank into surrender. In the 5th Massachusetts Cavalry there were 81 horsemen from Newton, who campaigned on the Virginia lowlands until the end. Besides these there were clusters of Newton volunteers in the 31st, amid its perilous Louisiana and Alabama campaigns; 17 in the 24th, marching and fighting in the Carolinas; and smaller groups in many other regiments. There were 65 in the Veteran Reserve Corps, 40 in the regular army, 21 in the Massachusetts batteries, and 41 in the Navy.

As Ordway said, in his poem on the dedication: —

> "The sons of Newton like their sires arise,
> And march, as did of old the minute-men,
> To find the nearest spot where danger lies.
>
> "And each true heart, and every noble soul,
> Like the brave heroes of an earlier day,
> Are ever first and foremost in the fray,
> When duty calls the roll,
> And honor leads the way."

For the rest, one may ramble for hours through the cemetery, up and down its Rose Paths and Violet Paths and Valley Roads, and look with sympathy on the monuments, with their inscriptions of hope and faith, and rejoice in the beautiful flowers and shadowy trees and sunlit hill-tops. And we will remember that all these thousands who have lived and loved and passed on, somewhere and somehow to enter the eternal peace of God, have but a little way preceded each one of us who remains here in the twilight.

Nonantum.

THE OLD NORTH VILLAGE, OR TIN HORN.— FULLER'S CORNER.— THE
BEMIS FACTORIES.— THE FIRST GAS-LIGHTING IN AMERICA.

About a mile north of Newtonville is the prosperous manufacturing village of Nonantum, bounded on one side by the broad meadows along California Street, and on another by the mild Charles River. It straggles rather widely over the generous plain, and lacks the cohesion which a few

North Evangelical (Nonantum Congregational) Church, Chapel Street, Newton.

more years of peace and prosperity may give it, but the houses are neat and comfortable, and the evidences of modest plenty appear on all sides.

The North Evangelical Church is a Congregationalist institution which owes its origin to a little Sunday-school, started in the Bemis railway station, in 1861. It received organization in 1866, and the Rev. Samuel E. Lowry became its pastor, meeting oftentimes with fierce opposition from the foreign industrial population, but winning their love and respect at last; and achieving a world of good among them. The pretty stone church in which the society now worships was built in 1872, of Newton-Centre stone, at a cost of $18,000; and the membership includes 67 persons, with 225 in the Sunday-school. The pastor is the Rev. William A. Lamb.

All the lands of Newton in this part belonged in the first times to Richard Park and John Fuller, whose farms covered, the one 600 acres, and the other 750 acres. The site of the Fuller farmhouse is still shown on the Ezra-Fuller farm, near the river; and the Park mansion stood on the Seth-Bemis place, until 1808, when it was pulled down. So in the seventeenth century and much later the region was known as "Fuller's Corner." The history of manufacturing at this point has some interesting phases, although it pertains to the Watertown side rather more than to this. It was about the year 1760 that David Bemis bought some 64 acres of riverside land here, and a few years later joined with Dr. Enos Sumner, on the Newton shore, and built a dam across the stream. The Sumner interest was sold out to manufacturers, who in 1779 erected a paper-mill here; and this factory passed under the control of David Bemis in 1781. Ten years later, David's sons, Luke and Isaac, inherited it; and the former ran it from the day of Isaac's death (in 1794) until 1821, a part of the time associated with Caleb Eddy of Boston. The machinery, moulds, and workmen were imported from Europe; and the value of this industry stood so high that, when the mills were burnt, the General Court made a special grant to insure their rebuilding. The grist and snuff mill that David Bemis founded descended to his sons Luke and Seth, the latter of whom became sole possessor in 1796, and began the manufacture of chocolate, drugs, and dyewoods, and (about 1803) of cotton warp, on which he made great profits. Five years later, the mills were at work on sheeting, shirting, ticking, bagging, and satinet, and turned out the first cotton duck ever made in America. The first ship that ever sailed under a snowy cloud of American duck was equipped from these mills. Here, also, they made woollen yarn, machinery, and fine ground-glass. In 1821 Seth bought the property of his brother Luke, across the river, and with him and others formed the Bemis Manufacturing Company, which until 1830 made satinet and cotton duck. Seth Bemis and Thomas Cordis then bought out the property, and ran it for seventeen years, Cordis leaving the concern after about half this period had passed. In 1847 Bemis sold the mills on the Newton side to William Freeman; and in 1860, ten years after Seth Bemis's death, his son Seth sold the Watertown mills also to William Freeman & Co., from whom they passed into the hands of the Ætna Manufacturing Company. The property had been in the Bemis family for over a century.

On Bridge Street, near California Street, is the home of the late Seth

Bemis, who died late in 1887, at the age of seventy-five years, having been in his day a prominent man in the railroad and manufacturing affairs of Massachusetts. George Bemis, another member of the Bemis family, at North Village, was a learned and versatile jurist, long time Solicitor for the Worcester Railroad, associate in the trial of Professor Webster for the murder of Doctor Parkman, and a first authority on international law. He made large bequests to Harvard College and the Boston Athenæum.

At this point illuminating gas was first used, as early as the year 1812, when Seth Bemis erected a building for its manufacture, and for a year lighted his factory with it, until the leakage of the unsavory material from its thin tin pipes became so offensive that the experiment was given up. During this period, wondering visitors came from far and near, to see the springing of clear white light from an invisible spirit of air. As a local historian poetically remarks: "It is a fact worthy of record, that carburetted hydrogen for illuminating purposes gleamed out over the waters of the Charles and irradiated the intervales of Newton two years before it was in use in England."

Near the Ætna-Mills station is the only rolling dam in America, over which the water falls with rhythmic precision. The only other dam of this kind in the world is at Warwick Castle, in England, and has cost fabulous sums of money.

In olden times the hours for beginning work in the Bemis mills were indicated by long and hearty blasts on a prodigious tin horn, whose echoes floated up and down the valley like

> "The sound of that dread horn,
> On Fontarabian echoes borne,
> That to King Charles did come."

In memory of this potent factor in the history of the glen, the northern village of Newton still bears, among the common people, the name of "Tin Horn."

The first bridge was built here by the Bemises before 1795, and its Watertown end several times succumbed to the angry floods of the Charles.

The long boulevard of California Street, which approaches the little glen of the bridge, was laid out in 1816, and traverses a lovely region, rich in corn and enwalled with maples, with views across the great grassy esplanade to the westward, and northward to the high hills of Waltham. The house at the corner of California and Nevada Streets was for a long time the home of Celia Thaxter, the poet.

On one side of Nonantum is the pleasant rural road of Crafts Street, traversing a region of farms, and passing down to the edge of the Newtonville Park.

The chief natural feature of the village is Silver Lake, an attractive sheet of clear water, without any visible outlet. Its ice was in olden times much prized by the citizens. Near the shore, on Nevada Street, is the handsome mill of the Silver-Lake Company, devoted to making solid braided cordage and steam packing, and employing a large force of workmen. Near by are the mills of the Nonantum Worsted Company, and other prosperous factories.

The population of Nonantum is not far from 3,000, mainly French Canadians, Irishmen, and Englishmen, engaged in the factories. The devotion of many of these hardworking fellows to "John Barleycorn" results in many shrewd devices to evade the local liquor-laws, and "the crathur" comes hither in innocent-looking flour-barrels and express-packages and is slyly peddled out in the purlieus of Bottle Alley and other streets, to the great obfuscation of the workmen. In good time, however, this nefarious traffic will yield to better influences, and Nonantum may become in every way a model manufacturing village, rejoicing on its fair sunlit plains.

West Newton.

A FAMOUS OLD SCHOOL.— BELL-HACK AND SQUASH-END.— THE SECOND CHURCH.— THE CENTENARIAN DOMINIE.— THE BLITHEDALE ROMANCE.— PINE-FARM SCHOOL.

West Newton is a bright village of 3,200 inhabitants, lying along the old Worcester turnpike and the Albany Railroad, where the Cheesecake Brook, escaping from the hills, wanders out over the plain towards the Charles River. It is a place of homes, free of manufactures, and abounding in quiet streets, where peace and contentment dwell undisturbed. On the south, beyond the quadruple steel bands of the railway and the park-encircled station, it has thrown a storming column of modern villas up the steep heights, and crowned their crests with far-viewing estates; and on the east and west it merges amicably into the environs of Newtonville and Auburndale.

Land at West Newton is from 5 to 75 cents a square foot; and house-rents range from $5 to $100 a month. There are 30 direct trains to Boston daily, and 20 indirect trains, by the Circuit Railroad. The fare, by package-tickets, is $9\tfrac{3}{4}$ cents. With such reasonable facilities for settlement and transportation, the future growth of the village must be rapid and satisfactory. There are ample church and school accommodations, the best of streets and roads, an abundance of good society, and an unusual dearth of illiteracy and other objectionable features. And in this matter-of-fact Arcadia, as in all the other villages of Newton, no liquor-saloon is allowed to spread its lures.

The old Second Congregational Church, West Newton.

The little stream which traverses the village rises near the ancient hilly domain of Deacon Staples, and winds away into the Charles, not far from

Watertown. In the good old days of the Colony it received the name of Cheesecake Brook, because a party of hunters rested at noonday on its sylvan shore, and regaled themselves on cakes and cheese. Along this placid little stream stretched the famous old Fuller Farm, acquired in 1658 by John Fuller, maltster and selectman, in whose will appeared the curious provision that none of his land should be sold to strangers until it had first been offered to the nearest kinsmen. His estate included a thousand acres, and was bounded on the north and west by the Charles River. It is on record that twenty-two of his descendants in Newton entered the army of the Revolution.

The Cheesecake Brook, curbed and confined within neatly-built stone walls, may properly be called the classic stream of the village. At a facetious entertainment at the City Hall some years since, the project was unfolded of deepening and widening this rivulet down to deep tide-water, thus to make the village a port of entry, with a Custom House and other appropriate accompaniments.

Ten rods north of Cheesecake Brook, and thirty rods north-east of the West-Parish meeting-house, stood the old home of Major Samuel Shepard, built about the year 1650. It passed into the possession of Deacon William Park, of Roxbury, who gave it to his son-in-law, Isaac Williams, an honest weaver, whom his admiring fellow-townsmen honored with the offices of Deacon and Captain, Selectman and Representative, and at the end (in 1707) saw him off on the road to Paradise with a military funeral, at which the Company of Foot paraded under arms. One of his sons was the Rev. Solomon Williams of Hatfield, whose son William Williams became one of the signers of the Declaration of Independence. Another son was Ephraim, whose son, Ephraim, born on this estate, was educated by his maternal grandfather, Abraham Jackson, and made many voyages to foreign lands, where, amid the polite society of Spain, Holland, and England, he acquired graceful manners and a valuable fund of general knowledge. At a later date, he commanded the Massachusetts forts among the hills of Berkshire, for eight years. In 1755, while advancing through the woods near Lake George, with 1,000 colonial troops (of the 8th Massachusetts Infantry) and 200 Mohawk Indians, he was defeated by the French army under the Baron Dieskan, and died on the field of battle. He had received a premonition of his coming death, and bequeathed his estate for the establishing of a collegiate school in the then savage wilderness of northern Berkshire. On this foundation the school was commenced, in 1790, and received incorporation as Williams College three years later. So that in a certain sense this famous Berkshire Athens, the birthplace of American foreign missions, is a child of West Newton, or, strictly speaking, a grandchild.

To this region came Dr. Samuel Wheat, in 1713, and settled as the village

1. Allen's Swimming Pond. 2 and 3. Residences of Instructors and Pupils. 4. Classical School.

N. T. ALLEN'S WEST NEWTON ENGLISH AND CLASSICAL SCHOOL.
Washington and Highland Streets, West Newton.

physician, succeeded twenty years later by his son, Dr. Samuel Wheat, Jr. The neighborhood was entirely agricultural, a group of well-tilled farms along the plain, with a range of savage hills to the southward. As late as the year 1800 there were but eleven houses within a radius of a mile from the present City Hall. Some of the aged men and women who lived in West Newton, forty and fifty years ago, used to tell to their children and

First Unitarian Church, Washington and Highland Streets, West Newton.

grandchildren the story of the strange and motley procession they once saw passing through the streets, when the prisoners of Burgoyne's army were taken to Cambridge. Professor Creasy calls the battle of Saratoga, fought on the 17th of October, 1777, one of the " Fifteen Decisive Battles of the World." Not far from 6,000 men were thus made prisoners of war, and thrown out of service in the British army. It marked the turning-point in the Revolutionary struggle. For the description of the march through West Newton, we are indebted to Benjamin F. Houghton, one of the old grocers of West Newton, who received the story by direct tradition from the elders. These prisoners, with their military escort, came down on the Framingham road, over the Weston Bridge, a little way above the present village of Auburndale, and thence by the street now known as Woodland Avenue. At the point where Woodland Avenue joins Washington Street, near the Woodland-Park Hotel, Jonathan Dix, then a boy, watched the way-worn multitude with eager eyes, as presenting one of the strangest sights he had ever seen. Arrived at the centre of West Newton, the dolorous procession was halted, to give the officers in charge an opportunity to go into White's tavern for a drink. The prisoners remained in the street, hungry and weary; and some of them presently fell to fighting with each other. One of the villagers ran into the tavern, and asked the officers to come out and stop the riot. The cool reply was, that they did not care what the prisoners did to each other; and the guardsmen finished their drinking at their leisure. Meantime the angry Britons, grenadiers and light infantry and dismounted artillerists, plying their swift shillelahs upon each other's heads, made such a Tipperary festival as West Newton has never seen since, and filled the air with resounding imprecations. It was a sad enough march, at best, as we may see from the account written by Mrs. Winthrop, an eyewitness: " The sight was truly astonishing. I never had the least idea that the creation produced such a sordid set of creatures in human figure,— poor, dirty, emaciated men. Great numbers of women, who seemed to be the beasts of burden, having bushel baskets on their backs, by which they were bent double. The contents seemed to be pots and kettles, various sorts of furniture, children peeping through gridirons and other utensils. Some very young infants, who were born on the road; the women barefooted, clad in dirty rags." On the night of Nov. 7, 1777, this mournful army encamped at Weston; and the next day, escorted by General John Glover, they marched across Newton to Cambridge.

Between Nickerson's Block and B. F. Houghton's store stands the ancient building which in the year 1760 was one of the chief taverns on the Natick road (the present Washington Street), with long lines of horse-sheds to the westward, a famous well (where Elm Street now is), and a cosey old tap-room, in which the landlord, Ensign Phineas Bond, served out good cheer in deep pewter tankards. Here the American, British, and German officers slaked their thirst; here Lafayette took a brief rest, and visited the tap-room, in 1825; and here the desperate highwayman, Mike Martin, was brought by his captors, after he had robbed Major Bray on the Medford road. In 1833, after the building of the brick hotel on Washington Street, the old tavern was bought by Seth Davis, and remodelled into a fashionable boarding-house. Of late years, it has been a tenement. The tavern comprised the middle part of the present building, and was a hip-roofed structure, broadside to the street, with the tap-room door where the bay-window now is. At the west end of this building, between it and Mr. Houghton's store, a gigantic elm may be seen, which was about ten or fifteen years old at the time the captive redcoats passed by. It was planted on this spot in 1767, though it had already received some years of growth probably before its transplanting. The tree was placed there by John Barber, who had kept the tavern before Mr. White took it. At one time, there was a summer-arbor built among its boughs.

Nickerson's Block, Washington and Cherry Streets, West Newton.

Early in this century, West Newton was one of the chief centres for the mail-stages, thirty of which passed through the hamlet daily, sweeping up, with great cracking of whips and shouting of drivers, before the doors of the village inn. On the site of Hunt's carpenter-shop, nearly a hundred years ago, stood the grocery store of Sol Flagg, whose pewter tankards — gallon, half-gallon, quart, pint, and gill — may still be seen in Houghton's store, after a good century of service.

From 1830, for twenty years or more, repeated and powerful efforts were made to divide the town of Newton into two towns, by a straight line running from Brighton Hill, just south of the Eliot Church and Bullough's Pond, leaving the Centre and Upper Falls in Newton, and forming a new town of West Newton, to include Newton Corner, the Lower Falls, and the villages along the Worcester Railroad. The West-Parish people objected strenuously to having the town-house at the Centre, and demanded that at least half the town-meetings should be held at West Newton; and this was as strongly objected to by the burghers of Newton Centre. Many an angry debate ensued; polemic pamphlets were issued; legislative committees came out to view the ground; and for a period longer than that of the Trojan war the citizens of the two sections made themselves unhappy over this singular contest. It cannot profit us greatly to follow the various steps of this intermunicipal war, or to recall how Thomas Edmands and one hundred and forty others of the Centre reported of their antagonists: "In the soil of Newton they sow thorns — We are laboring to cultivate the olive"; or how the Lower Falls tried to be set off to Weston, and Nonantum to Waltham, and Oak Hill to Roxbury; or how Newton Centre petitioned the Post-office Department to call it *Newton*, and to officially designate the "small village" two miles north as "Newton Corner"; or how, in despair, a part of the committee of the General Court, after being hauled about the town for three days, recommended that the town-house be put in the geographical centre, in the shaggy wilderness about Bullough's Pond. All these things seem as far past as the Wars of the Roses, or the siege of St. Jean d'Acre, and the hot combatants are sleeping in their quiet graves.

Nathaniel T. Allen, of the Classical School, thus traces the rise of the hamlet: "Previous to 1844 the village now known as West Newton was generally called 'Squash End,' and was inhabited by a sparse population, occupying some forty or fifty houses, mostly of ordinary size and architecture. In the spring of 1844, an impetus was given to the growth of the village by the removal of the Normal School from Lexington to the Fuller Academy. This event at once attracted families from Boston and vicinity to take advantage of the educational facilities afforded by the Normal School for their daughters and its model department for their younger children. When, in April, 1848, the writer became a resident here, the village contained the following distinguished persons among its citizens: Horace Mann, Rev. Cyrus Pierce, William Parker, superintendent of the Boston & Worcester Railroad, afterwards of the Baltimore & Ohio Railroad, and at the time of his death president of the Panama Railroad; Messrs. E. S. Cheseborough (Cheseborough afterwards distinguished himself by lifting up the city of Chicago to a level of several feet higher from the lake level) and William S. Whitwell, eminent engineers, engaged in introducing the Cochituate water into Boston; Marshall Conant; William B. Fowle, Sen. (founder Lancastrian School); Joseph W. Plimpton; Joseph S. Clark, D.D.; Captain Charles T. Savage; and Lyman Gilbert, D.D. With their equally distinguished wives, with such women as Elizabeth P. Peabody, Catherine Beecher, Harriet Davis, Madam Whitwell and her daughter Elizabeth, and others, they compose a notable company. Soon were added David Lee Child, with his noble wife, Lydia Maria Child; also Nathaniel Hawthorne and his family. It is easy to understand that such a galaxy would elevate the character of any community and attract the attention of other communities. We think the village owes much of its high moral and intellectual character to the impetus it then received through the influence of the above-named men and women."

In times of weariness Theodore Parker used to come to West Newton, and on one of the old farms in the neighborhood found congenial rest. In one of his letters he says: "Out here I have got comfort with the cattle; and the old horse knows me, and calls for hay; and I talk with the dumb beast, who is not deaf. The great long-horned oxen are pets of mine. The *pic* is one of my favorites also; and I speak to him every morning, noon, and night, and he answers me." From 1846 until his death in 1861, this little village was the home of the Rev. Dr. J. S. Clark, author of "A Historical Sketch of the Congregational Churches in Massachusetts from 1620 to 1858," and for eighteen years Secretary of the Massachusetts Home-Missionary Society. His house was at the corner of Chestnut Street and Hillside Street, and now (moved back and altered) is occupied by the Hon. Julius L. Clarke, formerly Massachusetts Commissioner of Insurance.

Another longtime resident (on Otis Street) was the Rev. Charles F. Barnard, the originator of free evening-schools in America. To him, more than to any other one man, Boston was indebted for its Public Garden. Henshaw Dana, the musical composer, whose long years of European study gave him wonderful mastery of the art of harmony, was a native of West Newton. A competent critic of Stuttgart wrote that "his songs are gems, but his compositions for the church are of special importance."

The West-Newtonians who aspire to the mild excitements of societies have formed the Newton Civil-Service-Reform Association, with 130 members; the Newton Assembly, No. 39, of the Royal Society of Good Fellows; the West-Newton Village Improvement Society, with 200 members, "to promote the beautifying of the streets and public grounds of the village, and to stimulate the citizens to care for and beautify their private grounds"; the West-Newton Women's Educational Club, with fortnightly meetings; the Newton Council, No. 859, of the American Legion of Honor; the Garden-City Lodge, No. 1901, of the Knights of Honor; the Triton Council, No. 547, of the Royal Arcanum; Branch No. 395 of the Order of the Iron Hall; Crescent Commandery, No. 86, of the United Order of the Golden Cross; Anglo-American Lodge, No. 75, of the Sons of St. George; and St. Bernard Court, No. 44, of the Catholic Order of Foresters.

THE SECOND CONGREGATIONAL CHURCH, WEST NEWTON.
Washington Street, opposite Highland, adjoining the City Hall.

At one time it was thought that the wealth and culture of West Newton demanded the establishment of a newspaper here; and (in 1878) the Newton *Transcript* was founded by the younger Henry Lemon, who managed and edited it until the spring of 1885, when the subscription-list was sold to the proprietor of the Newton *Graphic*, and its publication suspended.

The chief public institution is the West-Newton English and Classical School, whose history is worthy of a brief glance. When Judge Abraham Fuller died, in 1794, he left a bequest of £300, "for the purpose of laying the foundations of an academy in Newton." Through delays in settling the estate, the years passed away until 1832 before the building was erected, and in the following two years the school was taught by Master Perkins. The town then decided to abandon it; and after a period of disuse Master Seth Davis established his school therein, and remained for two years. At a later day, when it became necessary to give up the leased building at Lexington in which the State Normal School for Girls was domiciled, Horace Mann rushed into the office of the Hon. Josiah Quincy, at Boston, saying: "A chance for the highest seat in the Kingdom of Heaven for only fifteen hundred dollars!" The venerable Quincy rejoined: "That's cheap enough. How is it to be earned?" And Mann briskly replied: "We've got to move from Lexington. There isn't room enough. And I've found a building — the Fuller Academy of Newton — that can be had for that sum." Remarking that Mr. Mann's deed to him of a seat in the Kingdom of Heaven was almost as good as an actual possession thereof, Quincy drew his check for the amount, and gave the building to Horace Mann for the interest of education in this Commonwealth. Here, then, was the first Normal-School building owned by an American State, and the first permanent Normal School for Girls in the world. Mr. Quincy made it a promise, that when the property ceased to be used by the State, it should revert to Horace Mann; and when the Normal School was moved to Framingham, in 1853, the latter took the building, and sold it to Nathaniel T. Allen, who had been for some years at the head of the Model or Experimental School here. At the solicitation of Charles Sumner, Theodore Parker, Horace Mann, George B. Emerson, Samuel J. May, Rev. Dr. Thomas Hill, Dr. Samuel G. Howe, and other gentlemen, Mr. Allen and the venerable Cyrus Pierce opened in the old building a private school for boys and girls, as an academy and a training-school for college. The instruction is based on the principles of Froebel and Pestalozzi, and aims symmetrically to develop the body, mind, heart, and will. Here the first kindergarten in Massachusetts was established, in 1864.

The pupils of the West-Newton English and Classical School came from all parts of New England, from Texas and the Indian Territory, from the Far West and the Pacific States and the Spanish West Indies. Among the

RESIDENCE OF THOMAS B. FITZ.
Waltham Street, opposite Davis Avenue, West Newton.

former students have been Professors John Trowbridge, John Rice, and Webster Wells; the Hons. Parker C. Chandler, John Davis, Robert R. Bishop, and Francis Tiffany; Dr. Frank S. Billings; William E. Haskell, of the Minneapolis *Tribune;* William H. Dall, the explorer of Alaska; Joseph T. Clarke, the explorer of Assos; Joseph P. Davis, Chief-Engineer of Boston; Helen Ayres and Alice Curtis, the artists; and many prominent business-men of Boston and New York. Nearly a hundred of the students have come from foreign countries; 300 from States outside of Massachusetts; and 900 from Massachusetts towns outside of Newton.

On one occasion a lad from the South-west declined to study physical geography, because in that class there was a negro student. "But," said Mr. Allen, "what would you do if you fell into the river, and a black man saved you from drowning?" To which the boy answered: "As soon as I got ashore, I should knock him down."

An adjunct of the West-Newton English and Classical School is a snug little artificial pond, formed from the Cheesecake Brook, covering 5,000 square feet, and surrounded by fences and bath-houses. It has a depth of from one to five feet, and is used as a swimming-school, where hundreds of persons have acquired this useful art. Certain hours are reserved for men and boys, and others for women; and the villagers avail themselves of its privileges by small annual payments.

The old academy building still stands, at the corner of Washington and Highland Streets; and, after graduating nearly two thousand men and women, who have by its lessons met the world at an advantage, the busy hum of conning lessons may still be heard from its snug, old-fashioned rooms.

A little way to the westward of the Classical School was the home of Dr. Allston W. Whitney, one of the best brigade-surgeons in the Army of the Potomac, who passed many a dolorous month in Libby Prison. He it was who routed the fair members of the Culpepper Female Seminary out of their beds, late on the night after the battle of Cedar Mountain, in order that the mangled hundreds of his wounded soldiers might have their comfortable nests. In 1881 Dr. Whitney joined his old comrades, where

> "On Fame's eternal camping-ground,
> Their silent tents are spread,
> And Glory guards, with solemn round,
> The bivouac of the dead."

Not far from the school is the meeting-house of the Unitarian society, whose beginnings arose in 1844, in the hall of the village inn; and the organization was effected five years later, with the Rev. W. O. White as minister. He was son of Judge White, of Salem, and his wife was the daughter of Chester Harding, the artist. After him came the Rev. W. H.

Knapp (1851-53), Rev. C. E. Hodges (1854), Rev. Washington Gilbert (1855-57), Rev. J. A. Allen (1857-59), Rev. W. H. Savary (1860-63), Rev. John C. Zachos (1864-66), Rev. Francis Tiffany, and Rev. J. C. Jaynes. The meeting-house was erected in 1860, and twenty years later received enlargement by the addition of the tower and church-parlor. The vivacious red roofs of the building now make a high relief for the soberer tints of the village square.

All around the adjacent open place are the shops for the small commerce of the village, the ultra-Gothic points of the Robinson Block, and the spacious Pierce School. At the intersection of Washington and Watertown

William E. Sheldon's Residence, Highland and Hunter Streets, West Newton.

Streets stands the brick building erected by Seth Davis for a hotel, in 1831, and for a long time run by landlord John Davis, as the West-Newton Hotel.

The City Hall* is a large and uninteresting wooden building, with an open tower and a flag-staff, at the corner of Washington and Cherry Streets. Here, after its long warfare with Newton Centre, and a final hot skirmish with Newtonville, the village succeeded in establishing the civic temple of the thirteen hamlets, and so constituted itself the capital of the town. The building looks perkily modern, in its fresh paint and Mansard architecture,

* See illustration page 33.

but for all that it has annals of note. A view of it is shown on page 33. After years of consecration to evangelical uses, it was vacated by the Second Parish in 1847; and in the following year began to be occupied by the Model School, where young women who had learned the theory of teaching in the neighboring Normal School could practise on the children of the village, during their last term. The lower story was the home of the West-Newton Athenæum, where the assembled sages of the village exchanged views as to the questions of their day. In the long winter evenings, the local orators discussed the American Colonization Society, the Fugitive Slave Law, the Underground Railroad, the Higher Law, and similar topics; and the fearless radicalism of their views gave color of reason to the outsiders, who entitled the debaters "the Incendiaries and Radicals of West Newton." Parker, Sumner, Pierpont, Whipple, Starr King, and other orators of Freedom addressed the little band of heroes. Sometimes Abolitionist speakers in Boston were walled around by a body-guard of West-Newton yeomen, among whom, in an emergency, might have been found divers stout bludgeons, cut from the freeborn forests of their native hills. By such loyal guardsmen Wendell Phillips was more than once escorted, through howling hostile mobs, from the place of speaking to his home on Essex Street. When the magic sound of traitorous cannon in the Carolinas swelled this little forlorn hope of Freedom into over a million armed infantry, the prevailing question at the Athenæum was settled. But their earnest questioning of the times, the creeds, and the political economies has not ceased. Now it is a flaming Socialist who addresses them on the doctrines of his people; now an eloquent Irish orator, pleading for home-rule; now a Demosthenean woman, demanding suffrage for her sisters; now a Knight of Labor, setting forth the claims of the workingmen; now an orotund advocate of what he is pleased to call temperance, meaning abstinence. And on all these momentous subjects, perhaps the seeds of the American Civil War of the twentieth century, the conscript fathers of the village have much to say.

The City Hall has been enlarged and changed, since its adaptation to civic uses, and has heard many a sturdy debate on questions of local importance. The old men, rich in memories, may still remember momentous arguments on topics now forever settled by the logic of events; or hear Mason's fiery eloquence, in the dark days of the Secession War, when rising to his great peroration: " Millions of gold and rivers of blood will not compare with the influence of this question; for on its solution hang the hopes of civil liberty and civilization throughout the world for ages to come. Let it not be said that we of this generation have been unfaithful to the high and holy trust."

On the Fourth of July, 1876, the municipality celebrated in its City Hall the anniversary of American independence. After prayer by the Rev. Thomas S. Samson, and the singing of a hymn, Edward W. Cate read the Declaration of Independence, from the ancient town-book. Then "The Battle-Cry of Freedom" was sung; Mayor Alden Speare made an introductory address; the Hon. John C. Park delivered an oration; J. L. Ordway read an original poem, "One Hundred Years, 1776–1876"; and the school-children gave an historical drama. Afterwards the Doxology was sung, and the Rev. W. M. Lisle pronounced the benediction.

Adjoining the City Hall stands the great meeting-house of the Second Congregational Church. The old auditorium has been pushed backward to the Cheesecake Brook, and has had a new front put on, in handsome quaint, unecclesiastical architecture, bearing a low-spired clock-tower, and decked in the olive tints that this age affects. The first movings of local pride in West Newton began to upheave the placid surface of its rural life in 1760, when the tavern-keeper and the tanner and a yeoman were made a committee to arrange for building a meeting-house. They hired a minister for the double duties of schoolmaster on the six secular days, and preacher on Sunday. After diligent effort, by the year 1764, they built a meeting-house 43 x 30 feet in area; and, as a result of fourteen years of warfare, they succeeded in being set off from the First Church and made into a new parish.

The first pastor of the West Church was the Rev. William Greenough, a Yale graduate, who held the spiritual sway here for half a century, beginning almost with the foundation of the society, in 1781. The incorporation of the West-Parish society was resisted with determined energy by the older church to the eastward, and the running of the parish-line occasioned many bickerings. While the partisans of the two hostile Zions were marking out their boundaries, they fell into a hot dispute in the midst of a field of winter-squashes, through which the division ran, and, as ill fortune would have it, the line was found to cross one particularly huge squash, leaving its better half in the East Parish. The people of the latter region applied to the other the presumably opprobrious name of "Bell-Hack," and the yeomen of the West thereupon dubbed the old parish "Squash-End," which two terms of wrath became geographical expressions for half a century. Up to within forty years the West Parish was commonly called Bell-Hack "by those who are willing to betray indubitable marks of vulgarity and low breeding" (as its historian caustically remarked).

Mr. Greenough's old pastor, the Rev. Dr. John Lothrop, of the Cockerel Church in Boston, preached the installation sermon, before "a small house, and a little handful of people." His church gave the pulpit Bible to the new society; Mr. Greenough's father, Deacon Thomas Greenough, of Boston, presented it with "a christening basin, two flagons, and two dishes for the communion service"; and the First Church in Newton sent them four pewter tankards and one pewter dish. With this frugal store of church plate the sacrament of the Lord's Supper was administered, perhaps as acceptably as at any Pontifical High Mass in great Milan Cathedral, or under the majestic arches of Cologne. It was *naively* admitted that the meeting-house looked "like a barn"; and that the galleries, reserved for boys and girls and transient people, were "never very full"; and that the fifty windows rattled furiously on windy days, and on sunshiny Sabbaths admitted floods of glaring light through their blindless openings. The first church-bell was one given by an English lady to the town of Concord, from which it was bought by this parish, in 1828. It bore these solemn words, in high relief: —

" I to the church the living call,
I to the grave do summon all."

The Greenoughs were an interesting family of the old school, and many anecdotes are current of their singular and characteristic ways. Seeing some lads skylarking in the gallery of the church, Mr. Greenough put aside his sermon, and exclaimed: "Boys, behave in the house of God! You not only disobey your parents, but greatly offend your Maker." One day he demanded of a neighbor why he used profane language, and, being answered: "Because it relieves my stomach," he replied: "Your stomach must then be very foul." He refused to allow the word *Sunday* to be used in his family, saying: "I don't like to hear the word Sunday. Because the heathen worship the sun, they call it Sunday. Let us say SABBATH." It was indeed kept as a holy day, beginning at sundown on Saturday; and even the parsonage dishes had to go over unwashed until Monday. If the neighbors' children were seen in the road or the fields on that *Dies Iræ*, their parents were reprimanded smartly. The ever-ready hospitalities of the manse were hedged about with quaint restrictions, now-forgotten courtesies, and obsolete observances. No salutation was held valid unless the uplifted hat descended as low as the elbow. The good dominie's alms were given plenteously, but in secret, and with injunctions of silence. When Mrs. Greenough was testifying as a witness in the great Badger will case, Daniel Webster tried to confuse her and break down her testimony, fearing the effect her stately presence might have on the jury. Failing in several attempts, he finally took a huge pinch of snuff, blew a long blast before his bandanna handkerchief, and said: "Mrs. Greenough, was Mrs. Badger a *neat* woman?" She answered: "I can't say as to that: she had one *very dirty* habit." Webster said: "What was that?" And the witness replied: "SHE TOOK SNUFF!" Amid a wild roar of laughter from court and people, the great expounder sat down, and had no more to say to the quick-witted lady.

For over fifty years Mr. Greenough ruled his parish in the fear of the

RESIDENCE OF GEORGE COOK.
Waltham Street, near Derby Street, West Newton.

Lord, during which time he added 102 members to the church. His salary was £80 a year and 15 cords of wood; and his diocese included also the North Village, Auburndale, the Lower Falls, and part of Newtonville,— about forty families in all. He was not only a Yale graduate, but enjoyed an *ad eundem* degree from Harvard (whatever that may be). In his gown and bands he bore a strong physical resemblance to John Wesley; and in his small-clothes, shoe and knee buckles (which he wore long after all New England had gone into prosaic trousers), he presented a quaint and venerable appearance, which led the small boys of Boston to follow him about the streets in wonder. When the icy sea of Puritanism began to break up, under the first heats of the nineteenth century, this venerable dominie held his parish firm in the ranks of Orthodoxy, and turned its energies with strong effect into the new-born foreign missionary movement. The old church, with its eagle's eyrie of a pulpit, and steep galleries, and square box-pews, became a training-school of Christian heroes; and three of the greatest of our Congregationalist chieftains, Professors Park, and Shedd, and Stowe, of Andover, avowed that their first impulses toward the ministry came from Mr. Greenough's direct and earnest preaching. The old church received enlargement in 1812, 1831, and 1838, and was sold to the town in 1848 for $1,600. Mr. Greenough's parsonage stood on Washington Street, between the present Auburn and Greenough Streets, where the great elms that loving parishioners planted in its dooryard are its only memorials.

Mr. Greenough's colleague from the year 1828, the Rev. Lyman Gilbert, succeeded him in 1831, when the old pastor was called home to the Golden City; and ruled the parish until his dismissal, in 1856. The next two pastors, Joseph Payson Drummond and George Barker Little, died after short terms of service, and were succeeded (in 1860) by the Rev. Henry Johnson Patrick, the present incumbent. Several missionaries went out from this little rural church, which, of its own accord, also supported teachers among the freedmen and the Indians.

A little way to the westward stands Nickerson's Block, a commodious brick building, in whose chambers are the reading-rooms and library of the West-Newton Athenæum, a vigorous local senate which dates from the year 1849, and preserves amid its treasures the collections of several older literary societies. There are about 4,000 volumes in the library, which circulates perhaps 15,000 volumes yearly, and has also a well-supplied reading-room and a reference library. The West-Parish Social Library came into existence in 1798, and included Rollin, Plutarch, Goldsmith, Addison, Doddridge, Edwards, Paley, Franklin, Watts, and such other sterling old authors, for the most part unfamiliar, save by tradition, to the vast majority of modern readers, in this age of epitomes and compilations. Towards the year 1840 these venerable tomes were transferred to the Athenæum. Here, also, is preserved the quaint old library of the Adelphian Society, founded in 1830, and for many years kept in the entrance-room of Master Davis's Academy.

Cherry Street runs northward from the City Hall, across the Cheesecake Brook (which is here as large as the world-renowned Ilissus, at Athens), and intersects Webster Street, whose western reaches are occupied by a group of Gothic cottages dating from the year 1847. At the corner of these two streets is the home and estate of Nathaniel T. Allen, of the Classical School, which has been the abiding-place of hundreds of pupils. Here dwelt for the last 25 years of his life the celebrated Phineas Allen, who prepared Thoreau for college, and spent 67 years in teaching, the last 25 being at the West-Newton Classical and English School, conducted by his nephews. He had special charge of the Spanish students there.

On Watertown Street, in an ancient brick house amid lawns and orchards and flowers, dwelt Seth Davis, whose hundredth birthday was celebrated with great enthusiasm on the 3d of September, 1887, by the City Government, and school-children, and his old pupils, with addresses by Mayor Kimball and ex-Governor Alexander H. Rice, and a poem by the Rev. Dr. Samuel F. Smith. He was a lovely, clear-minded old man, with scarce-wrinkled and smooth-shaven face, and a smile full of brightness and vivacity. Seth Davis was a descendant in the sixth generation from Dolor Davis of Kent, who came to Cambridge in 1634; and a son of a soldier of the Revolution. He was born in Ashby, Massachusetts, in 1787, the year of the adoption of the Constitution of the United States, and reached West Newton in 1802, with twenty-five cents in his pocket, and all his worldly goods tied up in a handkerchief. At that time there were but five houses in the village. His subsequent labors as teacher, lecturer, trial-justice, county commissioner, etc., are a large part of the life of the town. His school-days covered a period of only twenty months; but good fortune threw in his way a copy of "Robinson Crusoe," whose perusal aroused in him a keen love of reading, out of which came notable results. In the century that he rounded out, he was never sick, and he attributed a great share of this immunity to abstinence from liquor and tobacco. In 1888 he was called upward to his reward. On Waltham Street, away back in 1812, Seth Davis established a famous private school, which was conducted with great success for nearly forty years. Among its pupils were Warden Gideon Haynes, Professor D. B. Hagar, B. F. Houghton, Phineas Adams, Governor A. H. Rice, J. Willard Rice, Seth Bemis, and other afterwards famous men and women. The legend is still extant how Hamilton Rice and Hagar caught the master's pet cat in their rabbit-trap, and left the rueful Davis to wonder for twenty years what had become of his favorite mouser. When a pupil ran away, and was caught and brought back, he was anchored for some days with a ball and chain attached to his ankle. In order that he could watch his little flock, and still enjoy his favorite posture, with chair tilted back and feet on stove, Master Davis had a series of mirrors affixed to each of the walls of the school-room, whereby he became endowed with the vision of Argus. Governor Rice thus describes the room: "The school-house was peculiar in construction, and designed to promote good order and discipline, as it were, automatically, and thus to aid in dispensing with the labial tactics of Xantippe on the one hand, and with the birch-bark efficiency of Solomon on the other. The centre of the room was a clear space, and around the walls ran a series of stalls, each separated from another by a high partition, after the fashion seen in some eating-houses now; and in each stall was a short and narrow seat, so that its occupant could see no fellow-pupil except on the opposite side of the room, or at least beyond speaking-distance, while each and every one was visible to the master. I say that each one was visible to the master, though it is manifest that, when seated in his chair in the centre, the master's back must be towards some of the stalls on one or more of the four sides of the room. But while this fact is recognized as a physical necessity, it seemed then to have no practical importance; for any mischievous vibration behind him, though as delicate as the step of a velvet-footed mouse, seemed to reverberate upon his sensitive and expectant tympanum as the summons to an instantaneous and whirling jump that brought him, chair and all, face to face with the entrapped offender." When Lafayette passed through the town in 1825, he paused to see this temple of learning, and shook hands with some of the students. The master gave monthly scientific lectures to his boys, and for their instruction built the first orrery in the State. The old school-building now stands on Webster Street, and is the home of George A. Field.

In 1825 there were about thirty students in his school, including Isaac Sweetser of Charlestown, De Witt Clinton of New York, the Stedmans and Deans of Boston, and other likely lads, most of whom boarded with the master, and devoured great stores of hasty pudding and doughnuts, solacing their free hours with base ball, squirrel-hunting, skating and coasting. The Davis School now stands on the site of the ancient academy.

Thousands of trees were set out by Mr. Davis, beginning in the year 1811; and much of the sylvan beauty of the village is due to the now-venerable elms, oaks, maples, and evergreens which he planted in those early days. The huge maples before his house are from seed that he put into the ground over eighty years ago.

Master Davis was one of the *patres magnanimi* of West Newton, whose cause he championed most vigorously in the long legislative and legal conflicts of 1833-49, as against the aggressions of Newton Centre; and pub-

RESIDENCE OF GEORGE B. WILBUR.
Waltham Street, near Derby Street, West Newton.

lished a singular history of Newton, devoting four pages to the annals of the town, and all the rest (an' there be enow) to a pitiless excoriation of the oligarchs of the Centre. Subsequently, he became a leader in the temperance movement, in 1826; and in all other good works stood actively conspicuous. Dr. Smith thus characterized him, in his poem: —

> " Friend of our early youth and riper age,
> The citizen, the patriot, and the sage,
> Blessed with an eye to see, a hand to do,
> A heart to throb, a soul, both large and true,
> Man of the present, treasury of the past,
> How has thy life been honored, to the last!
> Of old traditions, thou, a matchless store,
> A walking volume of historic lore;
> Lover of nature in its varied moods,
> Its brooks and flowers, its fields, and leafy woods.
> A thousand trees, set by thy loving care,
> Attest thy taste and toil which placed them there."

The West-Parish burying-ground was set apart and given to the town in 1781 by Colonel Nathan Fuller, a gallant old Continental soldier, who commanded the rear-guard in the disastrous retreat of Sullivan's army from Canada, with signal valor and intelligence. It has been made over to the city by the Second Congregational Church, and now enjoys the same care that is given to the other Newton cemeteries. The first man to be buried here, the pioneer and vidette of all that came after, was John Barber, the jovial tavern-keeper of the West-Parish, who (in 1767) set out the great elm-tree in front of the meeting-house. It was then a little sapling, which he brought from the woods on his shoulder. His home formed a part of the Old Tavern House which is still standing. In the west cemetery are the graves of the Rev. William Greenough and his two wives, Abigail Badger and Lydia Haskins, and his three daughters; also that of Deacon Joel Fuller, "whose influence in private and public life was very marked"; and Deacon Joseph Ward, father of Colonel Joseph Ward, of the Continental army. The names most frequent on the gravestones are those of Houghton, Jenison, Fuller, and Adams.

The horse-cars will take you in a short time from the railway station to Waltham, through a region of small cottages and fields, assuaged only by the views of the great green hills across the Charles. Presently the line reaches the stately buildings of the American Watch Company, and so on into Waltham, and out again to the foot of Prospect Hill.

On one side Waltham Street runs out by several pleasant and spacious estates, in a rich rural landscape. One of the finest places here is that of George B. Wilbur, on Walnut Street, near Derby. Another of the very fine places is the large estate of George Cook, the president of the Hallet &

Davis Piano Company. And still another, out in the Arcadian region toward Crafts Street, belongs to Vernon E. Carpenter.

There is naturally a colony of negroes on the outskirts of the village, which was in the old days one of the chief stations of the underground railroad, that vast beneficent conspiracy, which covered the Northern States with a network of places of refuge for escaped slaves. The colored population of West Newton supports the vigorous and enthusiastic Myrtle Baptist Church, organized in 1874, with the Rev. Edmund Kelley as pastor. For some years afterwards, the pulpit was occupied by students from the Newton Theological Institution, under whose ministrations the parish increased and grew strong. It has forty-seven members; and the pastor is the Rev. Jacob Burrell.

Washington Street runs out to the westward, to the Lower Falls, a broad avenue, winding through prolonged lines of noble elms. Beyond the railway track, it reaches the long green oval of Lincoln Park, near which stands an engine-house which has a handsome brick tower. At the corner of Washington and Prospect Streets was the home of the Rev. William Dall, afterwards a prominent Unitarian missionary at Calcutta, and a leader in the Brahmo Somaj. His son has since attained eminence as an explorer, under the auspices of the Smithsonian Institute; and his recent book, "Our Arctic Province," is the best account extant of Alaska. On Perkins Street is the home of the Rev. Francis Tiffany, the author of "Bird-Bolts" and other bright writings.

The plain little Gothic meeting-house on Lincoln Park belongs to the First Baptist Church, which was organized in 1853, in Newtonville, where it languished for several years, and thence flew away to West Newton. The church was dedicated in 1871. Its pastors have been the Rev. Joseph M. Graves, Rev. B. A. Edwards (to 1856), Rev. R. H. Bowles (1866–69), Rev. R. S. James, D.D. (1869–70), Rev. William Lisle (1870–75), Rev. T. B. Holland (1875–78), and Rev. O. D. Kimball (1883–89). The first contribution for the Home for Little Wanderers, in Boston, was made in this Baptist Church.

Not far away is the neat brick building of St. Bernard's Church, surrounded by such bravery of lawns and flowers as but few of our hardworking Catholic shrines can find time for. The corner-stone was laid in 1871, by Vicar-General P. F. Lyndon; and the dedication-sermon was preached in 1874, by the Bishop of Springfield. The Rev. Bernard Flood, the Rev. M. T. McManus, and the Rev. Laurence J. O'Toole have been the shepherds of this contented flock, which dated its beginnings from Father Michael Dolan's mission of 200 persons, established in Boyden Hall, at Newton Lower Falls. The building seats 850 persons, and cost $38,000, all of which has been paid.

West-Newton Hill lies south of the railway, and is traversed by pleasant roads, winding along its northern edge, and commanding attractive views across the valley to Waltham and Prospect Hill. Along this noble terrace are many modern houses, some of them very attractive, and a few almost grotesque in their forms and colors. On Hillside Avenue stands the home of the late Rev. Dr. Increase N. Tarbox, one of the foremost of New England's antiquaries and scholars. On the beautiful hill-road of Otis Street is the handsome house designed by Bertram Taylor for Edward B. Wilson, a Boston merchant. On Chestnut Street, near Margin Street, dwells George A. Walton, the agent of the Massachusetts Board of Education. On Highland Street, at the corner of Hunter Street, is the house of William E. Sheldon, journalist and orator, who has for many years been so prominent in the National councils of educational officers. His daughter, Miss Marian E. Sheldon, now conducts the famous girls' school at Adabazar, in Asiatic Turkey, and has translated several books into the Armenian language.

At the corner of Chestnut and Highland Streets, amid broad grounds, and with a noble prospect over the valley, stands the house which was for many years the home of the Hon. Horace Mann, the great founder of the educational system of Massachusetts. In this mansion dwelt the prince of our American authors, Nathaniel Hawthorne, who here wrote one of his noblest works. In his diaries Hawthorne makes but slight mention of West Newton, giving only here and there an allusion to snow-storms and awesome weather, and the advance that he made on "The Blithedale Romance." He lived with the creatures of his ideal world, with Coverdale and Hollingsworth and Priscilla and Zenobia; and the strange drama wrought itself out with the trist background of a New-England winter. If at any time he wished to deepen the local color of his scene, it was but a short hour's drive to the well-remembered meadows of Brook Farm, the Blithedale of the fantastic socialistic experiment in which he had been a participant some years before.

In his Life of Nathaniel Hawthorne, Julian Hawthorne gives this sub-acid description of the home of the family from November, 1851, to June, 1852: "A more dismal and unlovely little suburb than West Newton was in the winter of 1851 could not exist outside of New England. It stood upon a low rise of land, shelving down to a railway, along which smoky trains screeched and rumbled from morning till night. Lenox was one of those places where a man might be supposed to write because the beauty around him wooed him to expression. West Newton was a place where the omnipresent ugliness compels a man to write in self-defence. Lenox drew forth 'The House of the Seven Gables'; and in West Newton 'The Blithedale Romance' was composed; from which data the curious in such matters

THE RESIDENCE OF FREDERIC R. CUTTER.
Chestnut Street, West Newton.

may conclude what kind of environment is the more favorable to the artist." The two chambers on the sunny side of the house Hawthorne used as a study, and here he composed his magnificent sentences, while walking up and down the floor, in an undeviating track. Hour after hour, day after day, his slow footsteps wore away the carpet, while he recorded the deeds and words of the children of his fancy. Between the windows, inside one of the rooms, grew a great arbutilon, whose pendulous shower of golden drops gave him sweet intimations of summer and nature, amid the deepening gloom of winter. Hither often came Whipple, to discuss the story with him; and it was due to his solicitations that the complex and ghastly tragedy that the author had devised for the closing scene received important modifications and became less terrible.

Opposite the house thus made famous is the beautiful home of Charles Robinson, Jr., the lawyer (ex-mayor of Charlestown, and brother of ex-Governor Robinson), notable for the rare and delicate flowers in its gardens and conservatories.

On Temple Street, curving along the heights to the westward, is the mansion of Fisher Ames, the lawyer. Here also is the summer residence of the Hon. Horatio King, Postmaster-General of the United States during the latter part of Buchanan's administration. He and Judge Holt were the only War Democrats in the Cabinet, and it was largely due to their activity that Washington enjoyed immunity from a rebel occupation. Mr. King has been a resident of the National capital for 52 years, and spends his long summers at West Newton, near the home of his son, Henry F., one of the most conspicuous residences in this district. From the tall towers of this house, which is almost at the summit, at the corner of Putnam and Temple Streets, can be had glorious views of several of the surrounding villages.

In his description of West Newton, Mr. James T. Allen thus speaks of the noble view from the heights: " No one who has stood on these hills in spring-time and watched the morning mists from the Charles creep up the slopes of distant Prospect Hill, in Waltham, or lie in silvery masses over the parent stream below, whose hidden meanderings they thus betray, — no one who at noon of summer has rested the weary sight with the thick masses of foliage that, in their luxuriance, partly hide the distant hamlets or nearer dwellings on every side — or again, in autumn time, has caught the reflection of the setting sun in the gorgeously arrayed colors of these same masses of foliage,— no such privileged person, I say, need sigh for Naples before he dies."

After Chestnut Street has pluckily climbed the heights, it escapes as soon as it can from Queen-Anndom, and stretches away to the southwest, through a delightful region of forests. At a long mile from the village it reaches the Pine-Farm School, a building rising on the right, beyond the cross-roads, with 26 acres of farmland and woodland pertaining to it. This is a pleasant charity, founded by the Children's Aid Society of Boston, in 1864, "to provide temporary homes for vagrant, destitute, and exposed children, and those under criminal prosecution of tender age in the city of Boston, and to provide for them such other and further relief as may be advisable to rescue them from moral ruin." More than 500 boys, between the ages of 8 and 13, have thus been rescued from the slums of the metropolis, and brought out here, where the pure air and good associations of this upland home are quick to sweeten the hard, surly, pallid expression of the city poor. Besides receiving many of the lacking elements of a common-school education, the lads are trained in singing, and in carpentry, and more than all else in the practical work of farming, so that after a year and a half of discipline and instruction they are sent out to work on farms in New England and the West. There is no suggestion of the penal colony about the place. The boys have their liberty; can receive visits from friends; are clad in no degrading uniform; and are scattered among the various classes in the Congregational Sunday-school at West Newton. They come here bad, many of them taken out of the prisoners' dock, by Uncle Cook and other kind-hearted men: they leave the Home for the fair hopes of a new life, transplanted from the hot-beds of vice to the pure air and honorable industry of the country. The officials of the institution are the Superintendent and Matron (Mr. and Mrs. Moore), the farmer and his wife, the seamstress, and the laundress; and these unite to make a fair Christian home for their wards. But rarely do the lads straggle back to the dangerous city. They see that the world has given them a chance, and they improve it, with brave earnestness.

One large and sunny room is used as a library, where the well-worn books and magazines bear witness to the continual and happy use to which they are daily put. The upper story of the house is in two spacious and airy halls, in which (on a hard-wood floor) are the snug little iron cots of the boys, each with a stool by its side. Everything is neat, orderly, and comfortable; and the stigma of repression nowhere appears. The healthfulness of the place and its *régime* is seen from the fact that not a single death has occurred here, from the beginning. The President of the society for many years was the Rev. Dr. Rufus Ellis; and the Vice-Presidents, James Freeman Clarke and Robert Treat Paine, Jr.

Opposite the Pine-Farm School is the Raymond estate, where, many years ago, Harriet Beecher Stowe and Lydia Maria Child used to board, in search of that retirement and that environment of natural beauty in which high inspiration might come to them for their great works of composition.

Here Mrs. Child could carry on her studies, and use her pen, without much danger of interruption If any one will glance at her record, as an author, he will see that her pen was kept very busy. Yet in the intervals of her work she desired kindred companionship, and Mrs. Harriet Beecher Stowe was often her guest for weeks. Very likely the two ladies were thoroughly agreed in filling the larger portion of each day with continuous work, enjoying their hours of relaxation all the more, because of the labors accomplished. Here also Mrs. Child entertained the celebrated Fredrika Bremer, during her visit to the United States in 1849–1851.

Fuller Street, named after one of the old families of Newton, runs from the Pine Farm westerly into Washington Street, which it strikes a little north of the Woodland-Park Hotel. Several years ago this street, then a narrow country road, was widened to fifty feet and the grade improved. It now ranks among the best roads in Newton, and is a favorite resort for cyclists and pleasure drivers. The view westward from near the School — the two lines of trees leading the eye over to the Weston hills — and the views of Beacon Hill and Wellesley to the south are especially fine. Fuller Street is bordered by fruit grounds and market gardens, among which is the small-fruit farm (next house to the School on the south side) of Rev. N. P. Gilman, Editor of the *Literary World* and Assistant-Editor of the *Unitarian Review* of Boston.

Pine Farm School, Chestnut and Fuller Streets, West Newton.

Auburndale.

THE PRETTY RAILWAY STATION.—PIONEER FARMS.—PIGEON'S BATTERY.
SAINTS' REST.—SWEET AUBURN.—A NOTED ARTIST.—VILLAGE NOT-
ABLES.—FAMOUS SCHOOLS.—A TRIO OF CHURCHES.—A PRO-
VINCIAL INN.—ISLINGTON.—THE WINSLOW AFFAIR.

"Crow's Nest" at Lasell Seminary.

Undoubtedly, one of the loveliest villages in America is Auburndale, occupying a peculiarly advantageous position between the shaggy hills that enwall the upper Cheesecake glen and the picturesque bays of the Charles River, which bends gracefully around its bold plateau, in curves of surpassing beauty. It is the home of perhaps 2,000 people, who find here tranquillity combined with scenic beauty, and a climate delightfully free from the malignant east winds that so often scourge Boston. The sanitary condition of the locality is almost perfect, with admirable drainage, a copious water-supply, concrete sidewalks, and an enlightened public vigilance.

The charm of the place begins as soon as the visitor alights from the train, for the railway station is one of the prettiest on the line, a long, low structure of stone, in massive and attractive architecture, pleasantly bordered by verdant lawns. The architect of this dainty temple of travel was the famous H. H. Richardson, the foremost of Americans in his profession. Emerging from the broad arches of this handsome building, one sees on all sides the scattered houses of the village, embowered in trees and engirdled with gardens, favored by a fertile soil and genial climate. The local society, being made up of professional and city men, escapes all rural provincialism, and is in a good sense select, without clannishness.

Before threading its leafy aisles, we may languidly glance at the scant and peaceful history of the place. The domain of Auburndale originally pertained to William Robinson, who had a farm of 200 acres here in the seventeenth century, and bequeathed it to his sons. One of these lived in the Bourne house, afterwards Whittemore's tavern, on the road to the bridge; another on the site of the Seaverns house; and still another in the house afterwards occupied by the village poor, and now standing on

Auburndale Station of Boston & Albany Railroad.

Auburn Street, between Melrose and Lexington Streets, opposite the railway station. The town's poor were for many years let out, to be boarded by certain of the citizens; but in 1818 the town bought from Captain Joel Houghton the old Henry-Pigeon House, paying $2,500 for the buildings and 43 acres of land; and this pleasant domain was for many years the abiding-place of those whom Fortune had frowned upon, or forgotten.

Another of the pioneers was Alexander Shepard, Jr., who built the so-called Crafts house, about the year 1765. Some years later, in company with several other Newton men, he went away into the Northern wilderness, and founded the town of Hebron, in Maine.

John Pigeon, who came hither from Boston about the year 1770, received distinction as an active patriot in the Revolutionary days, a Delegate to the Provincial Congress, and in other ways offensive to the Lion of England. Particularly in that at his own costs he bought two field-pieces and presented them to the town, which raised a company of artillerists to work them, in case the red-coats took a promenade toward Nonantum. Although himself a slave-holder, John Pigeon was such an ardent champion of liberty, that he became Commissary-General of the 8,000 Massachusetts soldiers encamped at Cambridge, before Washington arrived to take command of the army. His son was Henry Pigeon, who died in 1799, aged 40, leaving a farm of 150 acres, with 2 houses, the whole being valued, in those Arcadian days, at $4,311. The Rev. Dr. Lyman Gilbert one day called on the Rev. Charles Du Marisque Pigeon, who was living at the Newton-Centre Female Academy, and told him that there was a great chance to make money by buying land at the then budding settlement of Hull's Crossing. Mr. Pigeon remarked that he was averse to ministers engaging in speculation; but soon afterwards, visiting his father's farm, he resolved to make an attempt there. Moved by love for his old home, he succeeded in starting a small hamlet on this site, and inducing the railway to stop some of its trains here, in 1847. An earnest attempt was made to give the new settlement a peculiarly Evangelical character; and it won from the light-minded the title of "Saints' Rest," on account of the number of clergymen who came here to live, exhausted in their long battle with the Prince of the Powers of Darkness. The Rev. Dr. Clarke was urged to move up hither from his home at West Newton, "among the world's people and the Unitarians"; but he dryly remarked: "I don't know but what I like a sprinkling of the world's people," and so remained in his old place. The Rev. Mr. Pigeon, a native of the soil, and his neighbors, the Rev. Messrs. Partridge and Woodbridge, both connected with "The New-England Puritan" (and who settled here more than forty years ago), held many consultations as to the name which should be applied to the budding hamlet; and finally settled upon AUBURNDALE, as if from some pleasant association with Goldsmith's poem: —

"Sweet Auburn, loveliest village of the plain."

According to the practical turn of manifest destiny in New-England nomenclature, it should have been called *Pigeonville*, or *North Newton;* but happier counsels prevailed, and about the year 1845 this euphonious Auburndale (or Auburn Dale, as it was often written) became the local designation. Dr. J. C. D. Pigeon, of Roxbury, a son of the sponsor of this village, says: "While my father was in Harvard (class of 1818), his favorite resort, during leisure hours, was Mount Auburn; and he soon noticed a similarity between those hills and the shady slopes about his native place. When he first came into possession of the land where Auburndale stands, he wrote of it as 'Sweet Auburn'; but, feeling bound to recognize the not inconsiderable proportion of valley, he modified the name in various ways, finally fixing upon the name as it now is."

In the year 1848 William Jackson organized a company that bought up much of the Auburndale tract, and laid it out in streets and avenues, which were speedily occupied by new-comers from other towns. Up to that time there were but six houses in Auburndale and Riverside, including the farmhouses of the Bourne, Ware, and Washburn families. The population rose to 698 by the year 1865, and to 1,258 by the year 1878. The growth of the village has thus been steady and healthy, and it now numbers not far from 2,000 souls, dwelling amid the surroundings of a rich and park-like country.

The public spirit of the community is kept up by several active little societies, under whose auspices sweetness and light are cultivated like precious flowers. The Auburndale Village-Improvement Society watches after the adornment of the streets, with lawns and trees and shrubbery: "to create and encourage in the community a spirit of improvement which shall stimulate every one to seek to make his own surroundings more attractive; to attend to matters affecting the public health; and to provide such entertainments as the Board of Government shall think proper." The long winters are enlivened by the entertainments provided by the Star Lecture Course. A poet familiar with the village avers that,

> "The citizens are amiable, the clergymen are 'nice';
> All welcome a stranger cordially,
> And none of them put on airs,
> So you need not fear in that respect,
> And you may be helped by their prayers."

The flowery avenues are the home of pleasant charities, in their kind; and sometimes in a single season 2,500 bouquets are sent from this little suburb to the hospitals and the poor of Boston. The village also has an influential Women's Christian Temperance Union, holding monthly meetings in the Congregational chapel.

Here was the summer-home of Albert F. Bellows, the well-known artist in water-colors, whose works were celebrated all over the world for their gentle poetry and harmonious and quiet tones, reflecting in some strange way the almost feminine urbanity and kindliness of the artist himself. He had been for many years a student and painter in Europe, and became an honored member of the New-York and Brussels Water-Color Societies, and the New-York, Philadelphia, and London Societies of Etchers; but he found no scenes more satisfying than the landscapes and hamlets of his native Massachusetts. Whatever his Paris and Antwerp teachers imparted to him of skill in art, he enriched by an admiring study of English rural scenery, and applied the resulting method to New-England meadows and riversides and forests. His home at Auburndale was with his son, Dr. H. P. Bellows; and here, in the year 1883, he died.

Another citizen from Auburndale, who from this rural plaisaunce passed upward to Paradise, in 1859, was Dr. William A. Alcott, cousin of Amos Bronson Alcott, and himself the author of more than a hundred books, "The Young Man's Guide," "The Young Woman's Guide," "The Young

J. Willard Rice's Residence, Grove Street, near Centre Street, Auburndale.

Husband," and similar works of counsel and instruction. His avowed object in life was "the prevention of vice, disease, and poverty"; but up to the time of his death it remained unfulfilled. Here for a time dwelt the Rev. M. J. Cramer, the Dean of Boston University, and for many years United-States Minister to Denmark. He was a brother-in-law of General Ulysses S. Grant, and maintained most friendly relations with his illustrious kinsman.

In Grove Street is the fine large estate and good old-fashioned home of J. Willard Rice, of the famous Boston firm of Rice, Kendall & Co., paper merchants, and brother of the Hon. Alexander H. Rice.

On Rowe Street is the quiet little home where William H. Crane, the celebrated actor, was born and passed the years of his youth, ere yet he had met his double in Stuart Robson.

A pleasant old-fashioned house in one of the oak groves was for years the home of Charles S. Pratt, the author, and his wife, the "Ella Farman" of the pretty magazine called "Wide Awake." On Hancock Street dwells Deacon C. C. Burr, of the A. B. C. F. M., and a large holder of Mexican Central and Atchison Railroad stocks; and not far off, on Grove Street, is the estate of the late Charles A. Sweet, the banker. Major David T. Bunker, a veteran officer of the Secession War, and a citizen of this village, recently died while United-States Consul at Demerara. Fannie Buss Merrill, now a well-known New-York journalist, was a native of Auburndale; and for some years Elizabeth M. Gardner, now an eminent artist in Paris, dwelt here. Another longtime resident was Dr. Eben Tourjée, the head of the New-England Conservatory of Music. On Hancock Street is the home of the Rev. S. W. Dike, who has for many years waged valiant war against the evils of the divorce system, of late such a deplorable factor in American life. Another citizen is the Rev. Dr. S. Eliot Lane, who took a prominent official part in the pacification of the Carolinas, after the close of the Secession War. Here, also, dwells the Rev. F. E. Clark, the founder of the Societies for Christian Endeavor, which have latterly spread all over the world, and number their members by hundreds of thousands.

On Central Street, near Fern Avenue, is the pretty home (designed by Edwin J. Lewis, Jr., the Boston architect) of Professor Julius Luquiens, professor of modern languages at the Massachusetts Institute of Technology, and also at Lasell Seminary.

The little red school-house on Auburn Street, which was the first educational building in the hamlet, has been succeeded by a group of important and active public and private schools, such as can be found in few other places of equal size in the world. The Williams School-house, not far from the Congregational church, on Hancock Street, is a spacious and commodious new building, quite the handsomest of the schools of Newton, in its quaint Old-English architecture, accented with clambering ivy. Miss Delia T. Smith's Riverside School, on Evergreen Avenue, occupies the house built by the Rev. C. D. Pigeon, about the year 1848, and afterwards the home of General J. F. B. Marshall, for twenty years a resident of the Sandwich Islands, and commissioner from that insular kingdom to the other insular kingdom, Great Britain.

The former Auburndale Home School stands on high ground, in a retired part of the village, and was owned and conducted by James Bird, A.M. It used to be an expensive and carefully conducted boarding-school, for a limited number of lads, who received the advantages of a home and family training and supervision. A few years ago it was given up, and it and the companion house across the lawns and roadway are now conducted as charming suburban boarding-houses, by Theodore W. Fisher. These places are on Seminary Avenue, back of Lasell Seminary, and are known as Oak Ridge. They are situated amid delightfully picturesque scenery, and are much frequented by families from Boston and vicinity.

Lasell Seminary Grounds, Seminary Avenue, Auburndale.

Miss Williston's Home, on Melrose Street, is a beautiful little charity, where a dozen or more poor children are kept, at a nominal board (or none at all), and taught industry, self-support, kindness, and sweetness, in addition to the usual (and not always so beneficial) educational studies.

Lasell Seminary for young women dates its origin from the year 1851, when one half the present spacious building arose on the hill-top over Woodland Avenue. Professor Edward Lasell, its founder, did not live to see its full development, which was carried forward (after his death) by his brother, Josiah Lasell and George W. Briggs, Esq. From 1864 until 1873 the property was held and conducted by Professor C. W. Cushing. In 1873, the Seminary was bought by ten Methodist gentlemen, and reopened under the care of Professor Charles C. Bragdon, the present incumbent; and it is safe to say that there is no school of the kind in New England that holds a higher rank. The building is large and comfortable, with broad views over the country, and sunlight in every room. Among the special features of interest are Dr. William J. Rolfe's Shakespearean instruction, careful topical and reading courses in history, experimental work in the natural sciences, efficient facilities in teaching art and music, the practical study of the modern branches of book-keeping, phonography, and telegraphy.

There is also a three-years' course in cooking, resulting in many loaves of capital bread and other delicacies of the table; and another branch of the curriculum initiates the girls into the mysteries of dress-making and the construction of bonnets. To all these acquirements is added that of physical culture, in the handsome new gymnasium, bowling alley, and natatorium, and in the boats on the river, under the intelligent direction of professional teachers of these specialties.

The object of Lasell is not to make bookworms or blue-stockings, still less to develop cooks or dressmakers or athletes; but to graduate first-rate, all-round women, full of practical knowledge for daily duties, and versed in Parloa and Redfern and Hollander, as well as in Virgil and Mendelssohn and Euclid. The Seminary has always about 115 boarding pupils, its full capacity, and a dozen or twenty day pupils, some of them from families that have settled at Auburndale expressly for the purpose of having their daughters educated here. The students are from thirty different States and countries. The building was doubled in size in 1881, to meet the increasing demand for accommodations; and in 1884 the gymnasium, one of the most perfect of its kind, was erected. Among the abundant art-treasures of Lasell is the Breton picture "Anxious Moments," ordered for the seminary by Professor Bragdon, from the studio of Henry Orne Ryder, an artist of Auburndale birth, now working in Paris.

Turning from the schools to their sister-institutions, the churches, we may find here several prosperous and active religious organizations, prolific in good words and works. The Evangelical Congregational society has a comfortable church on Hancock Street, with a parsonage adjacent. This society was founded in 1850, with 34 members; and built the church in 1856-57, at a cost of $12,000. In 1862, the spire blew over on to the roof, smashing its way down into the auditorium, to the great confusion and destruction of all things therein. Extensive enlargements and improvements were made in 1877-78. Among the clergy here have been the Rev.

LASELL SEMINARY AT AUBURNDALE.
Woodland and Seminary Avenues.

Sewall Harding, Rev. J. E. Woodbridge, Rev. C. D. Pigeon, Rev. Melancthon S. Wheeler, Rev. Edward W. Clark (1857-61), Rev. Dr. James Means, Rev. Augustus H. Carrier (1864-66), and Rev. Calvin Cutler, from 1867 until the present time. The church has 285 members, with 264 young people in the Sunday school. The clock in the tower was made in 1812, and for more than half a century told the time in the old Hollis-Street Church, in Boston. Among the present members of the society are missionaries and teachers in Spain, Corea, Turkey, Syria, South Africa, and five in India.

The Methodist church began in a series of prayer-meetings, in 1860; and after a series of slow advances and upbuildings the present Centenary Methodist-Episcopal Church was erected, in 1866-67. Its clergy have been the Rev. J. Emery Round (1862), Rev. Solomon Chapin (1862-63), Rev. Henry V. Degen, Rev. B. Otheman (1864), Rev. C. W. Cushing, Rev. Mr. Townsend, Rev. Mr. James, Rev. J. R. Cushing (1872), Rev. Daniel Steele (1873-75), Rev. J. M. Avann (1875-76), Rev. William McDonald (1876-77), Rev. Andrew McKeown (1877-80), Rev. Charles Parkhurst (1880), Rev. J. W. Bashford (1881-83), Rev. E. R. Watson (1884-85), and Rev. W. Rice Newhall (1886-87). The society moved from John Mero's parlor to an unoccupied school-house, and thence to the village hall; and when that was burnt, it erected its present house of worship. The organist and musical director for many years was the well-known Dr. Eben Tourjée, of the New-England Conservatory of Music, longtime a resident of the village.

Episcopalianism in Auburndale and West Newton was a plant of languid growth; and after its suspension, in 1858, thirteen years passed by without the regular recital of the Litany and the Nicene Creed in this little hamlet. But in 1871 worship according to the Anglican form was re-established here, with wardens and vestrymen and all, in the Village Hall at West Newton, and (in 1877) the chapel of Lasell Seminary. In the year 1880 a piece of land was bought; and the society acquired the brownstone of the then recently demolished Rowe-Street Baptist Church, in Boston, and transported it to Auburn Street, in Auburndale, where the stones of the old Baptist temple have been re-edified into a shrine where Bishops and Priests may intone their ancient liturgies. It bears the name of the Church of the Messiah, and was opened for services in 1881. The Rev. N. G. Allen was the first rector (in 1858), followed, after a long interval, by the Rev. C. S. Lester (1872-73), Rev. H. W. Fay (1873-75), and Rev. Francis W. Smith (1875-77), after whose rectorate the pulpit was for some time occupied by the rectors of neighboring parishes. The Rev. Henry A. Metcalf is the present rector of the parish.

In 1888 the Vestry began the erection of a new and handsome Early-English-Gothic church to form two sides of a quadrangle with the present chapel. When this edifice shall have been finished, it will be a great ornament to the lovely village.

AUBURNDALE CONGREGATIONAL CHURCH.
Woodland Avenue and Hancock Street.

The Home for Missionaries' Children, on Hancock Street, was informally established in 1868, when Mrs. Eliza H. Walker, widow of a missionary at Diarbekir, Turkey, settled here with her four children, in a house built for her by her father, the Rev. Sewall Harding. Here are accommodations for a score or more children of missionaries in Japan, China, India, Africa, and the South Seas, who attend the Newton public schools, and receive those advantages of civilization that cannot be found on the distant outposts of Christianity, where their parents are stationed. Much of the housework is also done by these children, who thus learn practical lessons of self-reliance and industry. When their parents return to America, on furlough, they frequently sojourn here, to be near their children, in the heart of a peaceful Christian community. The children are in part supported by an allowance of from $120 to $150 each, given by the American Board; and efforts are being made to buy and endow the institution, as a permanent home for these wards of the Church Universal. For over sixty years the American Board has made appropriations for the children of missionaries; and there are many wise men who hope that in time a great institution may arise here, like that at Walthamstow, near London.

Auburn Street runs down from the railway station to the picturesque stone bridge that crosses the Charles River to Weston, in a beautiful sequestered and embowered glen. It was laid out in 1729, as "a way from the fording place in Charles River, against the town way in Weston, to the county road that goeth from the Lower Falls to Watertown." Here rose (near the bridge) the gray old walls of the Whittemore Tavern, opened by Nathaniel Whittemore as early as the year 1724, and a busy place on the day of the Concord battle, whose artillery firing reverberated over the quiet valley.

Farther down the stream, and north of Auburndale, is the beautiful promontory, between the main stream of the River Charles and a long bay, occupied by Islington, the estate of the late Colonel Royal M. Pulsifer, of the Boston *Herald*, whose great and hospitable mansion rises amid groves of fine old trees, and looks down on blue water on either side. About a dozen years ago, this point was purchased by the Rev. Ezra D. Winslow, it being then held of little value, being in the condition reprobated by Massachusetts farmers as "sprout land." The dreadful career of this Winslow is the great moral tragedy in the quiet annals of the village. He had been an efficient chaplain during the Secession War, and afterwards turned his energies to preaching, journalism, trading in real estate, and various speculations on a grand scale. He settled at Auburndale, and was very active, erecting the Haskell and Pulsifer houses, and others, and in every way furthering the development of the place. Genial, generous, interesting in all ways, he was in and of the best society, and every one looked upon

CHURCH OF THE MESSIAH, AUBURNDALE.
Auburn Street, near Rowe Street.

him with respect and admiration. He had a luxurious home, and a lovely wife, whom he married at the age of nineteen, she being then but seventeen. Suddenly, and without a premonition, this prosperity crumbled to the ground. In the dead of winter, he fled across the ocean to Amsterdam, a defaulter and forger for vast amounts, the destroyer of fortunes, the wrecker of banks. The business men of Boston could hardly credit the magnitude and turpitude of the crime. He took refuge in Brazil, and finally in Buenos Ayres, where, blotting out the memory of the wife who had accompanied him in his European flight, he married a woman of that country, and resumed his old avocations of journalism and speculation.

The Bridge over the Charles, connecting Weston and Auburndale.

He still remains there, as earnest in the new life as aforetime in the old; while his true wife faded away and died amid the glens of Auburndale.

Afterwards Islington forgot its oldtime memories in the gladness brought in by the Pulsifer family and their thronging guests; and on many a summer's eve the grounds, illuminated by myriads of lanterns, were given up to garden-parties and joyous *fêtes*. The career of the lord of the domain was one of wonderful success, from the year 1861, when, at the age of eighteen, he entered the office of the Boston *Herald*, in which, within four years, he became junior partner. In the year 1879 he was elected Mayor of Newton. The details of Mr. Pulsifer's lonely death in the Islington mansion, late in the year 1888, after disastrous business complications, are still fresh in every one's memory. Mr. Pulsifer's great interest in public matters, and his admirable social and family traits, endeared him to a host of people.

Near the Islington estate is the great house once occupied by Abner I. Benyon, a well-known financier of Boston, and President of the Pacific National Bank — who some years since got into trouble, in a business way, and took refuge in hospitable Canada.

In this same region, near the little oval park, stands the Tanglewood estate, of happier memories, occupied by the Hon. W. B. Fowle, who was born in 1826, the son of a prominent educator, who lived for many years at West Newton. In the Secession War he held a captaincy in the 43d Massachusetts Infantry, and commanded the military post at Beaufort, S.C., in 1862-63. After the close of the war, he settled in Auburndale, and during the years 1878 and 1879 held the mayoralty of the city.

The Auburndale Watch Company was founded about the year 1875 by Mr. Fowle, for the manufacture of rotary watches; and its shops stood in a wild and secluded glen on the Weston shore, some ways below the bridge, and reached by a regular ferry-boat. The success which was hoped for this enterprise, in a region so favorable for watch-making, somehow failed to come; and the works were converted into a factory for manufacturing thermometers. In 1884 the factory and its machinery were sold.

Among the other citizens of Auburndale there are several who have achieved distinction. Raymond L. Bridgman, the author of "Ten Years of Massachusetts" and correspondent of the New-York *Evening Post*, dwells on Hancock Street. Up on the hill, towards Captain Charles E. Ranlett's, is the home of Edward E. Hardy (Alpheus Hardy's son), in the most charming part of this garden-village.

Auburndale merges into its maritime suburb of Riverside and its highland dependency of Woodland without perceptible change or barrier; and so we will e'en move across into other little chapters, to set forth the charms of these localities. In passing, let us add a bit from one of Miss Guiney's lyrics, probably derived from her Charles-River boating: —

"Far hills behind,
  Sombre growth, with sunshine lined,
    On their edges;
  Banks hemmed in with maiden-hair,
  And the straight and fair
    Phalanx of sedges:

"Wee wings and eyes,
  Wide blue gemmy dragon-flies,
    Fearless rangers;
  Drowsy turtles in a tribe
  Diving, with a gibe
    Muttered at strangers;

"Wren, bobolink,
  Robin, at the grassy brink;
    Great frogs jesting;
  And the beetle, for no grief
  Half-across his leaf,
    Sighing and resting.

"In the keel's way,
  Unwithdrawing bream at play,
    Till from branches
  Chestnut-blossoms, loosed aloft,
  Graze them with their soft
    Full avalanches."

In these Johnsonian lines a poet of the region praises the bonnie Doon of his native glens, the bright Charles River: —

> "Shade of Sir Isaac and the angler's god,
> Here couldst thou sit and gently troll the rod;
> Here, 'midst the pictures of our winding stream,
> Would meditation mount and reign supreme;
> And fancy, startled by its scenes so fair,
> Would call the angels down, and seat them there.
>
> "Its gentle waves through miles of verdure flow,
> Anon o'er falls they leap, 'mid rocks below;
> Its music strikes our ears like soothing sound
> Mellowed by distance, and the hills around;
> Its fame's acknowledged; even Choate could pour
> An avalanche of eloquence upon its roar;
> While the Hyperion Poet, in gentler style and tone,
> Has made it classic, by a power his own.
>
> "Scenes such as these, Fair Charles, are on thy breast;
> They fire the lover, and they soothe the opprest;
> They thrill the soul, to nature's beauties prone,
> And bring new comforts to the sad and lone.
> On thy fair banks the Indian maiden wept,
> As in his bark canoe her lover from her swept;
> Here she prepared their simple meal of maize,
> While he weired out, for fish, its shores and bays."

Woodland.

THE WOODLAND-PARK HOTEL.— WILLIAM DEAN HOWELLS.— THE SHORT HILLS.— BURGOYNE'S ROUTE.— VISTA HILL.— EDWIN B. HASKELL.— NEWTON COTTAGE HOSPITAL.

Woodland, sometimes called Woodland Park, has only within a few years begun to be recognized as a distinct village, as one of the fifteen villages which collectively make up the incorporated city of Newton. Woodland is still to most people only a part of Auburndale, but it promises in time to work out for itself a clearly defined village, the forerunners of which are the pretty station and the famous hotel of the same name.

Woodland station is a quaint and cosey little structure of Braggville granite and brownstone, finished inside in spruce in its natural colors, and cypress. About it are pleasant and extensive grounds, with a pretty pond, fed by a never-failing spring.

Less than a mile from Auburndale station, by the lovely Woodland Avenue, and about half a mile from Woodland station, on the Circuit Railway, is the chief public house of Newton, the Woodland-Park Hotel, well-secluded from the adjacent rural roads, and standing on an elevated plain, with a charming view of the far-away Blue Hills of Milton. It is a handsome Queen-Anne building of considerable size, with abundance of picturesque dormers, gables, and verandas. The entrance hall is thirty feet square, with heavy ceiling beams overhead, and floors and wainscots and a grand stairway of quartered oak; and from thence the visitor may pass into the airy and comfortable dining-room; or the richly-furnished parlor, with its interesting paintings; or enter upon the road to the billiard-room; or ascend the stairway to the three stories of chambers overhead. The hotel was erected in 1881–82 by Messrs. Haskell, Pulsifer, and Andrews, of the Boston *Herald*, and Mr. Frederick Johnson, as a suburban boarding-place, near one of the fairest and most comfortable of Massachusetts villages. The climate of this locality (like that of Wellesley Hills, a few miles to the westward) is very beneficial in certain diseases of the throat and lungs, too common in Boston; and several of the best physicians of the New-England metropolis have been in the habit of advising their patients to go to Florida or Auburndale, during the inclement seasons of the year. The sanitarium thus formed by genial climatic influences, a fortunate isle of safety in a wild sea of wintry east winds, naturally became in due time fashionable, a little Massachusetts Nice or Mentone. The first lessee and present proprietor of the house is Joseph Lee, a Virginian, sometime a butler in the United-States Navy, who has won a renown extending over four counties, for the ingenious excellence and variety of his cookery, a form of carnal temptation to which the most Browningesque and Theosophic of Bostonians are peculiarly susceptible. It is averred that Mr. Lee serves the only genuine Philadelphia chicken croquettes and dressed terrapin in all New England.

At certain seasons of the year, the assassin-like Spring and the perilous late Autumn, the hotel fills up with families from the Back Bay, the Faubourg St. Germain of Boston, whose delicate residents find security here from throat and lung troubles, and an environment of good manners and correct genealogies, while still within a half-hour's ride of their tall red-brick or brownstone homes. Mr. Howells has spent several long seasons here, and perhaps amid such favorable surroundings made the preliminary studies for his Bromfield Corey and the Rev. Mr. Sewell and Miss Vane. Of course, no Silas Lapham could have entered those Queen-Anne portals; and as to Bartley Hubbard or Lemuel Barker,— we regret to say that all our rooms are engaged for the season.

Mr. Howells has used the fortunate term, "Short Hills," to denominate this region of bold knolls and sharp little ravines; and it seems more than likely that before many years shall have passed, it will become as beautiful artistically as the famous Short Hills of New Jersey.

Opposite the hotel, a hundred years ago, stood the famous old Stimson mansion, near the site later occupied by the Atkinson place.

Not far distant, near Unity Place, is the beginning of a long glacial moraine, which curves away to the westward, and crosses the line of the railway. Washington Street runs away from the front of the hotel, to West Newton, on the north-east; and toward the south-west to the pretty stone station of Woodland, on the Circuit Railroad, and then on to Newton Lower Falls. And nearly in front the lonely country road called Fuller Street winds away across the Cheesecake glen, and alongside Beacon Hill, to the Pine-Farm School, of which some mention is made on a previous page.

Woodland Avenue in 1750 was the range-way over which the Worcester turnpike passed, on the way from the First Church to the Weston Bridge, and for many years held its place as one of the most important highways in the county. Over this rugged road marched the forlorn battalions of Burgoyne's captive army, English infantry, Irish linesmen, and Hessian yagers, the latter attended by droves of women, bearing huge bags full of camp-equipage and babies. In later years this road was well-nigh discontinued, especially after 1809, when the new Worcester road was built, by the Upper Falls. But within a decade it has been revived, as a beautiful rural avenue, lined with the estates of the Johnson, Priest, Hackett, Pemberton, Butler,

WOODLAND PARK HOTEL, JOSEPH LEE, PROPRIETOR.
Washington Street, corner Woodland Avenue.

Pickard, Young, Barnes, and other families, and overarched by noble old trees.

On the high knoll of Vista Hill rises the mansion of Edwin B. Haskell, for a long time one of the three fortunate owners of the Boston *Herald*, and for twenty-five years editor of that paper, who has assembled here a rare treasury of fine paintings, including a portrait of his daughter, by Makart, the great Austrian artist, and fine examples of Gabriel Max, Diaz, Defregger, Lambinet, Vedder, Hunt, and other masters. From this high place may be seen points in sixteen towns, with Bunker Hill, the Blue Hills of Milton, and many another famous landmark of Massachusetts. The mansion on this lofty mound of glacial drift was built about the year 1870, by Ezra D. Winslow, and passed into the possession and occupancy of Mr. Haskell two years later.

Opposite Vista Hill, on Vista Avenue, is the home of the famous young poet, Louise Imogen Guiney, daughter of the late General Guiney, of the Massachusetts infantry in the Secession War. Near by, on the same avenue, are the handsome estates of Messrs. Deming, C. S. Roberts, and H. A. Priest.

A little way south of the Woodland-Park Hotel, on the road to Newton Lower Falls (which is but a mile from the house), is the Newton Cottage Hospital, a recent and benignant foundation of the citizens. It was first suggested by the Rev. Dr. George W. Shinn, in 1880, and received incorporation in the following year. In 1884 the institution acquired nine acres of the old Granville-Fuller estate, on Washington Street; and in 1885-86 the building was erected, from plans by William P. Wentworth, the architect. The furnishing of the hospital came from the tireless efforts of the Ladies' Aid Association. The erection of this beneficent institution has been due to the interest taken by the chief people of the city, old and young, who have planned and labored and given money for its advancement with great enthusiasm. Mrs. Elizabeth T. Eldredge gave $10,000 towards it; Mr. Joseph R. Leeson, of Newton Centre, gave $7,000; and a score of others each gave $500 or more. The municipality also has aided the enterprise; and several of the large corporations have contributed to it. The hospital stands on high ground, in a quiet, healthy, and airy situation, and has already proved a great blessing to many scores of sick or injured persons. Much of its success has been due to its esteemed treasurer, George S. Bullens.

RESIDENCE OF EDWIN B. HASKELL.
Vista Avenue, Woodland.

NEWTON COTTAGE HOSPITAL.
Washington Street, near Beacon Street, Woodland. [View in January, 1889.]

Riverside.

THE NEWTON NAVY.— THE PLACID RIVER CHARLES.— A FEW BITS OF POETRY.— THE BOAT CLUBS.— COUNTY ROCK.— THE CARNIVAL IN SEPTEMBER.— AN OLD-FASHIONED APOSTROPHE.

Turning away from these high and breezy plains, let us visit the bright pleasure port of Newton, not far away. Riverside, a station of the Albany Railroad, is indeed a charmingly picturesque point, where the Auburndale plateau bends away, to let the Charles River sweep by, with the broad emerald meadows of Weston and the craggy heights of the legendary Norumbega beyond. The great railway throwing off here its spur-track to Newton Lower Falls, and the Circuit Railway to Newton Centre, afterwards crosses the river on a high bridge, and fares away towards Natick and Nebraska. Here the river is narrow and still, flowing between high grassy banks embroidered with sweet-brier and daisies, and among cool and shadowy thickets and groves, where the young people, in their pretty boats, enjoy the charms of *solitude à deux*. The scene can hardly be better described than in the words of the kindly Chamberlain, whose "Listener" chapters, in the Boston *Transcript*, suggest the sweetness and strength of Charles Lamb: —

"It is to be doubted whether any other large city in the civilized world has, within easy access to its heated human masses, a reach of river at once so attractive and so quiet as the Charles River between Waltham and Newton Lower Falls. The entire river has its delights, but below the dam at Watertown the navigator is subject to the exigencies of the tide, and, moreover, the shores are not of the wooded sort that the boatman loves to see as he floats along. Beginning at the watch works at Waltham, there is a stretch of river four or five miles long, taking in the windings, that is without rival anywhere for pleasure-boating purposes; a deep, clear river, with shores lined everywhere with vegetation. Riverside commands the whole stretch, and it is there that the excursionist from the city leaves the train and gets his boat. Below Riverside the river is entirely placid, and the low woods and thickets everywhere touch the stream, except where an occasional residence reveals a bit of lawn. Above Riverside there is a little more of wildness, with here and there a fallen trunk, over which luxuriant vegetation has scrambled, jutting into the stream, and making incomparable nooks of shade, in which our boating parties seem to have a strong and perfectly natural propensity for mooring their boats while they read or dream. Here, too, the current flows more rapidly, making navigation a bit more interesting, though it is still perfectly safe. Above the Newton Falls there is still more of lovely river, and through Dedham there are river views quite as beautiful as anything in this stretch which borders Newton, Waltham, West Newton, and Wellesley; but the Charles there is scarcely so easily accessible as it is at Riverside, and this strip will probably always be what the Seine at Bougival is to the Parisians, and the Thames from Putney to Mortlake to the English. And, compared with these hilarious resorts abroad, what a placid home of quiet respectability the Charles is!"

At Riverside are the club-houses of the Newton Boat Club and the Boston Canoe Club, with the Partelow and Robertson boat-houses, where visitors may hire yachts, canoes, wherries, lapstreaks, randans, Whitehall boats, steam-launches, and other craft. As a local poet has sung: —

> "You will find the public boat-house
> Very near where you leave the train,
> While midway down the river
> Another is seen again,
> That belongs to the Newton Boat Club,
> And from its central 'float
> Many a lad and lassie,
> Taking canoe or boat,
> Have drifted down toward Waltham,
> Telling the old, old tale
> Of a love they bore each other,
> Of a love that should never fail.
>
> "Others not quite so romantic,
> Because not as far along,
> Spend their boating time in a social way,
> Singing portions of popular song;
> For the fellows are very attentive
> In paddling young ladies about,
> And it quite often occurs they escort them to town,
> Taking the late cars out."

The house of the Boston Canoe Club is oddly enough placed on the top of a hill, west of the river, with a broad veranda overlooking miles of the winding stream; and has a great brick fireplace in its main room, surrounded by pictures and trophies.

The Newton Boat Club was organized in 1875, to encourage boating on the Charles River, and other forms of physical and social culture, and as much as possible of goodfellowship in all other ways. The club-house stands amid picturesque grounds, and has a bowling-alley and dancing-hall attached, and other conveniences for merry days and evenings. There are about 200 members in the club, active and honorary, and its house is but a few minutes' railway ride from any of the Newton villages. It contains many handsome boats, shells of all kinds, Rob-Roys, and canoes, with lockers, landing-stages, and other essentials; and on pleasant summer afternoons and holidays, and on fair moonlight nights, the river in this vicinity is dotted with rowing parties, pleasure-boats, birch-bark canoes, and occasional little steamboats. In June they have the annual races, in Rob-Roys, shells, birches, pleasure-boats, and tubs; and if the stroke-oars do not land them among the reedy margins, or the canoes do not spill out their solitary

Newton Boat Club House on Charles River at Riverside.

crews, the boats usually reach their goals before nightfall. For the Newton navy resembles that of the United States, in that it is more to be counted on for contemplative comfort and sedate conviviality than for indecent and unseemly speed; and the high and shadowy wooded banks, and cool nooks between the islands, and beautiful riparian estates, invite to philosophic drifting and a placid lengthening of the happy hours of the voyage. The boating-ground is about five miles long, from Waltham up to where the rapids come down near County Rock, a midstream bowlder on which the Norfolk and Middlesex county lines converge; and one may row across Maple Bay, and Crehore Bay, or drift along the rippling reaches of Lake St. Francis, with easy oar.

Occasionally, in September, a spectacle is presented here that not even Venice in her palmiest days could have far surpassed. On an appointed night the steamer *White Swan* starts up river from Waltham, followed by upwards of 400 boats, of every variety, from leaky yawls and crazy rafts to costly cedar shells and aboriginal canoes, and the kerosene steamers of the newspaper reporters. Every boat is belted with lines of lanterns, and filled with joyous monarchs of the wave; and from sundry islands and moored rafts salvos of artillery, rockets, golden rain, Japanese fires, fiery colored stars, and other pyrotechnics flame across the black sky, while the great estates along the shores, and the railroad and corporation properties, are brilliantly illuminated. On the river there are thousands of people, with myriads on the shores; and the music of military bands is taken up from point after point, as the magnificent *cortège* moves up to Fox Island and Islington, following the *White Swan* as its Bucentaur, Newton Boat Club, Boston Canoe Club, Arlington Canoe Club, Somerville Boat Club, Waltham Canoe Club, Upper-Charles-River Boat Club, Aurora Canoe Club, Harvard Club, and others, each with from a dozen to fifty boats in massed column, their oars and paddles keeping time to the sweet music of the bands and the choruses of the rowers, whose charming boat-songs reverberate from the forested banks and the island thickets. Here and there advance small Chinese junks, floating light-houses, miniature *Mayflowers*, Spanish galleons, lit up by Roman candles, mines, bombs, water-rockets and other pyrotechnics, and by myriads of Chinese lanterns strung along the shores, in lines and groups and masses. Vast crowds from Boston and other cities come hither to enjoy the fairy scene; and in 1886 the Governor and his staff inspected the procession from Riverview, and no fewer than 3,000 persons assembled on the Pulsifer estate alone.

The *White Swan* is a small but commodious steamboat that makes several trips daily, in summer, from the bridge at Waltham, past the Watch Factory, Lily-Point Grove, and the gentlemen's estates above, and ends its quiet voyages at the stone bridge near Auburndale and Weston.

This expanse of river has been thus happily described by an enthusiastic writer: "Within ten miles of Boston, there is a stretch of river scenery that cannot be surpassed in the United States, and which cannot easily be equalled. Until within a few years this lovely spot has scarcely been known beyond the limit of the inhabitants who have quietly taken possession of the elegant sites on either bank, and beautified and adorned them for their own pleasure. Many who have travelled through Europe affirm that for quiet beauty it is not equalled. One familiar with our Southern streams is reminded of the Yazoo, with the deep green and luxuriance of the foliage on the banks and the quiet of the waters. At sunset, the river is alive with canoes, row-boats, shells, and sail-boats, filled with ladies and gentlemen, adding, with their delightful music, greatly to the natural charms of the scenery."

Nor can we forget the enthusiastic words of Oliver Wendell Holmes, who once astonished a committee of the Massachusetts Legislature by saying: "You need not go to the Rhine nor to the Bay of Naples for scenery; you have it in perfection on the River Charles." Another philosophic writer has remarked that, "The man who has made up his mind that life is not worth living, ought to take a canoe-

Lasell Seminary Boat House at Riverside.

voyage on the picturesque Charles before he shuffles off this mortal coil." For in these peaceful glens are the fairest scenes of the little river which has been more beloved by American poets than any Mississippi or Columbia of the great West, flowing through thousands of long miles. Longfellow's "To the River Charles" and Lowell's "Charles-River Marshes" are perhaps the best of these hymns of the flowing stream, and their sweet pastoral music gives a peculiar interest and distinction to the scene, and the sentimental interest is deepened by the reflection that on those rugged and imposing heights across the river Professor E. N. Horsford has discovered the remains of the ancient city of Norumbega, that prehistoric metropolis about which the old French discoverers romanced so enthusiastically, like Marco Polo after he returned from the land of Prester John. Only some fragments of its old defences remain, as if to show how their martial invincibility outlasted all the constructions of peace, of worship, of love.

The only manufacturing in this vicinity is of so unusual and delicate a kind as to merit the name of an art. Down by the old Weston bridge the Partelows (H. V., A. E., and A. B.) have a factory for making all sorts of small boats, from steam-launches of extraordinary swiftness down to cedar

Partelow's Boat-house and Boat-livery, Riverside, Newton.

canoes, floating as lightly as egg-shells. And so apt and skilful are these artificers, after many years of experience, that they could no doubt fashion and fabricate to order a Thames wherry of the old style, or a Venetian gondola, or a Nile dahabeeyeh. Many of the best boats in use around Boston, especially those on the upper Charles, were turned out at this well-known shop, and now float on the calm inland waters of Longfellow's river. The Partelows also carry on a boat and canoe livery, and provide for the resident or the transient visitor a luxurious ride on the picturesque stream.

NEWTON LOWER FALLS.
BIRDSEYE VIEW OF THE VILLAGE AND SURROUNDINGS
[From Photograph loaned by Dr. C. F. Crehore.]

Newton Lower Falls.

A PAPER-MAKING GLEN.— NEWTON'S FIRST POST-OFFICE.— FAMOUS PAPER-MILLS.— A MASSACHUSETTS MAGNATE.— OLD ST. MARY'S.— A FINE OLD COUNTRY-SEAT.— OUTER BEACON STREET.

Newton Lower Falls is one of the quietest and most tranquil of hamlets, nestling about the sides of a deep little glen, in which the Charles River makes a sudden leap downward. The beauty of the ancient falls has given place to the geometrical regularity of water-power dams, whose hydraulic force is utilized by several busy mills. On the bluff above, surrounded by a circle of graves, stands the crossless and rather Methodistic appearing Church of St. Mary, the modest shrine of the local Episcopalians, with a few venerable houses near it, and a pleasant street curving away along the ridge. Above the dam is the aqueduct of hammered granite which conducts across the river, high up on its round arches, a stream of crystalline water for the use of Boston. The vicinity of the stream is occupied by the works of the Dudley Hosiery Company; the shoddy mills of Cordingley; the paper-mills of Crehore, Rice, and Wiswall; and a group of machine-shops. The river makes three falls, one of sixteen feet, and another of six feet, each of which is crested by a dam, wherewith to utilize the water-power. From the foot-bridge near the Crehore mill, a picturesque cascade is visible, during the season of high water. The distance from the Lower Falls to the Upper Falls, either by road or by river, is about two miles. Some part of the stream between is navigable; but canoe-men who are out for the circum-navigation of Boston usually have their boats carried by wagon from below the Lower Falls to the bridge above the Upper Falls, whence they have a clear course for many miles.

Standing on the top of Falls Hill, east of the hamlet of Newton Lower Falls, we are at the point where the colonial road-makers, building the highway westward from Boston, ceased their labors, reporting that probably no one would ever have occasion or desire to journey further inland in Massachusetts. They had no premonition of Worcester and Springfield, still less of Santa Fé and San Diego. But it was only a few years before the advancing skirmish-line of English civilization descended into this lonely glen, and occupied it. The first individual owner of land here was John Leverett, who received his grant from the proprietors of the common and undivided lands of Cambridge, and in 1703 conveyed four acres to John Hubbard of

Roxbury. This industrial pioneer erected here in 1704 iron-works, forge, trip-hammer, and fire-hearths, and filled the glen with new and unaccustomed sounds. Jonathan Willard, the patriarch of the village, came in about ten years later, as a smith and bloomer, and dwelt here for half a century, acquiring a large interest in the works. Near the falls was the Wading Place, in the old days used as a ford by the wagoners of the remoter western settlements.

The local magnates of that period are now forgotten, save by the antiquaries, and but few of their names have come down to us. From about 1750 for many years the village tavern was kept by Colonel Ephraim Jackson, a lieutenant in the wars against the French, and afterwards a minuteman. When the great war for independence from Britain began, he put on his martial uniform for the last time, and fared away to the Northern campaigns, receiving the billet of Lieutenant-Colonel of the 10th Massachusetts Continental Infantry. He was destined never again to see the tranquil glens amid which the Lower Falls make ceaseless music, for in the dreary winter cantonments of Valley Forge he found his death.

Joseph Davenport, the village clothier, lived on the west side of Beacon Street, and had a large family, for whose support and education he furnished the local gentry with waistcoats and breeches and coats, and top-coats, withal. His son John was one of the founders of Bridgton, Maine, and sent four stalwart sons into the Continental army and navy, three of whom died in the service of the young Republic.

The country store was kept, late in the last century, by John Pigeon, a son of the man who gave two cannon to defend Newton from British foragers. In those ancient days the chief secular organization was the Cataract Engine Company, whose sturdy members often dragged their little machine to the neighboring fires with much uproarious enthusiasm.

It was expected that this locality, with its valuable water-power and busy factories, would become the chief place in Newton, a great manufacturing centre, with a dense and active population; and for this reason the United-States authorities established here the only post-office in the town. Up to the year 1820 every one in Newton who had letters to send journeyed over to the Lower Falls, or else went to Dedham or Watertown.

When this century dawned on the tranquil little village, it had but ten resident families. In 1823 there were 33 dwelling-houses and 405 inhabitants; in 1837, 493 inhabitants; in 1847, 560; in 1850, 627, with 80 dwelling-houses. In 1872 the roll had risen to 940, and probably it will never far pass that number again.

The chief distinction of the place is its paper-manufacturing, in which it has for nearly a century held a conspicuous place. The ancient colonial paper-mills at Roxborough, near Philadelphia, were founded in 1690; and

ST. MARY'S EPISCOPAL CHURCH, NEWTON LOWER FALLS.
Concord Street.

the industry began in New England thirty years later, when the mills at Milton were established.

The pioneer paper-mill was erected here in 1790 by John Ware, a veteran officer of the Continental army, and brother of Professor Henry Ware, D.D., of Harvard College, one of the chief leaders (with Channing and Norton) in the great secession of the then new Unitarian sect from the old Puritan church. Messrs. Conant and Hurd afterwards became associated with Mr. Ware; and the works were acquired by Lemuel Crehore in the year 1832, after which Mr. Benjamin Neal became a partner in the concern. Since 1832 the mills have been entirely owned by the Crehores, and are now managed by Dr. C. F. Crehore. Their daily capacity is 1½ tons of paper, but of late years their product has been confined to press paper, and cards for Jacquard looms; and their output is less, owing to the greater power required in that branch of manufacture. The changes in the firm have been as follows: Hurd & Crehore, 1825; Crehore & Neal, 1834; Lemuel Crehore, 1845; Lemuel Crehore & Son (George C. Crehore), 1854; Lemuel Crehore & Co. (C. F. Crehore), 1867; C. F. Crehore, 1868; C. F. Crehore & Son (Fred. M. Crehore), 1883. The mills include the ancient stone edifices on Washington Street, near the Hamilton Grammar School.

The Curtises, Crehores, and Rices carried the paper business forward here with great enterprise, as rapidly as possible supplanting the old processes of hand-work by more modern and efficient methods. The first Foudrinier machine in America was set up and used here.

The stone buildings back of the Crehore Mills were built by Allen C. and William Curtis for paper-mills, in which, for many years, was made a considerable proportion of the book-paper used in the United States. They are now owned by W. S. & F. Cordingley, and devoted to the manufacture of shoddy and wool extracts. Across the river from the Cordingley works are the mills of the Dudley Hosiery Company, for the manufacture of merino shirts and drawers.

The Thomas-Rice Paper Company's mills, on the Wellesley shore, were originally owned by William Hurd and Amos Lyon. The Hurd mill passed through the ownership of Rice & Garfield, and the Lyon mill through that of Wales & Mills; and about the year 1862 they were bought by Thomas Rice, Jr., who had previously owned a small mill upon the present site of the Dudley Hosiery Mills. Their present product is about 2½ tons daily. In the Rice Mills the paper for the Boston *Evening Transcript* has been made, almost from the beginning, so that in this product alone the works have turned out paper enough to make a pathway more than a yard wide around the earth at the Equator. Or, if one shall attempt to estimate the mental labor called out to prepare the contents of these

WASHINGTON STREET IN NEWTON LOWER FALLS.
[The C. F. Crehore & Son Mill Property on the left.]

myriad of miles of newspaper lore, how vast and unapproachable doth the result become! What a solemn army of essayists, what tuneful broods of high-cornered "For the *Transcript*" poets, what wrathy "Old Subscribers," what philosophic editorial writers, what telegrams from Antietam and Sebastopol, what myriads of Notes and Queries, have been spread on those leagues upon leagues of virgin paper!

The mill at the lower dam was owned for many years by Joseph Foster, and is now the property of the sons of the late Augustus C. Wiswall (Clarence A. and Herbert M. Wiswall), who make nearly 2 tons daily of Manila, colored, and hanging paper.

Across the bridge is the mill founded by A. C. & W. Curtis long afterwards Allen C. Curtis & Sons, for the manufacture of paper; and now occupied by Richard T. Sullivan, for the making of shoddy and wool extracts. Near by is the chemical laboratory of Billings, Clapp & Co.

It may profit us to stroll down the village street, and renew the memories of some of the old residents, whose faith and energy built up such interesting industries here. The brown house now occupied by Luther E. Leland, at the junction of Washington and Beacon Streets, was owned for many years by Ellis Stedman, an oldtime paper-maker of the Falls. The house farther west on the high ground south of the road was built and occupied by Mr. Sparhawk, likewise a paper-maker in the employ of Messrs. Curtis, some fifty years ago. Descending Falls Hill by the Sherborn Road, one first encountered on the right the house of Mr. Durell, in the employment of Hurd & Crehore. Next came the residence of William Curtis and then that of Allen C. Curtis, the old and well-known paper-manufacturers. Subsequently A. C. Curtis built and occupied the handsome Ionic-porticoed house on the south side of the road, later owned by Henry P. Eaton, and beyond which the beautiful meadows of the Charles River stretch away toward the aqueduct, which here crosses the river on three fine granite arches.

In the triangle between Washington Street and the back road leading down to the Wales Bridge stood the ancient tavern of Colonel Ephraim Jackson, in later years occupied by Nathaniel Wales, and for many decades a favorite halting-point for the lumbering old Albany stages, in the days before railroads began. Opposite was the old village pump. Upon a branch way to the right lived Thomas Rice, Sen., the original house (much altered) being occupied by his grandson, Mr. Atherton. The residence of the late Thomas Rice, Jr., just east of this, a handsome square structure overlooking the village and river, is still occupied by his widow and son. The private way upon which they were built is now a thoroughfare, called Hamilton Street. The Grammar School occupies the site of the original village-school, a black, unpainted, wooden building of one

THE RESIDENCE OF DR. CHARLES FREDERIC CREHORE.
Pine Grove Avenue, Newton Lower Falls.

story. A part of its site is also upon the property formerly owned by Mr. Bemis, an old resident, who finally lost his mind and devoted himself to piling outside his fence every stone and pebble he could pick up in his enclosure. It is needless to say that the school-boys with praiseworthy perseverance pursued a return policy which rendered the old gentleman's task as enduring as that of Sisyphus. At the foot of the hill formerly stood a house whose chimney was almost on a level with the school-house, and proved a never-failing target for snow-balls, which occasionally would enter, much to the discomfort of good Mr. Marston, who occupied the premises. At the abandonment of the old school-house, a new one was built in front of the present location, notched into the hill, in the midst of a sand bank. In 1866 this was sold to Thomas Rice, Jr., selectman, and moved across the street, where it now forms the Methodist Hall, with stores and market below. The present school building was erected at that time, and the roads and grounds laid out. In the low wooden building between the Methodist Hall and the approach to the bridge was one of the village stores, kept for many years by Horace Starr, the son of the old doctor. Starr was (like the Curtises and other contemporaries) a valiant sportsman; and woodcock and partridges, rabbits, pickerel, and perch, were fairly plenty in those days. On the left is the stone and wood mill of the Crehores; and opposite stands the brown house, now belonging to the Dudley Hosiery Company, and for many years the residence of Amos Lyon, and subsequently of William Mills. Beyond Crehore's Mill one encounters first the old house formerly the residence of Solomon Curtis, one of the fathers of paper-making in the village; and then a small building formerly used as a shop. The old Hagar house comes next, beneath the ancient elm which has for many generations borne the public notices of meetings and auctions, lost and found advertisements, etc., and is said to be full of carpet tacks to an indefinite depth.

On the east corner of Grove and Washington Streets stands the ancient mansion of William Hurd, another of the pioneers in American paper-making. On the next corner is the old house once occupied by the village doctor, Ebenezer Starr, who married John Ware's daughter, and lived here from 1794 until 1830. It then became the home of Benjamin Neale, the venerable paper-manufacturer.

Near the church, at the corner of Washington and Concord Streets, is the great old colonial house inhabited by Miss Elizabeth P. Baury. It was built a century or so ago by Mr. Hoogs, and afterwards acquired for a debt by Samuel Brown, who deeded it to Dr. Baury. For a third of a century it served as the parish rectory, and extended its ample hospitalities to many famous Bishops and Priests, and to scores of army and navy officers. Across the street, the Crehore house, now tenanted by Dr. Baker; the William

Curtis house, occupied by his children; and the old Durant place, still in the ownership of his daughter, Mrs. William Wallis,— complete the street to the river.

Across the bridge (which was rebuilt in 1888–89), on the left, is the tall, dark, wooden house in whose hall the mysteries of freemasonry were wrought out for many years. Close to the railway, on the other side of the road, still stands the house used half a century or more ago as a tavern, under the sway of George Hoogs, who at times ran a fierce rivalry with

The Old Wales Bridge, Newton Lower Falls to Needham.

Wales's inn, at the other end of the hamlet, for the custom afforded by the Albany stages.

A little way beyond, on the right-hand side of the Wellesley road, is an immense and venerable elm-tree, under which (as a very popular tradition affirms) General George Washington once rested, and partook of a bowl of cooling punch.

The changes in the village appearance are not especially rapid, and the general birdseye view as shown on another page, although taken about twenty years ago, still quite accurately shows the village of to-day.

The village is connected with the outer world by the Newton-Lower-Falls Branch Railroad, diverging from the Albany main line at Riverside, about five minutes distant, and crossing the river twice in its short course, which ends among the factories. The trains on this branch were in old times run under the direction of the energetic General Stephen Cate, who became, in his way, the dictator of the line. In the great snow-storm of 1848, he made his passengers dig the train's way through mountainous drifts, and reaching Boston on schedule roared out to the town, in a voice audible as far down as State Street: "Yes, sir, the Newton-Lower-Falls express *always* arrives on time." In 1886 the railway company built a handsome station of stone, and the people on the west side of the stream thereupon began an earnest movement to have the name of the place changed to Wellesley Falls. But this innovation was sturdily resisted by many gentlemen; and the President of the railroad company became the object of a confusing cross-fire of petitions for and against.

The old parish-church is St. Mary's, one of the most venerable in the Protestant-Episcopal Diocese of Massachusetts, and a precious memorial of the past. It took its rise in the conversion of one of the chief men of the village to Episcopalianism, nearly eighty years ago. Mr. Elbridge Ware, having learned to love the Episcopal service during a sojourn at Morristown, New Jersey, on his return to Newton Lower Falls induced John R. Cotting, a lay-reader, to come over from Dedham, and officiate frequently in the village school-house. At that time there were but two hundred Episcopal clergymen in the United States, and eight in Massachusetts. After the church had worshiped for two years in unconsecrated places, on the Feast of St. Michael and All Angels, Sept. 29, 1813, this present temple was founded, with Masonic rites, the officiating clergymen being Asa Eaton and John S. J. Gardiner, the rectors of Christ Church and Trinity Church, then the only Episcopal parishes in Boston. Seven months later, it received consecration from Bishop Griswold. The architectural style of the interior was in some respects copied from the even then old Christ Church, in Boston, with its square columns and high box-pews, which still remain, to screen the drowsy communicants on long summer Sundays. For some years the pulpit was served by Boston clergymen, and lay-readers from Harvard University, among whom were the late Bishop Wainwright, of New York; Philander Chase, the pioneer Bishop of Ohio; Allston Gibbes, of South Carolina; and Cheever Felch, of the United-States Navy.

After the long depression caused by the War of 1812, St. Mary's opened her gates again, and called to her ministry the Rev. Alfred L. Baury, who held the pastorate for nearly thirty years, from 1822 until 1851, a period of steady and healthy increase for the little rural parish. He was the son of Louis Baury de Bellerive, a graduate of the French military college at

THE RESIDENCE OF THE LATE HON. THOMAS RICE.
Hamilton Street, Newton Lower Falls.

Brienne, and a gallant officer of the Continental army, by virtue of which he became President of the Massachusetts Society of the Cincinnati. His youngest son, Frederick F. Baury, became a naval officer in the Secession War, and was shot through the body while leading his gallant blue-jackets in the charge on Fort Fisher, in North Carolina. The venerable rector was a tall, graceful, and dignified gentleman of the old school, whose sermons were carefully modelled on the best works of the Anglican divines of the last century.

The rectors since Dr. Baury's day have been the Rev. Henry W. Woods, from 1851 to 1853; the Rev. Andrew Croswell, a famous Greek scholar, who married the daughter of Simon Greenleaf, the jurist, and ruled the parish from 1853 to 1856; the Rev. Henry Burroughs, from 1856 to 1858 (non-resident); the Rev. B. F. De Costa, the learned antiquary, and now head of the White-Cross Army, in 1859 and 1860; the Rev. Winslow W. Sever, 1860-64; the Rev. Joseph Kidder, in 1865-67; the Rev. Richard F. Putnam, from 1868 to 1875; the Rev. Henry Mackay, 1876-82; the Rev. Ben T. Hutchins, 1883-84; and the Rev. William G. Wells, the present incumbent, who became rector in 1885. Many Puritan families from Needham and other adjacent country towns used to attend the services here, beguiled by the pleasant and decorous liturgy. At last, however, they laid claim to the Sacrament of the Lord's Supper, although not duly confirmed as communicants; and the problems arising from this irruption of good-natured Dissenters gave many a hard nut for the Bishop to crack. However, the result of these Episcopal admonitions turned, the parish grew in power and in churchliness, and now the old church contains an elaborate chancel, with a reredos and dossel, and other true Anglican furnishings. A handsome carved stone altar, with its top and re-table of marble, carved with lilies, was promised in 1888, by Robert H. Slack, of New Bedford, as a memorial of his parents, oldtime parishioners of St. Mary's. A beautiful memorial pulpit was only recently given by Holker W. Abbott, the Boston architect and artist.

Dr. Holmes tells a charming story of a summer Sunday when among the worshippers at St. Mary's were young Alexander H. Rice (afterwards Governor of Massachusetts), Thomas R. Gould (in later years a famous sculptor), and Ralph Waldo Emerson, then a young Unitarian minister. After the service Emerson took the two lads into a forest, and said: "Boys, here we recognize the presence of the Universal Spirit. The breeze says to us, in its own language, 'How d'ye do? How d'ye do?' And all the waving branches of the trees, and all the flowers, and the field of corn yonder, and the singing brook, and the insect and the bird,— every living thing, and things we call inanimate, feel the same divine universal impulse while they join with us, and we with them, in the greeting which is the salutation of the Universal Spirit."

The land for the church and churchyard, two acres in area, was given to the parish in 1813 by Samuel Brown, a wealthy merchant of Boston. It sweeps well-nigh around the church, like a bit from dear old England, with its long lines of graves under the arching trees, and close to the sacred walls. In the centre is the cruciform monument of the sacerdotal Baury family; and in various places rest the remains of twelve soldiers of the Secession War, and also (in the lower corner) the slab of slate which marks the grave of Captain Zibeon Hooker, a soldier of the old Continental Line, whose drum was perforated by a British bullet at the battle of Bunker Hill. All of these are decorated with flowers and flags, on the annual Memorial Day. In this quiet cemetery rest the remains of Hon. Thomas Rice, Jr., the public spirited paper-manufacturer, for five years a member of the General Court, for two years in the Executive Council, and one of the most active agents in keeping the Massachusetts ranks full during the Secession War. He was for eighteen years a member of the Newton Board of Selectmen, and for twelve years just prior to his death the chairman of that Board. Here also is the grave of the late Frederick W. Rice, a later representative of the same family and firm. Here lies Dr. Albert A. Kendall, of the 12th Massachusetts Infantry, who was killed by a chance shot at Antietam, while binding up the wounds of his soldiers. Near the northeast corner of the cemetery, alongside the ancient monuments of his wife and daughter, is the unmarked grave of Sam Lawton, the veritable hero of Mrs. Stowe's "Oldtown Folks."

The Methodist church at the Lower Falls dates its foundation from 1867, and has its place of worship in Methodist Hall, which used to be known as Village Hall, before 1869. The pastors have been the Rev. John Wesley Coolidge (1867-69), Rev. E. A. Howard (1869-70), Rev. A. Caldwell (1870-72), Rev. W. Pentecost (1872-73), Rev. A. Baylies (1873-76), Rev. W. A. Nottage (1876-77), Rev. Andrew McKeown, D.D. (1877-80), Rev. W. S. Richardson (1880), Rev. John B. Gould (1881), Rev. C. M. Hall (1882-83), Rev. J. Gill (1884), and Rev. John B. Gould (1885-87). The church has about forty members.

Intimately connected with the paper-making industry is the most famous of the natives of Newton Lower Falls, Alexander Hamilton Rice, who was born August 30, 1818, in a house still standing here, and educated in the Newton schools. He graduated with high honors at Union College, Schenectady; but the precarious condition of his health rendered professional studies inexpedient, and he entered the paper business, amid whose details he had been brought up. Active in all the public affairs of Boston, its charities, schools, and trades, he became Mayor of that city, in 1856 and 1857, and then went into the United-States Congress, where he served the people for eight fruitful years, including the terrible period of the revolt of the Southern States. In 1876, 1877, and 1878 he held the high office of Governor of Massachusetts; and he is now one of the leading merchants and publicists of New England.

Another native of the Lower Falls was Lieutenant Walter H. Garfield, U.S.N., who sailed the blue seas in a gunboat during the Secession War, and afterwards went to Martinique as United-States Consul. In that fair island, but a year or two ago, the gallant sea-king surrendered to the All-Conqueror, Death. Here, also, was born Professor Daniel B. Hagar, the Principal of the Massachusetts State Normal School at Salem; and Dr. Henry Lyon, of Charlestown.

A short distance north of the village, near the little Pine-Grove station, is the noble old domain of the Crehore family, with an air of seclusion and dignity not usual, even in long-settled New England. This residence was built in 1848, and the estate was founded nearly half a century ago, by Lemuel Crehore, who came hither from the town of Milton, and was a gentleman of courtly manners and graceful hospitalities. It is now owned and occupied by his son, Dr. Charles Frederic Crehore, formerly a physician in Boston, but since 1866, the date of the expiration of his military service, devoted to the manufacture of paper, at the Lower Falls. A large part of this property belonged to the estate of Dr. Starr, early in this century. A portion of the noble pine-forest that once clothed all this region still remains, covering with its cathedral-like arches of solemn foliage the bluff that projects into the tranquil Charles River.

On the plateau above the sequestered little hamlet is the western end of that most famous of Blue-Book avenues, redolent with the odor of social sanctity, and sacred to the palaces of the Puritan *noblesse*, Beacon Street. With deferential respect to this august terminus the city fathers have erected tablets here, signifying that it is 9½ miles thence to Boston, 4 to Oak Hill, 4 to Chestnut-Hill Reservoir, 7 to Brookline, 5½ to Brighton, 6 to West Roxbury, 10 to Roxbury, 10 to Dedham, 2½ to Newton Corner, 2½ to Newton Centre, 1½ to the Upper Falls, Auburndale, Newton Highlands, Wellesley Hills, or West Newton; 3½ to Watertown or Waltham or Wellesley; 6½ to Natick, 12 to Framingham, and 35 to Worcester. In this its remoter western territory, Beacon Street is but a broad country road, winding whitely over a high plateau, with the blue hills of Wellesley rising beyond the valley of the unseen river, and on the other side the long rampart of Beacon Hill, its rich green slopes dappled by clumps and lines of stately trees. On either hand are low-lying old farmhouses, herds of cattle lazily browsing on the fat herbage, and (in their season) high cornfields aligned like infantry on a brigade dress-parade, or thickets of fragrant berry-bushes, by which the saunterer is compelled to loiter.

Waban.

THE RED CHIEFTAIN'S HUNTING-PARK.— THE INTRUDING ANGLO-SAXON DEACON.— A MERCHANT-PRINCE.— STRONG'S NURSERIES.—BEACON HILL.— THE COLLINS ESTATE.— A LANDSCAPE-PARK.

The railway station at Waban is a handsome little structure of stone, opened August 16, 1886, and surrounded by a charming park of lawns and shrubbery and ancient forest trees. It is about midway of the new Circuit Railway, which has thirty-five trains daily (and twelve on Sunday) thence to Boston. It was one of the last designs of the late H. H. Richardson.

The fine trees of this neighborhood, elms, oaks, lindens, and butternuts, are worthy of admiration; and the great pine-groves exhale a delightful

Woodward Street, Waban.

and healthful perfume, and add to the attractions of the natural scenery. Within a few minutes' walk are the emerald meadows of the Charles River, whose crystal current winds around the lowlands in long loops, affording easy facilities for boating and fishing. This is the tranquil and lonely reach between the Upper and Lower Falls, amid the most idyllic rural scenery.

Waban is intersected by what was formerly known as the Old Sherborn Road, later changed to Beacon Street, which is now one of the main arteries

of business and travel to Boston; it is crossed, also, by Chestnut and
Woodward Streets. The land is elevated and undulating, and the location
is extremely healthy. Fine old shade-trees lend variety, and afford a grateful shade, besides forming picturesque elements in the beautiful scenery
for which the place is noted. The drives and the walks in and about
Waban are as varied and diversified as can be found in this region. In
fact, throughout all Newton, "The Garden City," there is no place that
exceeds this in natural beauty. The view westward across the emerald

H. Langford Warren's Residence, Woodward Street, Waban.

meadows, from the wooded hill near the station, is famous for its rich
pastoral beauty, and includes many a silvery loop of the wide-winding
Charles River, beyond the ruined and long-abandoned glue-mills. It is
about ¾ of a mile from Waban to the Pine-Farm School; about a mile to
Newton Upper Falls, or to Newton Highlands; and somewhat farther to
Newton Lower Falls, or to West Newton.

Rising from the groves of pine and maple along the river, and the inter-
vening meadows, is a chain of bluffs, broken in the most picturesque and
often weird way by natural glades and amphitheatres. These bluffs reach
their maximum altitude in a broad plateau, from which stretches a most
bewildering panorama of natural scenery. To the left rises the quaint old

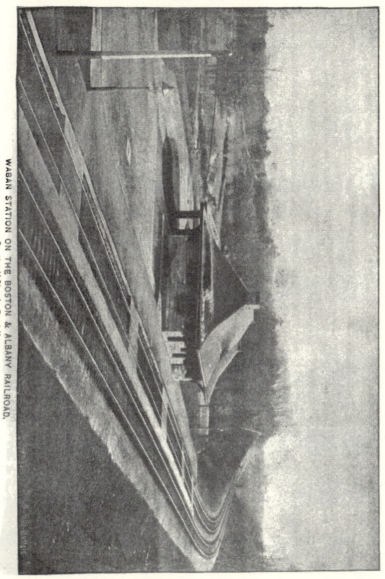

WABAN STATION ON THE BOSTON & ALBANY RAILROAD.
On the "Circuit Road."

village of Upper Falls, with that mighty production of modern engineering, Echo Bridge. Before one, through the pine tops, flows the sinuous, sparkling river; and beyond the meadows and the herds of feeding cattle, cornfields and villages, and away in the distance at the horizon loom the great Blue Hills of Milton. Turning to the right, we trace the river under the massive stone bridge of the old Boston Aqueduct, through the greenest of fields, and finally lose sight of it in a series of sharp bends as it approaches

Edwin P. Seaver's Residence, Woodward Street, near Chestnut, Waban.

the Lower Falls. Almost at our feet nestles the village, and over the housetops, through the curling smoke, we catch glimpses of Weston, Waltham, and Auburndale.

Beacon Street crosses the line of the Circuit Railway, near the exquisite Waban station, and only a little way from the spacious Almshouse, built about fifty years ago, and now about to be abandoned. Then it traverses the dull marsh-lands of Cold-Spring Brook, and the populous but architecturally unfortunate Hibernian settlement of Cork City ; and so on into

HOUSE OF CHARLES J. PAGE AND FREDERIC H. HENSHAW.
Woodward Street, Waban.

Newton Centre, hard by the classic strand of Baptist Pond. Here the bicycler must draw on his kid gloves and his best English accent, as he spins along the same supernal street to Chestnut Hill and Longwood and the Mill Dam, and so, in due time, to the Boston Public Garden, the State House, and King's Chapel.

But the æsthetic pilgrim will not so easily pass by the little Arcadian settlement of Waban, concerning which there are a few words to be said, howbeit the tranquil and pastoral beauty of the region fairly evades description. The name "Waban" was happily chosen to designate one of the most charming localities in Newton, embraced within Wards 4 and 5 of this prosperous and growing city. Tradition tells us that this was a favorite hunting-ground of Waban, the chief of the Nonantum Indians. Here, spring and fall, he encamped with parties of his braves, to hunt and fish along the banks of the Quinobequin,—the beautiful Charles River of to-day. Here they could find deer and bear, foxes and wolves, and a great variety of smaller game, and fish in abundance, wherewith to enrich the larders of their wigwams, and to content their squaws and pappooses, withal.

Later in the same century, the Waban region was the farm of Deacon John Staples, weaver, who came to Newton in 1688, at the age of thirty, and fulfilled the duties of town clerk, selectman, and deacon for many years. When he died, in 1740, he bequeathed to the church seventeen acres of land, "for the support of the ministerial fire"; a lot of Province Bills of Credit, for the poor; and a silver tankard, which is still used in the communion service. The farm passed into the possession of Moses Craft (in 1729), then to Joseph Craft (in 1753), and then to William Wiswall, Second (in 1788). To this place, many years ago, came David Kinmonth, the predecessor of Hogg, Brown & Taylor (now Beal, Higgins & Henderson), in the hope that the air of the pine-woods would restore his shattered health. The expectation failed; but, before his demise, the great merchant projected a capacious mansion, with a deer-park, and fronted his domain with a sturdy wall of stone. Subsequently the estate passed into the hands of William C. Strong, the well-known florist and nurseryman, who is now in occupation, dwelling in a spacious modern house with several gables, not far from the station. The old Kinmonth house, near by on Beacon Street, sometime the home of Captain Edward Wyman (brother of Dr. Jeffries Wyman), now belongs to and is occupied by Mrs. Marshall Scudder.

In the lovely glade back and to the eastward of these houses are William C. Strong's great nurseries, on the rich soil of an ancient lake-bottom, and sheltered from the cold winds by ramparts of hills and pine groves. Nearly forty years ago Mr. Strong carried on the business, at Nonantum Hill, in Brighton, where he had purchased the nurseries of the late Hon. Joseph Breck. Later he made heavy purchases of land at the

THE EDWARD JACKSON COLLINS ESTATE.
Beacon Street, Waban.

present village of Waban, where he now carries on his entire nursery business and makes his home. His products in trees, plants, and flowers have been long and favorably known; and he has attained an enviable reputation as President of the Massachusetts Horticultural Society and as Vice-President of the American Pomological Society and the American Horticultural Society, and as author of "Fruit Culture" and other books in this line. He has lately transferred his business to his home farm, where he has land peculiarly well-adapted to the work; and he is now confining his attention more especially to the production of the choicest kinds of hardy trees and plants. All the numerous novelties are here

Alexander Davidson's Residence, Waban.

tested, and either propagated and introduced or else rejected, as they are proved to be worthy or otherwise. It is well known that the country is flooded with pretentious novelties of no value, except to fill the pockets of unscrupulous dealers. This evil has undoubtedly been a serious hindrance to the advance of the interests of horticulture. By his trustworthy experiments and his impartial judgment, Mr. Strong is rendering a quiet but most important service to the public. Upon his grounds may be seen perfect specimens of all the most desirable kinds of trees, shrubs, roses, vines, and herbaceous plants suited to this climate. The quality of the soil and the location are so exceptionally fine, and the facil-

RESIDENCE OF WILLIAM R. DRESSER.
Chestnut Street, Waban.

ities for propagation are so perfect, that the finest specimens are offered at unusually low prices. The citizens of Newton and all others interested in horticulture will find profit in visiting this establishment, either for inspection or as purchasers. The place is easily reached by railroad either way, on the Circuit, the post-office address being Newton Highlands.

Recently evidences of real-estate development have become manifest along this beautiful undulating plain, where streets are being laid out across the pasture-lands and upland meadows, and new houses are rising here and there by the roadsides. Windsor Street has been built across the Strong estate, in a graceful curve and by easy grades, to the crest of Beacon Hill,

The New Dresser House at Waban.

which it follows, for a considerable distance, along the backbone of this far-viewing ridge. Here, where land is still sold by the acre (rather than by the square foot), it is hoped that a number of fine suburban estates may be established, to balance the architectural beauties of Chestnut Hill, on the other side of Newton. The hill had long been called Moffatt Hill, but with scant reason; and when the new streets were built to its summit, the name of BEACON HILL was bestowed upon it, in recognition of the fact that for a number of years the tall beacon of the United-States Coast Survey and the Massachusetts State Survey had been its most conspicuous feature.

Mr. Edward L. Collins, of Waban, has discovered the following facts

THE RESIDENCE OF WILLIAM H. GOULD.
Beacon Street, near Woodward Street, Waban.

about the first settler on this ridge : " In a conversation with an old resident I learned something of the unknown Moffat. As near as can be remembered, this Moffat 'squatted,' as he expressed it, on the top of the hill that bears his name. He was a very odd body, living quite by himself, with the exception of a horse, a cow, and a couple of dogs that occupied the same room in his miserable hut. Moffat associated with no one, save when he was obliged to buy provisions or some other dire necessity. Indeed, the neighbors knew nothing about him. He was as much of a mystery to them at that time as he is to those of to-day. As near as my informant remembers, it was some fifty or sixty years ago he lived on Beacon Hill; but whether he actually owned property there was not known."

Among the gentlemen who have founded their homes on this beautiful highland is Louis K. Harlow, whose etchings and illustrations are famous for their delicacy and beauty, and have given him a high measure of fame among our New-England artists. Halfway up the hill stands the house of Alexander Davidson, designed by H. Langford Warren, in a skilful adaptation of the old English style.

From the crest of the gracefully rounded hill, situated among the pastures and groves, one gains a charming view over many tall-spired villages, the picturesque hills of Waltham and Wellesley, bits of the distant Mounts Wachusett and Monadnock, with parts of Boston and the turquoise-tinted Blue Hills of Milton. Thence may be seen also the public buildings at Newton Upper Falls, the spires of the Highlands and the Centre, the theological buildings on Institute Hill, the round crest of Waban Hill, the Woodland-Park Hotel and Haskell estate at Woodland (Auburndale), Bear Mountain in Weston, Maugus Hill in Wellesley, Pegan Hill at South Natick, and the tall church of Highlandville, down in Needham. The hill rises 223 feet above the sea-level.

On the same side of the railway, and near Woodward Street, is the quiet and retired home of the Hon. Edwin P. Seaver, who has been for some years Superintendent of Schools for the city of Boston.

In this same vicinity stands the Tower house (so called), now the home of H. Langford Warren, a Boston architect. It is more than a century old, and was the home of the ancient pedagogue of this region. Opposite is a pretty house, planned by Mr. Warren, owned by Charles J. Page, and occupied by Charles F. Clement, of the Chilton Manufacturing Company. There are several new houses on Chestnut Street, including those owned by Charles J. Page, Frederic H. Henshaw, and William R. Dresser, of the Broadway National Bank, and Chauncey B. McGee (the Boston life-insurance agent), which were designed and erected by Mr. Warren, whose fine architectural taste has made a deep impress on the village of Waban, in the very dawn of its existence. Warren was one of the disciples of the late Henry Hobson Richardson, in whose studio he spent many profitable years.

Among the most actively interested villagers are the Dresser family, Mrs. Mary A. P., and her son William R., who are large owners of land and also the owners and builders of several of the most attractive residences.

The first house on the west side of the railway pertains to the Collins family, who are among the chief land-owners in this region, and one of the

Chauncey B. McGee's Residence, Waban.

largest, oldest, and most beautiful estates at Waban is the Collins property, which has been in the family for a hundred and ten years. Matthias Collins came from Marblehead in 1778, and bought one hundred acres of Joseph Craft, on the Sherborn Road, adjoining the farm of John Woodward. On his death, in 1785, the property was inherited by his only son, Matthias Collins, Second, who enlarged it by the purchase of seventy-eight acres of land adjoining. This whole estate he divided between three of his sons, Amasa, Edward J., and Frederick A. Collins, the latter of whom is now living, retired, at Waban. The late Edward Jackson Collins, who died July 25, 1879, was one of Newton's most respected sons. He had an established reputation for solidity of character, generosity, public spirit, and love for his native town. During the war, when so much money was required for the credit of cities and towns, he came forward to aid Newton, and, with his own personal indorsement of the notes of the town, established its credit, so that money could be raised without trouble or delay. Consequently, her quota was always ready. He filled acceptably many offices of trust, in the town, city, county, and State: was treasurer of Newton 21 years, treasurer of the Newton Savings Bank 25 years, director of the Newton National Bank 29 years, county commissioner 12 years, and represented Newton a number of terms in the General Court. The original Collins property, with its numerous additions, is again united in the fourth generation; and the entire estate is owned by the widow of the late Edward J., his son Edward L., and Mrs. Alice Collins-Gould, the wife of William H. Gould. It is a tract of land embracing over two hundred acres, extending from Beacon Street to Charles River, by which it is bounded for nearly a mile between Newton Upper and Lower Falls.

The Collins property, together with the contiguous estate of Samuel Hano, between the railroad and the river, and covering many hundreds of acres, is being laid out as a great landscape-park, by Ernest W. Bowditch, the well-known civil engineer, with winding drives, groups of trees, bits of shrubbery, broad lawns, and other natural beauties, heightened in effect by the crystalline river murmuring alongside. It is expected that this domain will be sold for residences, in such large blocks that no one can join the colony unless possessed of some means, so that Waban cherishes hopes of being, at some time in the far future, a sort of inland Nahant or Beverly Farms.

The river in front of Waban gives over half a league of good boating-ground, between Turtle Island and the first bridge at Newton Lower Falls; and there are several boats owned by the gentry who live in this vicinity.

Eliot.

THE CLARK, ELLIS, AND CHENEY PLACES.— HICKORY CLIFF AND ITS POET.— THE PLACE OF A VANISHED LAKE.— FAMOUS TREES.— AN ARCADIA OF THE FUTURE.

Between Newton Highlands and Waban is Eliot, where a new and highly finished station has recently been built for the Circuit Railroad, standing in close proximity to the junction of Boylston Street and Circuit Avenue. Boylston Street was once the turnpike between Boston and Worcester, and

Eliot Station, on the Boston & Albany Railroad.

sixty years ago was a thoroughfare of importance. The glory of the stage-coach has departed, but still near at hand stands the old toll-house, and the ancient hostelry, with its tall elms and luxuriant lilacs, to remind the passer-by of other days now fast being forgotten.

Less than five minutes' walk from Eliot station, along Boylston Street, will bring the traveller to the house long the residence of General Cheney, and now occupied by the Randall family. Close at hand, many years ago, the veteran machinist, William E. Clark, well known throughout Newton, had an establishment for the prosecution of his business, but no trace of that is now left. Within a stone's throw of the old General-Cheney house, embowered among lofty pines and hemlocks, in perhaps the most picturesque building-spot in all the Garden City, is the residence of Mr. Charles Ellis. This house was built by his father, who at one time owned and worked the iron-mills, which for more than a generation stood just below the bridge crossing the Charles River into Wellesley.

Southwest of Eliot rises a bold wooded hill, bounded along its southern brow by a regular wall of rock, often perpendicular, and sometimes running up into picturesque cliffs. This line of high escarpments, fringed with a hearty growth of young hickory-trees, gave reason for the name of "Hickory Cliff," applied to the adjacent estate. Here dwelt (until his death, in 1889) the gentle poet, William Peirce, many of whose works are familiar to the people of Newton. The following verses by Mr. Peircé give a pleasing description of the view from this hill-top, at the season when the falling of the leaves left the prospect clear: —

WINTER SCENE FROM HICKORY CLIFF.

"Deep is the snow on Hickory Cliff,
 And white the top of the Baptist tower;
The ice-bound river clanks his chains,
 And strives to shake off Winter's power.

"Dark are the pines on Prospect Hill,
 And frosty bright are Waltham's spires;
The sledded milkman homeward glides,
 Rich in his dreams of kitchen fires.

"Weston's and Wellesley's rounded backs,
 Shaggy with woods, look cold and still.
Deep in the gorge the silvery ice
 Fringes the snowdrifts white and chill.

"Dover, so blue in summer days,
 Seems to be robed in whitest wool;
While dimly the dome of Dedham shows
 'Gainst Milton's purple ridges cool.

"Gray are the woods on Oak Hill's crest,
 The shivering birches dot the plain;
The red roofs show no more their red
 Till Winter's mantle lifts again.

"But hark! the gust! I must begone;
 These arctic bees, the snowflakes, sting.
The poet's beard is stiff with ice,
 My frosty muse must fold her wing."

HICKORY CLIFF, THE RESIDENCE OF THE LATE WILLIAM PEIRCE.
Boylston Street, near High Street, Eliot.

The plain that stretches to the north of Eliot geologists tell us was once the bed of an extensive lake. Twenty or thirty feet below the surface, through clean sand and gravel, the dark ooze of the ancient lake is reached. Singular funnel-shaped hollows are scattered through the whole extent of this plain. Some of these are very interesting, and should be seen to be thoroughly appreciated. Quite large trees are growing on the bottom of a few of these natural earth-bowls.

The combination of hill and plain at Eliot is very marked; and few observers fail to see at a glance many natural beauties, to tempt the writer's pen or artist's pencil.

The march of improvement has always one drawback to some minds, in that not a few ancient landmarks are made to give way before it. Near Eliot station stand two venerable oaks, close together, twin bravers of a thousand storms. They are not quite the sole survivors among the trees of their date; but many a neighboring monarch of the ancient forest has within a short time been turned to ashes, notably a remarkable pine that has for generations stood as a tall sentinel over Boylston and Eliot Streets in this immediate region. At a third of its height from the ground it forked into two symmetrical branches, and was an object that caught the eye of every observer. Not far from it stood, until within a year, the old stone blacksmith's shop known for some sixty years back as a famous place for horseshoeing. Its last days were made troublous by some contentions in which the city of Newton participated; and the noted Belger case will not soon fade from the minds of those in the vicinity who are fond of legal hair-splitting.

It is but a few minutes' walk from Eliot to Newton Highlands, and it may be said that the station is within that village. But the extensive open spaces on the north and west form the site of the future hamlet of Eliot, which will extend from the Highlands to the Upper Falls, covering territory peculiarly adapted for residence-purposes, at once high, airy, and dry, and charmingly diversified in point of scenery.

Newton Upper Falls.

AN INDIAN FISHERMAN.— ANCIENT MANUFACTURES.— CHURCHES AND SHRINES.— OTIS PETTEE.— THE WATER-WORKS.— ECHO BRIDGE.— THE SUDBURY AQUEDUCT. — TURTLE ISLAND.— CANOE VOYAGES.

Newton Upper Falls is a manufacturing village of almost two thousand inhabitants, whose homes are scattered on and about the bold and lofty hills through which the Charles River cuts its way, breaking into a passion of rapids after more than three leagues of tranquil current. The other hamlets of Newton are more intimately connected with Boston; but this one has an independent life of its own, derived from its mills and workshops, and so can afford to lie outside of the Circuit Railroad. The houses that nestle along the slopes and perch on the heights are less ambitious than those of its neighbor villages, and have but few suggestions of modern architecture, household decoration, or the gabled glories of the so-called Queen-Anne era. Although in a score of ways exempt from the analogy, there is a certain sunny tranquillity and dignified repose about the place that gave reason for Mr. Howells to liken it to one of the ancient hill-towns of Italy, sleeping along its picturesque highlands, and overlooking leagues of dependent plains and glens.

The first recorded owner of the falls and the adjacent shores and islands and eel-weirs was Nahaton, a sagamore of the Ponkapoag tribe, who sold a part of it to one John Maugus, for a gun. The eel-weirs were built of stone, and rose three feet above the surface of the water. In a deposition made in 1760 as to events hereabouts, the witnesses bore this testimony: "Wee Never New aney Salt water fish to assend above said falls, nor do wee remember Ever to have heard our Predessors say that aney Salt water fish did ever assend above said falls. Further wee say, and Give it as our Opinion, that it is impracticable for the fish to Assend said Falls ever while wee consider it in the State of Nature." Nevertheless, the sagacious Maugus established his wigwams and eel-weir here, and got great comfort in catching and drying fish hereabouts, and finally bequeathed it to his son, John Maugus, from whom the English immigrants acquired it by purchase. In 1680 the people of Dedham bought the present township of Deerfield from the Sachem Nahaton (or Nehoiden), for £10 in money, 40 shillings in Indian corn, and 40 acres of land at the Upper Falls, and established Deerfield as a colony of Dedham (an unnatural relation, which did not endure). And in 1700 Nahaton sold the remainder of his domain at the Upper Falls, for £12, to Robert Cooke of Dorchester, who is strangely characterized in the deed as a "horn breaker." The antiquaries have failed to discover the meaning of this singular name.

In the old days, when unvexed by dams and sluices, the waters of the Charles made a precipitous descent of twenty feet here, and then fell twenty five feet in the next half-mile. Such a favorable water-power was not neglected by the practical colonists; and in 1688 John Clark came up hither from Brookline, and established a saw-mill (on the site of the present silk-mills), to make lumber withal for the incoming settlers. About the year 1710 a grist-mill and a fulling-mill were added to the local manufacturing interests, and there was further constructed a new and more practicable eel-weir. Nathaniel Parker and Nathaniel Longley became associated in the business with John Clark's two sons. John Clark sold half the saw-mill, the eel-weir, and two acres of land to Nathaniel Parker, for £57; and in 1725 Noah Parker, Nathaniel's son and heir, and one of the primeval Baptists, became possessed of the entire milling property and its appurtenances. His grandson, John Parker, was President of the United-States Branch Bank, and one of the solid men of Boston. The saw and grist mills and their adjuncts were sold during the Revolutionary War to Simon Elliot, a tobacconist of Boston, for £1,700. For thirty years or more Elliot, who was also Major-General of the Suffolk and Norfolk militia, conducted large snuff-mills here, with twenty mortars. He lived in the old Noah-Parker mansion, and had the largest snuff business in New England. In 1814 the property (screw-factory, wire-work, annealing-shop, and snuff-mills) passed into the hands of the Elliot Manufacturing Company, of which Frederic Cabot was agent; and seven years later they built a cotton-factory on the site of the old snuff-mills, Abbott Lawrence and Thomas Handasyd Perkins being among their number. Otis Pettee came to the Upper Falls in the year 1817, for the Elliot Company, and remained with them fifteen years, after which he started here a large workshop for making cotton-mill machinery. In 1840 he bought out the Elliot Company, and carried on the business himself until his death, twelve years later. He increased the capacity of the mills three-fold, and changed their product from sheetings to print-goods. After Pettee's death, in 1853, the property was acquired by the Newton Mills corporation, and greatly enlarged. Their output was from 12,000 to 14,000 yards of print-goods daily. At this time there were at the upper dam a cotton-factory with 14,000 spindles, and a mile above a steam-furnace employing 15 workmen on iron castings, and a machine-shop.

The lower part of the village, otherwise sufficiently unattractive, is adorned with lines of century-old elms, whose graceful hanging foliage

THE SECOND BAPTIST CHURCH, NEWTON UPPER FALLS.
Chestnut and Ellis Streets. [Before it was remodelled.]

overarches the road to Needham. The bridge on Elliot Street gives pleasant views down the picturesque rocky and foliage-draped gorge, with its rambling old brick mills, and the white Baptist church on the cliff above; and on the other side opens a quiet cove, with meadows and coppices beyond, and in the distance gracefully rolling hills, whose brilliant foliage makes a symphony of scarlets and bronzes in the still days of October.

On this bridge fifty years ago the credulous country-folk used to gather to watch for the "Baby Ghost," a wee spectre whom they thought ran at times across the blue waters, while the rocking of its cradle they fancied could be heard beneath the stream. The busy life of latter days has effaced the memory of this legend and its mysterious origin.

From the Hon. Thomas C. Amory's "Charles River," a recent volume of pastoral verse, following the stream from source to sea, and giving scores of pages to the Newton sections of the stream, we take but one stanza, describing this scene: —

> "'Midst the dark shadows of an ancient forge,
> All the more picturesque, — no rules control, —
> Below the bridge the waters gain a gorge,
> Between whose cliffs precipitous they roll;
> With bushes draped, the vale in breadth expands,
> Its bed descends till partly lost to sight;
> 'Midst tangled growth the lofty hemlock stands;
> The rapid slopes the snow-wreath flecks with white.
> The woods and rocks the grand and lovely blend,
> The widespread streams beyond new beauty lend."

The chief object in the view, of course, is the irregular pile of the Newton mills, which, after over sixty years of successful operation, were crowded out of operation by the sharp competition which made profits so low that the smaller factories could not exist. In the year 1884, therefore, they were closed, to the great loss of the village; and there were left only traditions of their palmy days, when Captain Moorfield, their old retired sea-captain agent, walked pompously up and down the yard, with thumbs in arm-holes, as if on his careening quarter-deck. In 1886 the works were bought by an enterprising silk-manufacturing company of New Jersey; and so perhaps in time the Upper Charles may rival the Passaic or the Rhone in its productiveness of the fine dress-fabrics that are adorned by the indwelling of America's maidens. The great quadrangle of weather-beaten brick mills is occupied by 130 operatives, spinning silks, silk yarns, filoselles, embroidery silks, and other goods of like character, the raw material for which is brought here in its original packages from France, Italy, China, Japan, and other far-away lands. Messrs. Phipps and Train, the heads of the company, have settled in the village, and are taking a kindly interest in brightening up the homes of the operatives, planting flowers, sowing lawns, and in other ways adding to the attractiveness of the streets.

Up to this point, before the dams were thrown across the river, came salmon and shad, alewives and smelts, tom-cod, and other sea-fish. The Indians had their weirs here, near the great mid-stream rock below the Elliot-Street bridge, and esteemed this commerce so highly, that they carefully reserved a part of the Needham shore to dry their fish upon. Although the tribe is extinct, this right is still legally intact; and every transfer of land on that tract must contain a clause specifying that the Indians may use the land for drying their fish upon. The ancient snuff-mill dam may be seen at low water, half-way from the bridge to the present dam, and partly supported on the great mid-stream bowlder. It includes the material of the Indians' eel-weir, stretching from the rock to the island, which latter has been filled in to the eastern shore. The Rock House was a cherished landmark of our red brethren, near the western shore of the falls.

At Newton Upper Falls began the opposition to the audacious attempt of Dedham to steal a river, which had met with some measure of success. It was away back in 1639 that certain enterprising Dedhamites cut a canal from the Charles River to East Brook, a tributary of the Neponset, and turned into it the full waters of the Charles, which there occupies much higher ground than the Neponset. One hundred and thirty-eight years later, Newton sent a worshipful committee to the Governor and Council, to prevent the filching of the entire stream from its natural course; and in 1807 another committee was chosen "to defend their natural rights against any invader that may attempt to turn said river out of its natural course." As General Elliot said in his petition to the town: "The proprietors of mills on Charles River are greatly alarmed for the safety of their property, having already suffered an incalculable loss, in the diversion of waters from the river; and he asks the Town to adopt measures which may tend to give aid and support in defending their property against further encroachments." The final settlement came only after much litigation, and many hard words between Newton and Dedham. It was a pure compromise, by which the ingenious hydraulic bandits of Norfolk County were allowed to capture one-third of the water in the river, to flow off through their Mother Brook, but were forbidden to seize the entire stream.

In the year 1800 there were but six families living in the village, which sixty years later had a population of 993, and in 1873 had 1,520. This influx of inhabitants has been drawn for the most part by the local factories, and has numbered a preponderance of foreigners, of that class of patient workers which has done so much to make New England what it is.

Near the crest of the Quebec-like ridge stands Sunnyside, the antique yellow mansion of Otis Pettee, rambling over its high terraces in luxuriant amplitude, and crowned by a little spire that recalls the colonial dignity of Mount Vernon. This house dates from the year 1828, when its farm-lands extended southward beyond the present railroad, and on them the senior Mr. Pettee built the great stone barn that is still standing down on Oak Street. The estate is now occupied by Otis Pettee, the son of its founder, and himself formerly an alderman of Newton. The stone barn was originally built as a silk mill. Although devoid of early scientific education, the elder Otis Pettee had a remarkable natural genius for mechanical invention; and his Gear Cone Double Speeder was pronounced by Professor Treadwell to be "absolutely perfect, because the principles of it are eternal, and can never be improved upon so long as the world stands." This speeder was for a long time in use in America, the mechanism being made here only; and in England also it conquered its place, although decried at first by the insular engineers. If the present sentence shall seem obscure to general readers, they will pardon it for the benefit of experts, namely: That this alone, of all existing machines, accomplishes (not by uncertain leathern belts moving upon conical drums, etc., but what always before was deemed impossible), by inflexible metallic gear-work and with the mathematical precision thus only attainable, all the relative movements, with all the changes in series by variables dependent upon other changes in series by variables, necessary not only for spinning, but for safely and accurately coiling on spools, etc., the delicate roping or roving, all by scientific yet the most simple arrangements, and adaptable for various degrees of required fineness.

Not far from the railway station, on the south, are the works of the Pettee Company, founded in 1831 by Otis Pettee, for the manufacture of cotton machinery. In 1839 they were burned out, in a great conflagration which destroyed $60,000 and lighted up the valley of the Upper Charles for leagues. In 1840 the works were rebuilt, employing three hundred men, and supplying machinery to the chief mills in New England and the Middle States, and as far away as Tennessee and Mexico. Between 1838 and 1850 a dozen great Mexican mills, at Tepic, Mazatlan, Colima, Guadalajara, etc., were fully equipped with machinery from this place. When it was proposed to utilize the water-power on the little brook that flows from the highlands toward Oak Hill into the Charles near this point, a local hydraulic expert objected that the stream wasn't worth a dam. But Mr. Pettee thought otherwise, and established here his cotton-machinery works, which, after the lapse of more than half a century, are still mildly prospering.

From the abrupt hillock near by, with an embankment at the top like a little reservoir, or a picket-station in Virginia, there is a capital view of the mills and their attendant ponds, with the Great and Little Blue Hills, leagues away up the valley, and the rugged heights of Wellesley nearer at hand.

ECHO BRIDGE, THE AQUEDUCT OF THE BOSTON WATERWORKS.
Across the Charles River at Newton Upper Falls.

The Cheney house, that stood opposite Pettee's boarding-house, near the south-west corner of Cheney and Mechanic Streets, was of heavy oaken timbers, wainscoted with oaken planks, as a protection against hostile bullets, which were to be feared in that remote day of 1702, when its foundations were laid. Joseph Cheney, Jr., brought from the woods one day two little saplings on his shoulder, and they have in ninety years grown into the noble twin elms now standing near the boarding-house. Joseph's son, General Ebenezer Cheney, was a representative to the General Court, a pew-owner in the First Church, and filled other positions of trust in the town. He had the orthodox number of twelve children, and died in 1853, at the age of ninety-four. The Cheney house long since vanished; but the great elms, its oldtime companions, remain to mark its site. Nearly opposite the Pettee place is the high-pillared mansion built by Dr. Samuel S. Whitney, afterwards the property of Dr. A. D. Dearborn, and for many years the home of Frederic Barden, the manufacturer, who died in 1877. It is now the home of Josiah B. Newell. To the eastward, Elliot Street climbs the slopes of Cottage Hill, which attains an elevation of 230 feet above tide-water.

On Needham Street, near the railway, are the buildings of the United-States Fireworks Company, from which the great Fourth-of-July pyrotechnic displays of the city of Boston have been furnished. To avert the danger of a general and disastrous explosion, the operations of manufacture are carried on in a number of small detached buildings, scattered at random through the forest.

On a noble situation high up on the ridge over the village stands the Methodist-Episcopal meeting-house, a plain old wooden building with a quaint little spirelet, and two great maple-trees in front. It was erected away back in the year 1827, mainly at the costs of the Elliot Manufacturing Company and Rufus Ellis, Esq., as a home for the Upper-Falls Religious Society; but somehow the rarefied air of these highlands failed to agree with the Unitarianism at first preached there, and the church fell into a fatal decline. Meantime, the Methodists, who had begun their services in an humble way in 1826, had waxed mightily; and in 1832 they were allowed to occupy the silent meeting-house alternate Sundays, and in due time they purged it of its Arian taint, and entered into peaceful occupation. For nearly two generations they have enjoyed the ministrations of their itineracy in this high-placed temple. Marshall S. Rice, the initiator of the Methodist experiment, early desired to buy the church for his brethren; and, on asking his wife what she should do if he so disposed of his little store of money, and then died, she answered, with brave spirit: "Buy the house. I don't believe you will soon be called to die, if you do; and, should it be so, I will support our children by going into the factory to work, if necessary." The thriving church received a bell in 1833; was enlarged in 1836; built a vestry in 1855; was renovated in 1860; got a new bell in 1861; an organ in 1863; a parsonage in 1865; and so has grown from decade to decade, with the adequate blessing of its Lord. The two great rock-maples in front were pulled out of the grass in New Ipswich, N.H., fifty years ago, being then about six inches high, and were brought down the country by Marshall S. Rice, in his chaise-box.

The incumbents of the Methodist pastorate have been Rev. Charles K. True, Rev. John Parker, Rev. Nathan B. Spaulding, Rev. Charles S. Macreading, Rev. D. K. Bannister, Rev. Joseph Dennison, Rev. Jacob Sanborn, Rev. M. P. Webster, Rev. Chester Field, Rev. Mr. Putnam, Rev. Z. A. Mudge, Rev. John Paulson, Rev. Edward Otheman, Rev. Newell S. Spaulding, Rev. James Mudge, Rev. Joseph A. Merrill, Rev. Joseph W. Lewis, Rev. William Pentecost, Rev. Augustus F. Bailey, Rev. James W. Morey, Rev. Jonas Bailey, Rev. Ralph W. Allen, Rev. William B. Toulmin, Rev. William J. Pomfret, Rev. Franklin Thurber, Rev. Charles T. Johnson (1880–82), Rev. A. F. Herrick (1883–85), and Rev. John Peterson (1885–89).

The white wooden meeting-house of the Second Baptist Society lifts its battlemented tower on a high bluff over the roaring river, whose perpetual melody ascends through the trees which spring from the steep incline, mingling with the burbling of the factory-wheels. The church dates from the year 1833, long before Texas and California became American soil; and the society was formed by fifty-five members of the original Baptist church in Newton. The first local meetings occurred in 1832, and the church was organized three years later. Its former bell once belonged to the Universalist society at Newton, on whose demise it passed into the possession of this church. It cracked a few years ago, and has been succeeded by a new bell, which now summons with melodious tones the people to worship their Lord. The building was remodelled and repaired in the year 1880.

The shepherds of the Baptist fold have been the Rev. Origen Crane (1836–39), Rev. Charles W. Dennison (1842–), Rev. Samuel S. Leighton (1846–47), Rev. Amos Webster (1848–54), Rev. Samuel F. Smith, D.D. (stated supply, 1856–64), Rev. William C. Richards (1865–71), Rev. Freeman T. Whitman, Rev. E. H. Jones, Rev. Thomas de Gruchy, Rev. Henry G. Safford, and Rev. B. L. Whitman. It is strongly hoped that this historic church may recover its ancient power and influence for good. Nearly four hundred members have been connected with it, but now there are but half as many members as at the time of its organization, fifty years ago.

Opposite the Baptist church is Winter Street, climbing up the eminence that in old times was known as Oyster Hill. Here, also, is the chief plaza of the village, with its iron fountain and tall elm-tree, and environment of somnolent shops.

In the old days the village was divided into two hostile parts,— the Upper Place, including the southerly part, and the Lower Place, which was over the hill towards West Newton. Never were such wars waged as those between the lads of these *faubourgs* in winter, when the air was brightened with flying snowballs, and thrilled with the cheers of storming parties. The tavern and its jolliest patrons were in the Lower Place (fitting though accidental designation), whereat the unco' guid of the Upper Place pointed the cold, unmoving finger of scorn. It was in those days that John Winslow wrote : -

> "Newton Upper Falls is split in two parts,
> Where we learn the sciences and fine arts.
> We have all sorts of trades, all kinds of trash,
> Machine-shops, cotton-mills, but not much cash."

The first Roman-Catholic services in Newton were held at the Upper Falls, in 1843, when Father Strain, of Waltham, began to celebrate Mass in a room in James Cahill's house. Father Bernard Flood was missionary here from 1852 to 1864, and secured an acre of land for a church-site, on which his successor, Father John McCarthy (1864-70), erected a large wooden church, which was dedicated by Bishop Williams in 1867. The next priest in residence was Father Michael Dolan, who settled here in 1871. Five years later, the enlarged St. Mary's Church received a service of rededication from Archbishop Williams, with a sermon by Bishop Healey of Portland. The building has 1,000 sittings, and the average attendance is 750. The priest in charge is Father Martin O'Brien.

The Universalist society was composed of 22 proprietors, who maintained the Rev. Samuel P. Skinner as their pastor from 1841 to 1845. The pulpit was then filled for two years by A. S. Dudley, a dentist, and William F. Teulon, a Canadian doctor, under whose ministrations the society melted away, and their church became Eliot Hall, used for some years by the Catholics, and also for lectures and other secular purposes, and being finally converted into a dwelling-house.

Another ecclesiastical institution (founded in 1886) is the Church of Yahveh, on Boylston Street, where the local believers in the Second Advent worship, under the direction of the Rev. L. T. Cunningham. It is a grim and singular-looking wooden edifice, with its odd title emblazoned across the front.

The local secular societies are the Quinobequin Association, with a library and fifty members, meeting every Monday evening at its hall on High Street; Home Lodge, No. 162, of Odd Fellows; Echo-Bridge Council, No. 843, of the Royal Arcanum; the Upper Charles-River Boat Club; and Good Templars, a temperance organization.

At the head of the glen, and not far from the handsome stone bridge

PUMPING STATION OF THE NEWTON WATERWORKS.
Newton Upper Falls.

whose triple arches join Newton and Needham, is the building of the Newton Water Works, whose architecture suggests that it is something more than the ordinary factory. This neat civic structure shelters a handsome little hall, with polished floor and timber roof, not unlike a chapel, and enshrining the great engines, whose mighty throbbing forces through leagues of underground iron arteries the river of pure water that supplies the homes of this wide-spread city. It is worth while to watch, for a few minutes, the almost noiseless motion of this tremendous piece of mechanism whose mission is so beneficent and useful. The grounds about the building are prettily laid out, and afford pleasant views of the winding blue river, out of which project huge weather-stained rocks. Here and there float little boats, indicating that on these still reaches of the sylvan stream there are available chances for navigation. Above, the Charles sweeps around a bend along which extend the embankments of the Filter Basin, like the tow-path of a riverside canal. The engine at the pumping-works is a pulsometer, built by the Worthington Pump Works, and can pump 5,000,000 gallons in 24 hours. There is also an auxiliary engine that can pump 1,000,000 gallons a day, used when the main engine is being repaired.

One of the first things Newton did to signalize its arrival at the dignity of a city was to begin arrangements for a water-supply. The people voted, 928 to 443, in December, 1874, to authorize the expenditure of $600,000 for the purpose; and Colonel Royal M. Pulsifer, the Hon. Robert R. Bishop, and Colonel Francis J. Parker were appointed Water Commissioners. It had been the original idea to get the water from Hammond's, Wiswall's, and Bullough's Ponds; but the commissioners recommended that it be taken from a well above Pettee's works, at the Upper Falls. This then was done; and in 1875 and 1876 fifty miles of street-mains were laid, and $766,000 had been expended. The reservoir on Waban Hill holds 15,000,000 gallons. The water supply was supplemented by seven artesian wells, sunk in 1886 by the Manhattan Artesian-Well Company, and capable of drawing from the great underground currents something like 300,000 gallons a day of pure water, at a temperature of 50 degrees.

The Upper-Falls Racquet Boat Club has its house and moorings alongside the Needham-Street Bridge. The navigation of the stream is unbroken for ten miles, from this point up to Charles-River Village, beyond Dedham, the current being very slight, and not without frequent shallows. Through these leagues, the silent and lazy stream flows amid a sylvan solitude, between luxuriant thickets and woods, and along the emerald edges of lonely meadows. Its shores are almost as uninhabited as they were three centuries ago; and the unknown river traverses miles of serried grass and fields of fragrant white lilies, through shadowy forests and silent meadows, and past lines of low rocky hills. By and by the high dome of Dedham

Court-House rises over the trees, with the spires and roofs of the capital of Norfolk County grouped about it. About half a mile before reaching Dedham, the narrow water-lane of Mother Brook turns off to the left; and here the boatman drifts swiftly downward, over grassy deeps and sandy shallows, carries his craft around five dams, and emerges on the Neponset River, near Hyde Park. The circumnavigation of Boston and Newton, ascending the Charles from the harbor to Mother Brook, and descending the brook and the Neponset to the harbor again, may be made in two days, the distance being about seventy miles. One of our best writers thus describes some phases of the scenery: "The downward voyage from Dedham is worth an Odyssey. The distance is $23\frac{1}{2}$ miles from Dedham to Boston, by the river, according to the accepted schedule. It is fair to assume that it is more than $23\frac{1}{2}$ miles from Dedham boat-house to the Union Club's house in Boston,— 25 miles, perhaps. And all but a mile or two of that distance is made up of as lovely river-scenery as is to be found anywhere. Starting from Dedham, one passes through a continuous garden. The river in the 6 miles down to Newton Upper Falls is lined with water-lilies. How wonderfully abundant they are! They dot the margin everywhere,— untouched, apparently, and looking as if they were unknown, so Arcadian is this region almost at our very gates. The canoes glide swan-like on the smooth surface between a double row of these lilies: their fragrance rises to the boats. Above them there is a hedge of sweet-brier, which, covered with its deep-pink roses, makes a marvellous background for the scene; and clinging close to the foot of the briers, shoreward from the lilies, is a line of some sort of water-flag, which, over leaves like the calla, bears a plume-like blue bloom. The meadow is dotted with graceful elms, and beyond are the hills, with woody tracts and pastures interspersed, and the shadows of fleecy clouds chasing each other across them. Now the canoes glide past the meadows; and the deep thickets sweep down over close to the shore, driving out, for a time, the sweet-brier garden, and overhanging the water, instead, with branches of oak and elm, past which the canoers brush their way in their placid voyage. Here and there are picturesque stone-arched bridges, and an occasional habitation; but the way is for the most part purely Arcadian. And there is nothing like a canoe voyage for enjoyment of such a scene. One seems to be half bird of the air and half water fowl, as he skims along placidly among such scenes. He forgets the steady, easy movement of his arms in handling the paddle, and seems to glide by a pure mental volition, noiseless except for the soft ripple of the water at his boat's prow. It is the poetry of all boating,— the most exquisite of out-of-door enjoyments."

The lovely rural scenery that surrounds the village was for a long time the delight of Ralph Waldo Emerson. When he returned from Europe, in 1833, he settled down with his mother in a quiet old farmhouse a half-mile from Newton Upper Falls. He wrote to a friend: "Why do you not come out here to see the pines and the hermit? . . . It is calm as eternity, and will give you lively ideas of the same. These sleepy hollows, full of savins and cinque-foil, seem to utter a quiet satire at the ways and politics of men. I think the robin and the finch the only philosophers. 'Tis deep Sunday in this woodcock's nest of ours from one end of the week to the other; times and seasons get lost here; sun and stars make all the difference of night and day."

The crowning attraction of the village is the famous Echo Bridge, a marvellous stone aqueduct on which the Sudbury-River water is carried across the Charles River, high above the stream, on its way to the thirsty throats of Boston. There is a path leading down from Ellis Street, near the Baptist church, alongside the aqueduct, with an enrailed platform just under the arch large enough to accommodate a dozen persons. The favorite word to hurl at the arch is JULY, and the serious charge of lie — lie — lie is thrown back as vigorously and almost as frequently as if the bridge were a political newspaper in campaign time. The human voice, on a still day, is rapidly re-echoed 18 times from beneath this arch, and a pistol-shot gives 25 repetitions. According to the highly imaginative engineer of the water-works, "A shout, of moderate intensity, is reverberated back with so many and so distinct repetitions that all the neighboring woods seem to be full of wild Indians, rushing down from the hills, and with their terrible war-whoop ready to dash into view, and annihilate all traces of the surrounding civilization."

This beautiful bridge was built in 1876 and 1877, of solid granite masonry, 500 feet long, with five arches of 37 feet span; one (over Ellis Street) of 28 feet; and the great segmental arch over the river, 130 feet in span, with a radius of 69 feet, and a height of 51 feet above the stream, or 70 feet to the top. There is but one larger arch in America. The foundations rest on solid rock, with a pressure of 16½ tons to the square foot. The arch is but 18 feet wide at the crown, and presents a very symmetrical and pleasing appearance, which is heightened by the sylvan beauty of the surroundings. The river below, still confused from its wrestle with the mill-wheels above, and its heady plunge over the rocky falls, flashes and darkens through the deep gorge, reflecting like a mirror the high hemlock trees above, and wimpling away around the fair wooded islet below. As Mary Blake says, in one of her charming suburban essays: "Like a properly trained athlete, the bridge runs on narrow arches across the level land, until one swift bound of unusual length carries it over the river. It is a place of enchantment. The fairy godmother of the place lives under the river-arch, with a chorus of attendant nymphs who echo your lightest whisper with true feminine pertinacity." Mrs. Blake thus narrates a subterranean voyage in the aqueduct, beginning at this point: —

"Under ordinary circumstances, to have a passage open under your feet in the solid rock, and a flight of steps take you down into the bowels of the earth, where a smiling gnome with a strong Milesian brogue invited you to step into a barge resplendent with waxen lights and floating on the bosom of a subterranean river, might shake your usually sober senses, but these were not ordinary circumstances. We were a party of adventurers, who, by the great kindness of the reigning powers, were allowed to go down into the main conduit of the Sudbury-River water supply, where it crosses the arches at Newton, and float down under the earth till we reached the light of day again at Chestnut Hill. When the opening through which we had descended had been closed, and we glided down the dark tunnel, with the flaring lights of innumerable candles fastened in tin reflectors to take the place of the bright spring sunshine, the situation was novel enough to suit even a modern spectacular dramatist. Fortunately, there was no such monster among us. Figure to yourself, as the lively Gaul would say, a clean, well-aired, brick arched aqueduct, nine feet in diameter, with a stream of clear, pure water, two feet in depth, flowing with almost imperceptible motion through the dark silence, and losing itself in the shadows. At every hundred feet a little numbered tablet of white porcelain divided the structure into sections, so that either cleaning or repairs could be carried on systematically and quickly. The gangs of men employed in labor of this kind can be subdivided, so that the work is accomplished in an incredibly short space of time. Twice a year the entire extent is carefully scraped and washed; and a constant supervision, with telephonic communication along the whole line, and expert examination, prevents the possibility of even slight damage. Through the entire length of 16 miles manholes and ladders give easy access at stated points, and a system of underground maps corresponding to the landmarks above makes it possible to locate any break or injury with great exactness. A complicated system of screens and floodgates at both inlet and outlet filter and control the flow, so that the mighty force is as gentle as a well-bred child, when it might easily be so terrible. The exquisite compactness and neatness of the enormous structure is a marvel to unused eyes; not a drop of moisture falls from the high, cleanly roof; both brickwork and cement look pure and fresh as if laid yesterday, and the clear, limpid water is transparent as crystal. The absolute absence of stale air or even the slightest odor is especially delightful to some who have regarded the trip from afar with the apprehension which clings to all unknown things. As we float swiftly on, helping the already swift current with long poles, a fresh breeze from the open gates at Chestnut-Hill Reservoir begins to play about our ears, a faint tinkle of falling water makes itself heard in the distance, and the brick sides and roof broaden and heighten into a picturesque cavern of stone where the aqueduct had been blasted through some rocky hillside. In such spots only an occasional dripping from the surface works its way through clefts and cracks, and we find umbrellas serviceable. Here and there lurk echoes of unearthly beauty; the artist's yodel comes back in a delicious diminuendo like the faint sweetness of an Æolian harp; a blow on the iron prow of the boat breaks in distant thunder against some distant angle; and O'Shaughnessey, sitting aloft in the stern in the glare of the candles, like a good-natured Irish cherub on an illuminated missal, pipes jigs and hornpipes and odd bits of gay melodies with quaint minor endings, which whirl back from the answering walls in a tumult of fantastic sounds. Just far enough behind to strengthen the picturesque effect of light and shadow the second boat, with its gay cargo and flaming headlight, followed us through the utter gloom; for any darkness of which we are conscious in the upper world is only relative compared with this intense blackness. . . .

"What concerns you and me is the precision, the thoroughness, the exquisite care, the constant watchfulness which day and night, summer and winter, with infinite thoughtfulness and infinite skill, is planning and perfecting, so that we may enjoy that best of all nature's blessings, good water. The next time you turn a faucet and see the precious stream which, in spite of grumbling and growling, is more presentable, more palatable and more healthy than that of nine out of ten of the other cities of the Union, think of the years of labor, the millions of money, the resources of science, the patient, watchful care that has been required before this plenteous indulgence was made possible for you. Think of the Sudbury aqueduct and the score of works connected with it.

"Meantime, we are nearing the end of our two-hour voyage. We have waked the echoes until we are hoarse; we have passed under hills and over valleys, skimmed beneath gentlemen's lawns and village streets, and now far off a point of brilliant white brightness shows through the darkness. What is that, O genial Shaughnessey? An electric light or a calcium? 'Faith, mam, it's a betther thing than ayther! It's daylight!' Nearer it comes and nearer until we float under the arch into the full glory of sunshine, and realize, as one can only realize who has been for a while deprived of its beauty, what it meant to the world when 'God said, Let there be light!'"

Near the north-east corner of Chestnut and Boylston Streets stands the house that from 1808 to 1850 was the village inn, dignified by the sonorous title of the Manufacturers' Hotel. Here the merchants and commercial persons who drove out from Boston on business at the mills, used to put up

THE WETHERELL ESTATE, RESIDENCE OF GEORGE H. ELLIS.
Eliot Street, Newton Upper Falls.

their horses and fortify their inner men. The Worcester Turnpike was built here in 1808, with its bridge across the Charles, its 600 shares of $250 each being nearly all owned in Boston, and turning out almost a total loss to the subscribers. Among the land-owners of this locality early in the present century were George Ticknor, Benjamin Guild, and Jonathan Mason, of Boston.

When Thomas Parker sold his works to General Elliot, he reserved four acres below the Falls, where, near the small island, he built a dam and saw-mill in 1783. This property passed in 1799 into the hands of the Newton Iron Works Company (Rufus Ellis, agent), who built a rolling-mill, a cut-nail factory (the latter in 1809), and a cotton-factory (in 1813). In 1821 Ellis became sole proprietor, and two years later formed the Newton Factories Company, for rolling and slitting bar-iron, and making cut nails and cotton cloth; and in 1835 the property reverted to Rufus and David Ellis. Fifteen years later, there were at this point a rolling-mill, which worked up 1,500 tons of bar-iron annually; a factory making 500 tons of cut nails; and a cotton-mill (on the Needham shore) with 2,000 spindles. Many years ago (about the year 1850), the cotton-mill was burned, and its lonely ruins now cumber the Needham shore. This mill was chiefly built of the timbers of a British ship, captured in the War of 1812, and brought into Boston and dismantled. Vast quantities of nails were sent hence to Cuba, to be used in the manufacture of sugar-boxes and similar works of utility. The rolling-mills were on Turtle Island, north of Boylston Street, and the nail-works south of the street. The rolling-mills were closed about a dozen years ago, when Frederick Barden died, and the mainspring of their action became motionless. The island is now occupied by paper-mills, in 1886 run by the Superior Wax-Paper Company, which collapsed, after a short tenure of life, leaving the village shopkeepers to mourn many unsettled accounts. Just across, on the Needham shore, in the wild little ravine formed by the outlet of the ponds, is the odd rocky grotto known as Devil's Den. This is, of course, to be expected; for poor must be the New-England town that has not its bit of a cavern, consecrated to his Plutonian Majesty.

From the bridge beyond Turtle Island you may obtain a charming view up the river, over a placid black mill-pond, which is shut in by picturesque rocky banks, and overhung by a wealth of various foliage. Above these, and closing the fair vista, rises the great gray and red arch of Echo Bridge. On the other side of the bridge is the resounding dam, with bright meadows opening out far below.

And so, amid the venerable colonial houses of the Lower Place, and in the presence of its strangely silent industrial Pompeii, we may take leave of Newton Upper Falls.

Newton Highlands.

A GROUP OF MODERN HOMES.— THE SANITARIUM.— ANCIENT TAVERNS.— THE TWO CHURCHES.— A COLONIAL FAMILY.— WELL-KNOWN CITIZENS.

The bright modern village of Newton Highlands stands on the breezy plateau which lies between Newton Upper Falls and Newton Centre, with the wooded heights of Cottage Hill on one side and Crystal Lake on the other, and on the south the beautiful and park-like open country opening

The Bethuel-Allen House, long occupied by Ralph Waldo Emerson, on Woodward Street.

away towards Oak Hill. On all sides the broad and quiet streets stretch away, lined with pretty villas and cottages, and presenting a pleasing scene of peacefulness and comfort. The rural beauty of the country, and the cheapness of land, have attracted hitherward many Boston families, whose nominal heads seek their daily avocations in the neighboring metropolis, while leaving the village authorities to guard their dear ones. Its high and dry location and sandy soil give this locality a singular degree of healthfulness; and physicians have for many years recommended it as a sanitarium for persons suffering from asthma and catarrh and other diseases of the throat and lungs. In 1886 the railway company built here a handsome and spacious stone station, nearly surrounded by pleasant lawns, drives, and walks. On all sides are heard the sounds of carpentry, where new groups of houses are being prepared for the incoming families of the next year and the coming decades. In the western edge of the village (as we have seen) is the new railway-station of Eliot, three-quarters of a mile from the Newton-Highlands station, and one mile from Waban. It is also less than a mile, by way of Eliot Street, from Newton Upper Falls.

Not many years ago, this village was but a small cross-roads settlement, in a region of farms, with two well-known taverns,— Bacon's (where Deacon Asa Cook afterwards lived) and Mitchell's (afterwards Thornton's), at the western corner of Centre and Boylston Streets. Near by were the shops of the blacksmith and the wheelwright, where the motive power of the western-county farmers could be repaired, what time the rugged yeomen themselves partook of the good cheer of the taverns.

The railway-station was first known as "Oak Hill," in allusion to the prosperous farming region to the southward. Afterwards they called it "Newton Dale," although a less dale-like place could not be found this side the Scottish marches. It was about the year 1870 that the straggling cluster of houses began to crystallize into a village with church and school and shops; and since that time its growth has been rapid and permanent.

From the site of the old blacksmith-shop at Woodward and Boylston Streets the distances are as follows: to West Newton, Newton Lower Falls, or Highlandville, $2\frac{1}{2}$ miles; to Grantville, 3; to Needham, $3\frac{1}{4}$; to Waltham, 4; to Wellesley, 5; to Dover, $6\frac{1}{4}$; to Natick, $7\frac{1}{2}$; to Weston, 8; to Medfield, $9\frac{1}{2}$. The blacksmith-shop was built in 1839, for Moses Crafts, with stone taken from a ledge on Dedham Street; and in 1886 it was demolished for foundation-stones.

In this vicinity is the home of Darius Cobb, the artist; and on Walnut Street dwells Walter Allen, the well-known Boston journalist.

The Congregational church was founded in 1871 and organized a year later, more than half its membership of 27 being of the families of Hyde, Woodward, and Stearns. The chapel was occupied in 1872, and the church in 1875, the cost having been $16,000. The pews are free; and the expenses of the society are met by voluntary subscriptions. The pastors have been the Revs. S. H. Dana (1872-77) and George G. Phipps (1877-89). The meeting-house occupies a pleasant and commanding situation, at the intersection of two of the principal streets, and looks out benignantly over the

RESIDENCE OF ALBERT F. HAYWARD.
Centre and Cushing Streets, Newton Highlands.

drowsy hamlet. Here the people enjoy their harvest festivals and corn sociables, and other pleasant reunions, besides the usual religious observances of the old Puritan faith.

The Church of St. Paul, under the pastorate of the Rev. Carlton P. Mills, has a handsome little temple on Walnut Street, frequented on Sundays and saints' days by the good communicants of the Episcopal faith, who are welcomed here to free seats.

One of the prominent residents of Newton Highlands is the Hon. J. F. C. Hyde, the first mayor of Newton, and a descendant of one of its seventeenth-century pioneers, a public-spirited and ever-active citizen, whose home-gardens show rare triumphs of horticulture. His house is in the eastern part of the village, toward Crystal Lake.

Near Mr. Hyde's place, at the corner of Centre and Cushing Streets, is the pleasant home of Albert F. Hayward, of Fobes, Hayward & Co.

Near the village, at the junction of the Dedham and Needham roads, is the South Cemetery, laid out in 1802, and used for many years for the burial of the Upper-Falls and Oak-Hill people,— the Richardses, Richardsons, Bixbys, Halls, Hydes, Wiswalls, Winchesters, and others. It was ceded by the proprietors to the town in 1833. Close to this old burying-ground lived the venerable Daddy Thwing, who used to entertain the country lads with stories of how he fought at Bunker Hill and in the old heroic days of the Revolution.

Well out on the road to Waban stands the Woodward farmhouse, one of the oldest hereditary places in America, having now remained in the possession of a single family and name for upwards of two centuries. John Woodward, the weaver, came hither in 1681, and built the house which is still standing, and occupied by his descendants of the ninth generation, having passed down to Ebenezer in 1716, to Deacon John in 1747, to Deacon Ebenezer in 1781, to Deacon Elijah F. in 1810, and so on to the present day. This family furnished many useful officials to the town and State, and dozens of soldiers for the Revolutionary and later armies. The old house is secluded from the public way, and may be reached by a lane diverging from Woodward Street opposite the alleged Beethoven Avenue. It is surrounded by century-old trees, and commands a charming view over the meadows of the Charles River to the westward.

The chief manufactory in the village is that of the Gamewell Fire-Alarm Telegraph Company, whose police-telegraph systems have lately been adopted in many American cities.

Newton Centre.

CHARLES DICKENS.— THE ANCIENT COMMON AND ITS CHURCHES.— NOON-HOUSES.— THE NATIONAL SONG.— BEACON STREET.— THE MOTHER CHURCH OF NEWTON.— AN OLDTIME DOMINIE.— MASTER RICE.— THE BAPTIST SOCIETY.— "BAPTIST POND," CRYSTAL LAKE.— NEWTON THEOLOGICAL INSTITUTION.— THOMPSONVILLE.— JOHNSONVILLE.

Along the "upper plain" of the ancient settlers, at the foot of Institution Hill, and covering something over a half-mile square of pleasant and diversified upland, sleeps the lovely village of Newton Centre, dreaming over its twenty-five decades of honorable history, and indulging in pleasing visions of its inevitably prosperous future. The rival villages of Newton and West Newton have long since passed it, in point of population and civic and ecclesiastical distinction; but the future is long and promising, and the air draws sweetly over this sunny highland terrace. On one side expands the bright shield of Crystal Lake, showing no traces of the myriads of sins that it has washed away in baptism; along the south stretches the long rampart of Institution Hill, with its garrison of Baptist theologians; and to the north the beautiful avenue of Centre Street winds away to the busier thoroughfares of the Corner. And along the semi-rural roads that converge upon the Common are the homes of 3,000 people, to whom, amid such restful scenes, come length of days and tranquillity of life. In rambling for an hour through this fragment of Arcadia, we may glance here and there at an old house or a modern villa, and recall a few quaint traditions, and yet leave much to be learned by the summer-day tourist from Boston or Yokohama.

We are not the first distinguished foreigners to explore this land of dreams. For on the 29th of February, 1868, the village was visited by a strange group of men, who called themselves the Man of Ross, the Boston Bantam, Massachusetts Jemmy, and the Gad's Hill Gasper. They are better known as George Dolby, James R. Osgood, James T. Fields, and Charles Dickens; and their purpose was a walking-match between the two first-named, coached by the other two, "for two hats a side and the glory of their respective countries." This contest was described at length, in cockney dialect, by Dickens, who announced as the turning-point "the little village (with no refreshments in it but five oranges and a bottle of blacking) of Newton Centre." The route led from the beginning of the Mill Dam to the Centre and back, over a waste of snow and ice, and in a bitter west wind. Dickens reached the Centre first, closely followed by Osgood, who finally won the match by seven minutes; and the victory was celebrated that night by a dinner at the Parker House, at which were present the two contestants, Charles Dickens, Mr. and Mrs. James T. Fields, Professor and Mrs. Charles Eliot Norton, Professor and Mrs. James Russell Lowell, Oliver Wendell Holmes and his wife, Thomas Bailey Aldrich and his wife, Howard M. Ticknor and his wife, Barthold Schlesinger, and Henry Wadsworth Longfellow and his daughter.

Dickens and Fields made a preliminary reconnoissance of the route before the contest, and the latter reached Newton Centre quite tired out, and sat on a doorstep with his illustrious guest, eating oranges, which (as they both agreed) were the only refreshments to be found in the place.

In remoter days, indeed, all visitors to this region were dependent upon the same pedestrian methods, unless they went by the fugacious buggy or the much-rumbling stage. But during the pastorate of the Rev. William Bushnell at Newton Centre, in the early forties, he devoted much time and energy to the planning of a railroad through his parish, from Needham to Boston. Many persons in Brookline opposed the scheme, as tending to ruin their gardens and bring undesirable persons among them; but the people in the Woonsocket region came to its help, desiring a quick route to Boston. Finally, Otis Pettee of Newton Upper Falls was induced to take hold of the enterprise, which from that time had an assurance of success. Mr. Pettee became the first president of this corporation, which received the names, successively, of the Air Line, the Charles-River Railroad, the Boston, Hartford & Erie, and the New-York & New-England. Two or three years ago, the Boston & Albany Railroad bought the line from Brookline to Newton Highlands, a distance of $5\frac{1}{16}$ miles, for $415,000, in order to finish out its great Circuit Railroad, which sweeps around through the Newtons. The Charles-River Railroad, from Brookline to Needham, began to run in November, 1852, season-tickets from Boston to Newton Centre selling for $35. Before this time, Bostonward passengers were carried from Newton Centre to the Corner by omnibuses; and a daily stage made trips from Newton Upper Falls through the Centre and on to Boston, the fare being $37\frac{1}{2}$ cents.

Centre Street was the old Dedham road, joining Watertown and Dedham; Boylston Street, the old Worcester Turnpike, dates from the year 1809; and Beacon Street came into existence in 1847-48.

It is but a short walk from the railway station to the Common, which may stand as the Forum of the village. This pleasant bit of park has been in the general service of the town for nearly 200 years, but the manner of its public acquisition is not known by records or other documents. There is a tradition that it was given to the people by Jonathan Hyde, and a part of it by Captain Noah Wiswall and his sons. Early in the last century, it was partly occupied by two noon-houses, erected by the selectmen, wherein, between the morning and afternoon services, on Sundays, the church-goers from a distance could eat their frugal bread and cheese, and quaff their refreshing cider. There were three or four of these noon-houses at Newton Centre, square one-story buildings, with fire-places in the centre, open on all sides, and supported on pillars, and with seats around the walls

Newton Centre Baptist Church, Centre Street.

for the uneasy rest of the sanctified. In these humble shelters the worshippers gathered, between the morning and afternoon services, to thaw out their half-frozen limbs and eat their simple luncheons, indulging the while in such neighborhood gossip as might be allowable on such a sacred and austere day. When this rather grim recess was over, the women replenished their foot-stoves, and prepared for the great discourse of the afternoon.

Close to the Common, also, stood the gun-house, in which the town kept the field-pieces presented to it by John Pigeon. At dawn on April 19th, 1775, a thundering detonation from these guns reverberated through the hills, and signalled the advance of the King's troops against Lexington and Concord. In response to this signal, the minute-men and yeomanry sprang to arms throughout the town; and in a marvellously brief space the companies were on their way to encounter the enemy. Here, also, at the corner of Lyman and Centre Streets, stood the quaint little powder-house, with its heavy brick walls, before which for many years the "trainers" of this region went through their martial manœuvres, captained by gaunt farmers and forensic selectmen. It was built in 1799, on the site of one of the noon-houses, and suffered demolition in 1850.

In the early part of the Secession War, a liberty-pole was set up by public subscription on the Common; and in the first flush of a lovely summer morning, after prayer by the Rev. Dr. Samuel F. Smith, the largest flag ever seen in Newton flashed up to its top. The halliards were drawn by the venerable Joshua Loring, whose birthday occurred before the Revolutionary War.

At the corner of Station and Centre Streets stood the town-hall, built in 1835, and, after the removal of the town-meetings to West Newton, used for lyceums and other secular gatherings, until about 20 years ago, when it was moved away, and destroyed by fire. During the darkest hours of the Secession War, at a great meeting held here, young Charles Ward came forward, and addressed the people, closing with the words: "If my country needs my services, I am willing for her sake to make the sacrifice." Within a brief year, he died of wounds received on the glorious day of Gettysburg, where he fought as sergeant-major of the 32d Massachusetts Infantry.

Near this site, and fronting on the Common, is the Methodist church, which began in 1875 as a prayer-meeting, a mission from the Methodist church at Newton Upper Falls, and was assembled in the engine-house at the corner of Station and Centre Streets. The church was organized in 1879, and dedicated its pretty meeting-house the next year, on land bought and given to it by the Hon. Alden Speare, upon the site of the old engine-house. Many Methodists in the town looked coldly upon the new enterprise, as tending to weaken existing churches; but Marshall S. Rice bequeathed $1,000 to it, provided the church could be built within a year after the bequest, and, with this stimulus and limitation, success was battled for and won. The society now has upwards of a hundred members. The first pastor was the Rev. George H. Perkins (1879-80), followed by the Rev. Bradford K. Peirce, D.D. (1880-84), the Rev. William Ingraham Haven (1884-86), and the Rev. William R. Clarke, D.D. (1886-87).

On one side of the Methodist church, upon the site of one of the ancient noon-houses, is the handsome Old-English building of the Rice School (primary), fitted with all the modern appliances and conveniences, and containing a portrait of the venerable Marshall S. Rice; and on the other is the great gray edifice of the Mason School (grammar), named in honor of David Haven Mason, an eminent lawyer and publicist, chief mover in the levelling of Fort Hill and the freeing of the Mill Dam from tolls, a prolific writer and gifted orator. A poor farmer's son, of New Hampshire, he fought his weary way through Dartmouth College, and, when his law-office in Boston was equipped, he had but 25 cents left, and no friends; but in time he rose to be United-States District Attorney for Massachusetts, succeeding George S. Hillard. Newton remembers him as one of her most valuable citizens, and thus perpetuates his name.

There were no public or private schools in Newton for well-nigh 60 years after its settlement, the children being taught at home, with some catechetical instruction at the church. In 1698 it was voted to build a school-house; and three years later the people resolved to have two, one at the meeting-house and one at Oak Hill.

Much of the beauty of the Common is due to the efforts of the Newton-Centre Improvement Association, which was originally a tree-planting society (founded in 1852), to whose labors we owe many of the fine rows of trees that shade the village streets. The Common was carefully graded and adorned in the years 1879–80, and now forms as pleasant and attractive a public square as can be found in many a long league. At a later day, the labors of the association took a wider range, and included regrading and planting the public lawns, improving the shores of Crystal Lake, and otherwise adorning the few waste places in their public domains.

Another prosperous secular society of this region is the Newton-Centre Gun Club, much devoted to practice with small arms, to the amazement and occasionally to the discomfiture of the wild animals and birds of the surrounding countryside. These sixty sons of Nimrod take much comfort also in annual dinners, and in bowling parties, and other happy diversions of a social kind.

Among the other societies which tend to make life pleasant here are the Newton-Centre Associates (Avery L. Rand, President; E. H. Mason, Vice-President); the Newton-Centre Young-Men's Lyceum, with 75 members, meeting fortnightly in the First-Church chapel; and the Neighbors, meeting monthly for social and literary entertainments. The secret fraternities that find so much favor in our democratic America have not as yet effected a lodgment here; and persons in Newton Centre who aspire to be Noble Commanders, Worthy Prelates, Chief Rangers, Regents, Dictators, Eminent Scribes, Orators, or Warders of the Inner Gate, must forsooth hie themselves at evening to the more secular villages elsewhere in Newton.

On the west side of the Common, near the local stores, stands the old meeting-house of the Baptist Church, which was moved to this place in 1886, and made into a public hall, when the new church was founded. The latter building is the pride of the village, in an architectural point of view, and stands near the Common. Some mention is made of it on a later page.

On the same side of the Common, just where Centre Street descends the sharp slope towards the little meadow below, stands the pleasant brown house which has for years been the home of the Rev. Dr. Samuel Francis Smith, a Baptist theologian and writer, and still better known as the author of our national hymn, "America." He graduated at Harvard, in Oliver Wendell Holmes's class, and has led a long and useful life as pastor, professor, editor, and hymn-writer. Among his productions in hymnology is the grand missionary song, "The Morning Light is breaking." At the recent celebration of his golden wedding, John G. Whittier wrote in praise of "his song of our country, which is sung wherever, on sea or land, in any part of the world, Americans are found"; and Dr. Holmes wrote this charming letter: —

My dear Smith,— I wish I could be with you at the home festival which crowns your fifty golden years of wedded life. There is no more beautiful record among those whose names are in our class-book than your own. And no one among them all, living on the earth or elsewhere, can or could greet you more warmly with every kind wish for yourself, your faithful companion, and all those nearest you who gather beneath your roof, than your affectionate friend and classmate,

OLIVER WENDELL HOLMES.

Many years before, the kindly Autocrat also wrote: —

> "And there's a nice youngster of excellent pith,—
> Fate tried to conceal him by naming him Smith;
> But he shouted a song for the brave and the free,—
> Just read on his medal 'My country,' 'of thee!'"

In 1842 Dr. Smith became pastor of the First Baptist Church at Newton Centre, at the same time editing *The Christian Review;* and this connection he retained for over twelve years. His most important prose work was the great "History of Newton," a constant companion during the preparation of this Handbook. For nearly half a century, Dr. Smith has been a citizen of Newton; and in his home are many rare old heirlooms and relics, Indian stone idols, personal mementos, and a great library.

The tune of "America" was composed by an Englishman, Henry Carey, who died in 1743; and it became a national melody in Prussia, England, and Russia. William C. Woodbridge brought home from Germany a number of school music-books, and gave them to Dr. Lowell Mason, who committed them to young Smith, then a student at Andover Seminary. To one of these German melodies, the youth fitted the words of a poem that he had

FIRST CONGREGATIONAL CHURCH, NEWTON CENTRE.
Centre and Homer Streets.

then just written, the now-famous "My Country, 'tis of thee." It was first sung, in public, in the Park-Street Church, Boston, on the Fourth of July, 1832.

TO THE REV. S. F. SMITH, D.D.,

AUTHOR OF "MY COUNTRY, 'TIS OF THEE," ON HIS EIGHTIETH BIRTHDAY, OCT. 21, 1888.

While through the land his strains resound,
What added fame can love impart
To his, who touched the string that found
Its echoes in a Nation's heart?

No stormy ode, no fiery march,
His gentle memory shall prolong;
But on fair Freedom's climbing arch
He shed the light of hallowed song.

Full many a poet's labored lines
A century's creeping waves will hide,
The verse a people's love enshrines
Stands like the rock that breasts the tide.

Time wrecks the proudest piles we raise.
The towers, the domes, the temples, fall,
The fortress crumbles and decays;
One breath of song outlasts them all.

OLIVER WENDELL HOLMES.

On Pleasant Street, which curves away from the Common to Homer Street, is the estate occupied until 1886 by Charles P. Clark, at that time general manager of the New-York and New-England Railroad, and now President of the New-York, New-Haven, and Hartford Railroad. Here, also, is the lovely estate of Mount Pleasant, owned by Charles S. Davis (formerly of the Hallet & Davis Piano Company), and notable for its luxuriant pine woods, and great ledges of conglomerate rock, and picturesque flanking knolls.

Homer Street runs off from the old meeting-house through a region of pretty homes, and then out to Bullough's Pond, overhung by heavily wooded hills. At the east corner of Cedar Street is the house which was occupied for many years by the Hon. David H. Mason. Just beyond Cedar Street, on the north, stands the pleasant Gothic villa and spacious estate of William Morton. Mrs. Samuel Clarke (the mother of James Freeman Clarke) received a broad domain hereabouts by inheritance, and on the brook Dr. Clarke built a mill, where he ground drugs, and made calomel, wherewith to heal the ailments of his neighbors. He also bleached wax, and manufactured other simples in use among the allopathic rustics of old-time Newton. Dr. Clarke's house was afterwards the home of Edwin F. Waters, of the Boston *Daily Advertiser*. After Dr. Clarke's death, Rufus Brackett converted the mill into a morocco factory.

The old farm recently occupied by the Rev. George S. Carleton, on Homer Street, was in more ancient times the homestead of Captain Henry King, a soldier of the Continental Army. After passing the pond, Homer Street traverses the wild edge of the cemetery, amid low woods, and curves gracefully among the low hills, past the massive stone embankment of Valentine Street, and so on, winding along the hills, with wide vistas of rural landscapes opening over the Cold-Spring valley, and farms and meadows delighting the view. Tempting wood-paths diverge into the contiguous forests; and away off on the left rises the spire of the Newton-

Associates' Hall, Centre and Pelham Streets, Newton Centre.

Highlands meeting-house, with the gray Baptist seminary crowning the heights still farther off.

Crossing the woodland cloister of Chestnut Street, the continuation of Homer Street is called Fuller Street, and assumes a French Imperial width and dignity. On the corner stand the buildings of the Pine-Farm School; and the road winds on, over hill and dale, with the pleasant ridge of Beacon Hill across the glen on the left, crowned with its Coast-Survey pole. Beyond the great Towne villa, high secluded among its sombre trees, the road descends to the level of the Cheesecake Brook, and soon reaches the Woodland-Park Hotel.

Beacon Street curves away to the eastward, from Newton Centre, a broad, firm highway, winding between rocky and forest-covered knolls, and giving occasional broad views over the country to the southward. Where Grant Avenue breaks away to the north, the long green embankment of the Sudbury-River Aqueduct is seen, with the picturesque half-stone country-house of Bertrand E. Taylor, the well-known Boston architect. Higher up on the ridge is the new house of Charles Copeland, the artist, whose illustrations of "Marching through Georgia," and other national melodies, are of such high excellence.

Farther along, on the north side of the street, above the low cliffs that beetle over the road, surrounded by forest-trees and picturesque crags and all the native flowers of New England, stands the massive square colonial-looking mansion of the Hon. Robert R. Bishop, sometime President of the Massachusetts Senate, and a prominent figure among the political leaders of the old Bay State. The ancient woodsmen's tracks have been utilized for driveways through the greenwood shade; and the natural features of the place, glacial bowlders, huge protruding rocks, dells fragrant with wild flowers, and clumps of lordly trees, have been preserved with wise forestry. On this estate is the Indians' Oven, where a crag arches over the greensward far enough to make a small grotto, in which half-a-dozen wayfarers might gain shelter. At the gateway, on the east side of the entrance to Mr. Bishop's grounds, and running thence along Beacon Street, rises a series of remarkable ledges of slate, in which the stratification is plainly visible, with all the folds and plications and contortions which were made during the ages when our Mother Earth suffered agony from fire and water and internal upheavals. These cliffs, bearing their silent witness, are draped with delicate festoons of trailing green, with the crimson sprays of barberries, and the velvety cushions of rare mosses, and crowned with tall and shadowy trees.

Beyond the Bishop place, on the right, towers the graystone castle of the Dupee family, with its ivy-mantled *porte-cochère*. From this house one gains a broad view over the woods and glens to the southward and eastward, and out to the ever-present Blue Hills of Milton. A few rods beyond, Beacon Street crosses Hammond Street, near Dr. Slade's place, and begins to descend toward the Chestnut-Hill Reservoir. Off to the right, within a short distance, are the patrician estates of Chestnut Hill, the homes of the Lees, Lowells, Saltonstalls, and others.

Turning backward to the village, in a charming vine-clad and embowered place at the corner of Centre and Gibbs Street, we may find the Baptist Home for Children of Missionaries, built in 1881-82, and already one of the most successful institutions of its kind in the country. It has a salaried superintendent, and the affairs of the Home are carried forward with admirable skill and care.

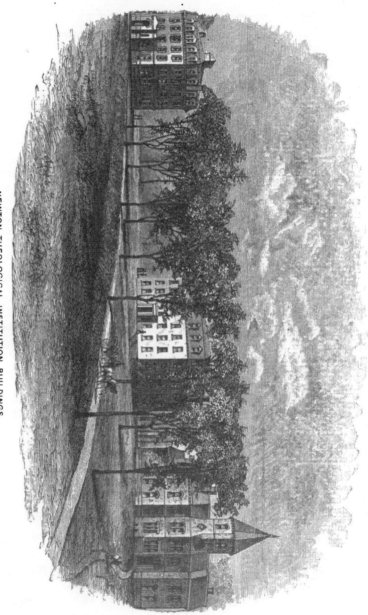

NEWTON THEOLOGICAL INSTITUTION BUILDINGS.
Institution Avenue, Newton Centre.

The venerable mother-church of the city, "The First Congregational," rises over pleasant lawns and a charming environment of trees, at the corner of Centre and Homer Streets. Its dark Gothic walls harmonize with the forest-like surroundings, and the spire rises above the maples, pines, and elms like the topmost spray of some more ancient natural growth. Successive enlargements of the church, in the direction of breadth, have given it a low and almost rambling appearance. The interior is comfortable, with good acoustic properties; and it may be many years ere the parish possesses a stone church and a debt. In writing of the old Cemetery on Centre Street we have spoken of the early history of this church, and have seen how the families in the southern part of the town strove against the parish, to secure the removal of the meeting-house, after sixty years of stability in that locality, to a place more convenient for them. This question of the site of the new meeting-house became of such importance that it was referred to the General Court of Massachusetts, whose committee journeyed to Newton, in 1715, and chose the site now so occupied. Six years later, the town appropriated for the cost of building the Bills of Credit issued by the Province to defray the expenses of the disastrous Canada Expedition, when Sir William Phipps's fleet and army were beaten back from the mighty ramparts of Quebec. The old meeting-house was sold; and the new one, lighted by diamond panes of glass, and with seats around the wall for the boys, passed into service, in 1721. It was not so hospitable to strangers as its modern successor; for Captain Edward Durant, a wealthy Bostonian who had moved out here with his retinue of slaves, and paid £1,800 for a farm, was not allowed to build a pew. In those old days, the people were assigned to seats in three grades,— by rank or dignity, by parish-rates, and by age, but "not to degrade any." Many of the pew-rents were paid in Indian corn, and other products of the soil; for at that time money did not abound in Newton.

Hither came the great evangelist, George Whitefield, in 1740, and preached before as large an audience as could assemble in the little church. Nor did all the Christian men of the town hold to his manner of doctrine; for many there were who objected to it as not becoming, while others made haste to avail themselves of the glad tidings of great joy that he brought to them, to the manifest enlargement and quickening of the church. Among these were two members of the oldest families of Newton, Jonathan Hyde and Nathan Ward, who became ordained preachers and gathered congregations of "New Lights," one in Brookline and the other in Newton, and were hard put upon with persecution by their former brethren. The great evangelist met here with some such triumph as he found on Boston Common, where his audience consisted of 23,000 persons; and some such opposition as encountered him at Newbury, where he was stoned, and rose up boldly against it, crying: "I have a warrant from God to preach; my seal" (holding up the Bible) "is in my hand; and I stand in the King's highway."

In the year 1758 the succession of the pastorate fell upon Jonas Merriam, the last minister to be settled by the entire town, who, after a tranquil rule of 22 years, passed quietly beyond the veil. During his incumbency Tate and Brady's version of the Psalms was added to the musical treasures of

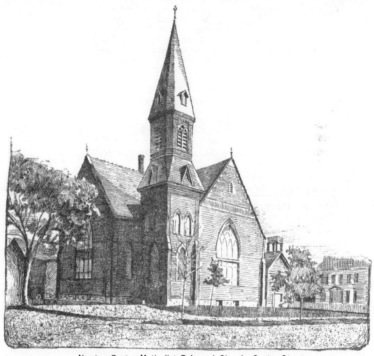

Newton Centre Methodist Episcopal Church, Centre Street.

the church, and efficient choristers led in the new-fangled melodies. This period also witnessed the secession of the West Parish, and the formation of the First Baptist Church. In 1761 the ingenious John Rogers (a descendant of the famous martyr of Smithfield) made and presented to the town the clock that still adorns the church, after having ticked away the seconds for a century and a quarter, perched on the front of the gallery. In 1764 it was voted: "That trees be set out to shade the Meeting-house, if any persons will be so generously minded to do it." In 1776, according to the decree of the authorities of Massachusetts, the Declaration of Independence was read aloud from the pulpit of the First Church in Newton, by the Rev. Mr. Merriam, and then recorded upon the town book by Abraham Fuller, the town clerk. As it is set forth in Increase N. Tarbox's poem: —

> "Just a century has departed
> Since those farmers, honest-hearted,
> In this ancient town of Newton
> Were in special session met,
> Summoned by the State's suggestion,
> Called to meet that mighty question,
> Whether they would bear the burdens
> Of Old England's growing debt.
>
> "They were gathered, as was fitting,
> In their place of Sunday sitting;
> For no house could be too holy
> For the work they had to do:
> And their pastor's prayer ascended, —
> Prayer where hope and fear were blended, —
> Asking God to guard and guide them,
> All their fearful journey through."

Ten rods from the meeting-house stood the emblem and sign of authority of the Church Militant, in the form of a pair of stocks, wherein to clap such luckless wights as were guilty of misbehavior during divine service. One who had often eyed them with juvenile terror thus described them, in 1876: "They were made of two pieces of white-oak timber, about eight feet long, clamped together with bar-iron at each end, through which holes were made, of various sizes, to fit human legs." From time to time, a committee of the church was chosen to see to the repairs of this bit of Inquisitorial machinery.

The affairs of the church were sagely administered by the freemen of Newton, assembled in open town-meeting, and regulating all details of their spiritual democracy, from the calling of the minister to the least events of parish finance. In the deacon's seat stood an hour-glass; and it seemed but a cold and unedifying Sabbath service when this measure of time was not turned at least once during the sermon. From 1770 to 1790 the Psalms according to Tate and Brady were used; and after that date Dr. Watts's Hymns came into favor. The next minister after Mr. Merriam was Jonathan Homer, who ruled the parish from 1782 until 1839, during the last twelve years of which his failing energies were assisted by a colleague, the Rev. James Bates. This gentleman was dismissed, finally, in deference to the wounded feelings of Dr. Homer. The new meeting-house, erected in 1805, resembled the old Dorchester church on Meeting-House Hill. There were the singers' seats, the groups of pews for the Newton-Female-Academy girls and Master Rice's boys, and the negroes' bench; and on the floor the pews of Kenricks and Cabots and Wards and Bracketts and Jacksons and Wiswalls and other local clans of good Christians. During the sweeping storm of the Unitarian defection, this church stood firm by orthodoxy, although Dr. Homer was suspected of irregular views as to the Atonement and the Trinity. The services here at the death of Washington were very impressive, every attendant wearing a strip of black crape on his left

Mason School, Centre Street, Newton Centre.

arm, while Dr. Homer officiated; and below the pulpit were two bass-drums draped in black. One of the original hymns then sung was: —

> "Mourn, mourn, mourn, mourn,
> O Americans, mourn!
> Washington's no more —
> Fair Liberty, in sables drest,
> With his lov'd name upon her urn,
> Washington — the scourge of tyrants past
> And heir of princes yet unborn,
> Round him her faithful arms shall bend."

The church-goers of Newton had sought the sanctuary throughout 170 years without the admonition of a church-bell, when, in 1810, Dr. Channing's Federal-Street Church, in Boston, presented them with the bell which they in turn had received from the Brattle-Street society in 1773. But the line of religious duties had grown so natural to the worshippers that they hardly needed its brazen admonitions. It is said that even the old horse of Deacon Elijah F. Woodward had in the course of many years become so familiar with the routine of Puritan devotion that, when he heard the plaintive notes of the Doxology, he was wont to leave the horse-sheds and move quietly around to the chapel-door, to be in his proper place to receive the venerable Deacon.

Dr. Homer was accustomed to preach in cap and bands, and also in black cotton gloves, always much too long in the fingers, and gifted with a way of limply waving at the congregation, as the good dominie advanced toward the tenth and fifteenth heads of his long extemporaneous discourses. After a pastorate of over 57 years, Dr. Homer retired from the pulpit, in 1839, and remained as pastor emeritus for four years, at the end of which time came his funeral exercises, conducted by Dr. John Codman of Dorchester, and attended by all the congregations of the town, they having given up their own services for the purpose of paying the final honors to their territorial shepherd.

In the pastorate of William Bushnell, which covered the period from 1842 to 1846, 31 members were allowed to go out to form the Eliot Church. The meeting-house had become rather cramped and uncomfortable, and many of the parishioners wanted to have a new one built, but were resisted by the conservative members. These, however, found themselves overborne by the pastor's celebrated sermon from Ezra vii.: "Blessed be the Lord God of our fathers, which hath put such a thing as this into the king's heart, to beautify the house of the Lord which is in Jerusalem." All opposition ceased after this eloquent discourse, and in 1847 the new meeting-house was dedicated. Yet the society had been so far weakened by wholesale dismissals to new parishes that it was unable to support its minister, and found itself obliged to let him depart. In 1847, Daniel Little Furber became pastor of the First Church in Newton. The organization was then so weak that some members proposed to unite it with the Eliot Church, and others wanted to move it to the Upper Falls. But new life came with the new pastor and meeting-house, and the organization throve mightily. During the first 30 years of Mr. Furber's ministry, the church received 448 members into its communion; and, in the twenty years from 1856 to 1876, its benevolent contributions amounted to $45,000. The Rev. Theodore J. Holmes was installed in the pastorate October 24, 1883, and Dr. Furber became pastor emeritus. The old church of 1805 was remodelled and doubled in size in 1869-70, to meet the growing demands for pews. Up to the year 1880, the church had received 1,175 members.

The Sunday School was commenced in 1816, to study the Bible and the Assembly's Catechism, with Deacon Woodward as its head. Subsequently,

RESIDENCE OF JOSEPH W. PARKER.
Lake Avenue, near Laurel Street, Newton Centre.

the older scholars were carefully taught in the mysteries of "Watts on the Improvement of the Mind," and such as showed proficiency received Bibles as rewards of merit. Among other lessons learned was that of patriotism; and, out of the band of young men who went from this church into the Secession War, six died on the field of honor. The Sunday-School movement grew into great proportions, and is now finely organized throughout the city. The Sunday-School Union of Newton was formed in 1838, to advance the cause, and to qualify the teachers for higher efficiency. The six schools originally composing it have grown to 25, with a membership of nearly 4,000, each school reporting to the Union at each quarterly meeting, and making annual contributions. 123 members entered the army during the Secession War, and 19 of these died. Within a year or two, the Congregational Club has been formed, to make a fraternal bond of union between the seven Congregational churches of Newton.

Leaving the old church, we may stroll along Centre Street, to the northward, in the direction of Newton, and observe here and there a noteworthy feature of the scenery. This immediate region is one of the oldest-settled parts of the city. Jonathan Hyde, a young Englishman, came to Newton in 1647, and acquired in this neighborhood an estate of several hundred acres, from which he gave for the public use lands for a training-field and a school site, mere fragments of his great farm, which was bounded on the south by Crystal Lake (then known as Wiswall's Pond). Hyde was the most important of the early real-estate men, and got great gain in buying and selling land in those old days. His mansion stood about 70 rods north of the Centre Meeting-house; and here he reared a good colonial family of twenty-one children.

Just north of the meeting-house, between three streets (Centre, Homer, and Grafton), is the triangular estate once part of Sergeant Jonathan Hyde's great domain, about the middle of the seventeenth century. In 1736 this pleasant triangle was sold to Ephraim Fenno, a cordwainer, of Boston. Subsequently, it became the home of the Rev. Joseph Grafton, pastor of the First Baptist Church in Newton from 1788 to 1836, when he "was taken from his United People after an Unbroken Communion of 48½ years" — as the old grave-stone in the Centre-Street Burying-Ground avers. He was one of the original trustees of the Newton Theological Institution, and President of the Missionary Society. He bore the reverent name of Father Grafton; and many are the quaint anecdotes preserved about him. Once, at a public dinner, being annoyed by the swearing of a young man near him, he rose straightway, and exclaimed: "Mr. President, I move you that no person at the table have permission to utter a profane oath, except my friend, the Rev. Dr. Homer!" This playful allusion to the saintly old Congregationalist divine silenced for that day the ill-speaking youth. After preaching a missionary sermon, and just before the collection, he remarked: "And now let every gentleman feel in his pocket, and every lady in her purse, and see if there be not there a piece of money, as there was in the mouth of Peter's fish." On another similar occasion, he complained that there were many who seemed willing to cast their bread upon the waters, but they always wanted to have a string tied thereto, so as to draw it back. He combated the dancing-school, which had drawn away the young people from his parish singing-school, saying: "John the Baptist lost his head by dancing"; and when his

Bertrand E. Taylor's Residence, Beacon Street and Grant Avenue.

venerable wife endeavored to mitigate this asperity by saying that in her youth she, too, had been a dancer, he gravely remarked: "Well, my dear, you won't do it again." The Rev. Dr. Sharp, of Boston, had arranged to preach for him, but was unable to come; whereupon he rose up in the pulpit, and said: "In music, every note is either a *sharp* or a flat; and I am afraid you will have a flat to-day." Being called to mediate, in a troubled church, he was amazed to see one of the sisters get up to state the case; and he lucidly struck at the heart of the controversy by saying: "Ah, I see how it is: the hens crow."

He was wont to work in his fields or walk in his garden while rehearsing the sermon for the ensuing Sunday, with great affluence of expression and gesture. "I get many lessons in the field to be carried into the pulpit," he affirmed, making even his hand-toiling hours tributary to his greater work of the pastorate. Yet, with all his parochial dignity, he carefully avoided dogmatism on uncertain points; and, when some of his people brought a group of knotty problems in eschatology for his solution, he playfully replied: "I cannot answer you as to these things; but ask some young theologian, and he will tell you all about them."

During the War of 1812, Father Grafton used to come out on the Common, when the local militia were on parade; and, mounting a cannon-carriage, he would pour out such an intense and earnest prayer as to profoundly move the rustic soldiery, drawn up in a hollow square around him.

About the year 1840 Father Grafton's house was removed to Mill Street, where it was burnt two or three years later. In 1860 the estate came into the possession of the late George C. Rand, founder of the famous Boston printing establishment of the Rand Avery Company, which passed out of existence in 1889; and a part of it is now occupied by the handsome modern estate of his son, Avery Lewis Rand, facing on Centre Street.

Opposite the Rand estate, high on the terraced bank, is a venerable white house which has a notable history. The old Prentice farm, bought by James and Thomas Prentice in 1657, and bequeathed to the Rev. John Prentice of Lancaster, was bought in 1742 by Henry Gibbs, a wealthy gentleman of Boston, who moved here to be near his brother-in-law, the saintly John Cotton. He built the picturesque old mansion-house which still adorns the wayside; and in its halls he exercised a generous hospitality towards the Provincial aristocracy, as became the grandson of Sir Robert Gibbs of Merrie England. When he died, he bequeathed the house to his widow, with the condition that it should never be made a tavern, and expressing a wish that it might become the home of some gentleman of the dissenting faith, who might aid the minister of Newton. In another clause he aimed a shot at the poor old Church of England, bequeathing a sum of money towards the support of preaching among the Indians, provided that it should not be of the prelatical sort. For over twenty years his widow, Madame Gibbs, dwelt here, active in all charities, and furnishing free medicines to the poor people of Newton. This venerable Lady Bountiful died in 1783, and left the estate to John Eddy, the husband of her daughter Ann. Afterwards the old mansion became the home of Marshall S. Rice, long time town clerk of Newton, who after the year 1827 set out the trees whose grateful shadows still console the wayfarer. The two huge maples in front were brought by him in his chaise-box from New Ipswich, N.H., when but a foot high. Mr. Rice came to Newton in

THE RESIDENCE OF CHARLES C. BARTON.
Beacon Street, near Centre Street, Newton Centre.

1824, and opened a popular private school, through whose courses of study more than a thousand boys worked their arduous way. His life covered the long span between 1800 and 1879, for twenty-seven years of which he officiated as town clerk.

One of his daughters married Alvah Hovey, the President of the Newton Theological Institution; and another became the wife of the Rev. C. H. Carpenter, one of the most successful of those who bore the Gospel to the Karens, in Burmah. A little way to the eastward, near Summer Street, stands the great Marshall S. Rice chestnut-tree, the area of whose shade is a hundred feet in diameter.

A little to the north, nearly opposite the Speare estate, stood the Newton Female Academy, founded in 1830, and opened in 1831, its teacher being Miss Leach, who received the munificent sum of $350 a year. The attendance from Newton and outside increased so rapidly that it was found necessary to build a boarding-house, where the day scholars also could get their dinners for ten cents each. Elbridge Hosmer, Deacon Ebenezer Woodward, the Rev. John B. Hague, and Deacon Bartholomew Wood were among the dominies here.

The Rev. E. H. Barstow changed the institution into a boys' school, and conducted it for nine years, until 1860, after which the academy disappeared; and its old home became a dwelling-house, which still remains on the same site, alongside the ruined cellar of its sister building.

In 1866 the boarding-house building was bought, for $10,000, for a Home for Orphan and Destitute Girls, mainly petty criminals from twelve to sixteen years old, its matron being the celebrated war-nurse, Rebecca R. Pomroy. On Christmas of 1866 the institution was dedicated, and within less than two years one of its inmates set it on fire, so that it was reduced to ashes. In 1872 the work was abandoned as impracticable.

The north corner of Grafton and Centre Streets is occupied by a broad lawn, on which in old times stood the First-Parish parsonage, occupied successively by the Rev. Messrs. Smith, Bates, and Bushnell. This building and the larger mansion of Dr. Homer were removed across the broad fields to the westward, and may now be seen on a rural road that runs nearly parallel to Centre Street from Mill Street to Grafton Street. The first house on Grafton Street, bounding one side of this corner lawn, is the home of Dean Huntington, of Boston University, a nephew of the celebrated Bishop Huntington. Just beyond is the home of the Rev. Dr. D. L. Furber, the pastor emeritus of the First Congregational Church.

Near the corner of Grafton and Centre Streets stood the Homer estate, in the old days of great extent and dignity, but long since passed away, its only memorial being two thorny acacias, which shaded the walk to Dr. Homer's front-door, and may now be seen midway between the Speare and

Nickerson mansions. On the same site stood the more ancient house of the Rev. Jonas Merriam, fourth pastor of the parish, an amiable and quiet man, and slow of speech, whose chief efforts were for charity and peace. When he came to be buried, the town provided half a barrel of beer and half a cord of wood for the funeral. Jonas Merriam graduated from Harvard in 1753, and settled here in 1758, where he died after a tranquil pastorate of over twenty-two years. His mother-in-law, Mrs. Fitch of Brookline, came to live with him, but did not bring with her that peace with which modern paragraphers fail to credit ladies in that position of brevet motherhood.

Mellen Bray's Residence, Institution Avenue, Newton Centre.

One of their chief points of contention was a negro slave, who had borne in her native Congo-land the name of Loquassichub Um, and in her Newtonian existence was known as Pamelia. It was the pleasure of *La Belle-Mère* to beat and pummel this unfortunate maiden when she felt aggrieved at the general events of life; but the mild dominie highly disapproved of these unchristian chastisements, and at last, when on one occasion Pamelia was receiving an unusually severe drubbing, he bought her of her irate mistress for $100, and forthwith set her free. Her gratitude was so strong that she refused to leave the parsonage, and so there she dwelt until the minister died, many years later.

Dr. Homer was descended from an old maritime family of Boston, and graduated at Harvard in the class with Rufus King, James Freeman, Seth Payson, Eliphalet Porter, and Judge Dawes. He was an indefatigable student in Greek, Latin, and Hebrew, and the various versions of and commentaries on the Bible. He learned the Spanish language after he had passed his sixtieth year, and in the retirement of his rich and valuable library spent many happy years. There was many a long discussion in the old parsonage when his Unitarian friends, Dr. Pierce and Dr. James Freeman, endeavored to lead him into the new sweetness and light of liberalism or his orthodox brethren, John Codman and Joseph Grafton, with weightier arguments, held him and his parish fast to the old standards of faith.

Mrs. Homer exercised a continual and almost motherly solicitude over her eccentric husband, who for years after her death used to speak of her as "a very angel about the house." The parsonage was always open to the poor and needy; and more than thirty homeless children were taken in there, at different times, and fed and clothed until places could be found for them. The pastor's heart was as tender and consecrated as St. John's. He was even reported to have stopped his carriage on a hot summer day, and clambered painfully out, to remove from the roadway a toad, and convey him to a cool and shady place.

The estate of the Hon. Alden Speare, ex-mayor of Newton, and a prominent official of the Atchison, Topeka & Santa Fé Railroad, is on the west side of Centre Street, just beyond Grafton Street. Alden Speare came down from Vermont to Boston in 1844, when nineteen years old, and began his business career, which has been crowned with so much success and honor. In 1864 he moved to Newton, taking the old George S. Dexter homestead, on part of the Rev. Dr. Homer's estate. He was mayor of Newton in 1876–77. In the year 1884 he endowed with $40,000 the Emma-Speare-Huntington Professorship of Liberal Arts in Boston University.

The next large estate, with a French-roofed brown house, pertains to Thomas Nickerson, an old-time shipping merchant, sometime President of the Atchison, Topeka & Santa Fé Railroad, one of the originators of the Mexican Central Railroad and its first president, and a prominent citizen of Newton. Opposite, the great cloister of Ward Street opens away under the maple-trees. Farther on, beyond a broad debatable ground, at the corner of Mill Street, is the high-gabled mansion of Arthur C. Walworth, with its great *porte-cochère*. Mr. Walworth received a scientific education in Paris, and is connected with the Walworth Manufacturing Company. He married a daughter of the late Hon. Gardner Colby, and has represented Newton in the Massachusetts House of Representatives for two years, 1887 and 1888.

RESIDENCE OF ARTHUR C. WALWORTH.
Centre and Mill Streets, Newton Centre.

In this vicinity, also, is the fine old estate of the Lorings, with its broad lawns and dignified gray house. Farther to the eastward the great Linder estate beautifies Cotton Street, which diverges at the old burying-ground. The beautiful avenue of Centre Street stretches away to the northward for over a mile to the Newton railway station. Some of its attractions are spoken of on preceding pages, which also describe the old burying-ground and the estates adjacent.

Let us turn back to the village green, and make another excursion, along the quiet streets in the opposite direction. At the southwestern corner of the Common, where Beacon Street runs off toward Waban and Newton Lower Falls, is the new house of worship of the Baptist Church, the mother-church of many others now flourishing throughout Middlesex and Norfolk.

The growth of the Baptist faith in Newton was slow, and amid many discouragements and persecutions. In 1729 Jonathan Willard, and in 1749 Noah Parker, joined the little Baptist church in Boston, the singular fact being that they were the chief men at the Lower Falls and Upper Falls, respectively. Four more Newtonians accepted the Baptist faith in 1753; and from that time for over twenty years they made frequent and unavailing petitions to be freed from pedobaptist parish taxes. But the local church was not to be disestablished so easily, and added their Baptist corn and wood and tithes to its own fund with annual regularity. In 1780 Elhanan Winchester, an eloquent preacher of the new faith, came into Newton, and assembled a church, which before the end of the year had 73 members. Not a long time ensued, however, before the zealous Winchester advanced to embrace the doctrine of universal salvation; and it became necessary to vote out of the church 15 of his followers into this new heresy. The first meeting-house was built alongside Baptist Pond, on land given by Noah Wiswall, and received its dedication in 1795. For many years it remained unplastered, with seats made of rough boards laid across carpenters' "horses," and with a pulpit of unplaned planks. Fifteen years passed before the society could afford a stove, whose cost was £11 14s. 10d. The salary of the first minister, Caleb Blood (1781-88), was £60 a year and "the loose money," which was the euphemistic term given to the income from the contribution-boxes. It was recorded on the church-book that "the singing, in a general way, be carried on by reading a line at a time in the forenoon, and a verse at a time in the afternoon." Apparently, "the loose money" failed to produce large dividends; for, after a few years, Mr. Blood found himself unable to get a living, and so moved away, into the remote wilds of the Green Mountains, and was succeeded by the Rev. Joseph Grafton (1788-1836), who remained as shepherd of a growing flock for nearly half a century, during which period 567 persons were added to the church.

In the old meeting-house it was the custom for the families to spend their Sunday noon-hour in the great box-pews, spreading each their frugal luncheon on a chair in the middle of the pew, and discussing in the mean time the points of the morning sermon, or perhaps even topics of a less spiritual character. The venerable Father Grafton was wont to go from group to group, during these almost sacramental feasts, taking an apple here, and a piece of cake there, and so on until all had partaken, when he would say: "Come, friends, it is time to go to the prayer-meeting," and so led his little flock to new services of devotion and of peace. Father Grafton was relieved of his pastoral charge, at his wish, in 1835; and his successor was the Rev. F. A. Willard (1835-38), who led his people to a new church, his last sermon in the old one being from the text: "If Thy presence go not with me, carry us not up hence." The removal was made to bring the meeting-house into a place of greater convenience for the people near the Newton Theological Institution; and the positively grim simplicity of the new temple is indicated by its pastor's words: "In the erection of this house, we felt bound to study that plainness in the finish which is alike demanded by Christian frugality and good taste." The locality of the new church was indicated as "by the training field." After the two years of Mr. Willard's pastorate, the church remained without a settled minister until 1842, when the Rev. Samuel F. Smith took the vacant office, and retained it 12 years. The Rev. Oakman S. Stearns succeeded him for another 12 years (1855-68); and his successor, the Rev. W. N. Clarke, remained from 1869 to 1880, and was in turn followed by Rev. Edward Braislin (1881-1886). The present pastor is the Rev. Lemuel C. Barnes, and the membership is about 400. In 1836 the society abandoned its old shrine (which is now a dwelling-house, nearly opposite Henry Paul's house, on Centre Street), and occupied a larger meeting-house. In 1856 and again in 1869 this structure was remodelled; and in 1886 it was moved away, to be replaced by a handsome church of Gloucester granite and Longmeadow red sandstone, for whose construction Gardner Colby left the munificent sum of $25,000, augmented later by large contributions from the Hon. Levi C. Wade and other parishioners. The edifice was designed by John Lyman Faxon, an architect who for years made a study of the best churches of Europe, and has applied many of their features here, including the rounded chancel, the triple arched doorways opening into a *loggia*, the delicate Byzantine carvings and frescos, in scroll and leaf work, the rich symbolism of Christian art, and the brilliant memorial windows. Even the gas-fixtures are reproductions of ancient Byzantine lamps; and the Biblical allusions seen everywhere on arches and tilings are so unmistakable in their allusions that, if a Venetian of the age of Dandolo or a burgher of mediæval Avignon could enter these precincts, he would instantly recognize the use and purpose of the place. There are three rich memorial windows, to Gardner Colby ("The Resurrection"), Charles S. Butler ("The Ascension"), and Father Grafton ("Paul preaching at Athens"); and the green damask upholstery and antique oak fittings of the interior make a rich and artistic effect. Another handsome building, of similar architecture and materials, projects from the back of the church at right angles, and contains the chapel and other parish rooms. The tower is at first square, and then octagonal, and adjoins the beautiful *loggia* on the front of the church. The seating accommodation of the church is adapted for seven hundred people, and the chapel will accommodate three hundred. The cost of the structure was in the vicinity of $90,000.

Beyond the new Baptist church are several pleasant little streets in the vicinity of Crystal Lake, better known as "Baptist Pond," on one of which (Crescent Avenue) is the home of the Rev. Dr. Bradford K. Peirce, once a State senator and for many years editor of the Methodist paper, *Zion's Herald*. Here also dwells the Rev. Dr. William Butler, a retired missionary, whose labors in India and Mexico highly advanced the cause of Christ. On the same street dwelt the Rev. Dr. Edward Cooke, for many years President of Lawrence University in Wisconsin and Claflin University in South Carolina. He died in 1888. The estate of Joshua Loring, President of the Blackstone National Bank, is on the same street.

The snug and cosey little Unitarian church, a little way south of the Common, with its rich storied windows, dates from the year 1880, and is the spiritual home of a society formed in 1877, and ministered to, from the first, by the late Rev. Dr. Rufus Phineas Stebbins, and since his death (in 1885) by the Rev. Horace Leslie Wheeler, a graduate of Harvard in 1881 and a young pastor of great promise. The church has about a hundred members. Close to this site stood the old town pound, which, after incarcerating countless vagrant and derelict cattle, was finally closed and sold in the year 1848. In recognition of this important public institution, the present Cypress Street in ancient days bore the name of *Pound Lane*.

Crystal Lake, or Baptist Pond, now forms one of the chief natural ornaments of Newton, and covers an area of thirty-three and a half shining acres of clear and limpid spring water, happily free from weeds and vegetation and aquatic plants. Its south bank is formed by the long railway embankment, which cuts off its lower bays; while on the west is the bit of woodland traversed by Lake Avenue, and all through which are inscriptions signifying that land may be purchased here, on application to a certain well-known real-estate agent. Along the remaining shores, and notably on the north, are groups of pretty villas, with pleasant rural surroundings, and looking out on the cheerful bright water. Down this side extends a substantial sea- (or pond-) wall, with a little esplanade; and off-shore are the moorings of the Baptist-Pond navy, which includes more than two-score boats, from the most perilous little craft with oars up to cat-boats and sloops that might safely make the run out to the Bermudas — in tranquil weather. There are also boats here for public hire; and in the one-mile circuit of the pond you may get a capital bit of exercise. On the Fourth of July there are prize scull-races here for boys and girls, tub-races, and other trials of skill and strength. At evening bonfires flame along the shores, and processions of illuminated boats move over the water, and every coigne of vantage in the neighborhood has its crowd of delighted spectators. But let not the frivolous Bostonian think that he can wantonly disport himself on these Baptist shores; for boldly inscribed tablets sternly warn him and his kind that "All persons committing the following offences will be prosecuted according to law. Bathing without a bathing-suit, discharging firearms, profane swearing, disorderly conduct, disturbing the peace."

A poetic writer says that "Sailing or rowing out here, and looking up the height, the scene is German or Italian in its bold and romantic character. The hues in the stone of the Institution chapel, and its architecture, embracing a heavy tower, give it, set upon the wooded hill, an air of age, and recall the castle sites on Como, or one of those still-inhabited religious habitations which rise upon the banks of the Danube."

Nature provided a comfortable outlet for the pond on the east side, near the old Wiswall farmstead; but about two centuries ago certain enterprising mill-owners dug a deep channel from its north side down to Smelt Brook, hoping thereby to augment the water-power on that busy little stream. Their schemes went all a-gley, however, and nought now remains of their hard work, except a nearly obliterated trench, near the Loring estate.

In 1871 Messrs. Rand, Hyde, Bishop, and six other gentlemen, forming the Newton Black-Bass Club, leased the pond from the Massachusetts Commissioners for Inland Fisheries for the term of twenty-five years, to be stocked with black bass from Plymouth, and protected by law against the casual hooks of the village youth. A hundred bass were put into these quiet waters, but they and their descendants were so wary that they enjoyed all the sport, and their would-be captors went home divers times with light and empty baskets. In 1877, therefore, three thousand land-locked salmon were added to the finny population, quite literally, for the bass came forth, with great joy, and devoured them, every one. A year later, the clubmen brought a few score of white perch, and set them loose in the pond; and their prickly backs sufficed for defence against the monopolistic bass, so that they increased and multiplied greatly.

In ancient times this Baptist sea bore the name of Wiswall's Pond, in remembrance of the first ruling elder of the church, who came here in the year 1654, and dwelt on the border of the pretty lakelet for nearly thirty years, until (in 1683) he was summoned to join the church above. A fair domain of a thousand acres "and a great pond" was granted by the General Court to John Haynes, Esq., as early as the year 1634. The next year he was chosen Governor of Massachusetts. In 1636, Haynes migrated to Connecticut, where he also served a year as Governor, and on his death in 1654 the pond estate went to his heirs.

Elder Thomas Wiswall was one of the first immigrants from England, and had been a town-officer in Dorchester before moving further afield to Newton. His house stood in a delightful situation, on the south shore of the pond, and was described in the inventory of his estate as: "lower lodging room — chamber over — fire room — chamber over — and the cellar." Here the good elder performed or prepared for his duties as assistant-pastor and catechist. And here, doubtless, he had many a bout with his valiant second wife, she that was born Isabel Barbage, of Great Packington, in Warwickshire, and who, after his death, strove against his sons for her dowry. To quiet down the spirited widow, the magnates of the settlement, Prentice, Bond, and Trowbridge, assembled in committee, and finally got her under discipline, Prentice, the stern old trooper, compelling her to retract certain rash assertions, and then dryly counselling her "to set a watch before her mouth, and keep the door of her lips." One of the Elder's sons was Ichabod, who received an education at Harvard and settled at Duxbury, and united in himself the sufficiently diverse offices of parish minister, astrologer, and agent, or ambassador, from the Plymouth colony to the Court of England. Another son was Captain Noah Wiswall, who fell in a long Sabbath-day battle against the Indians in New Hampshire, when his command was defeated and nearly annihilated. The grandson of this unfortunate hero, Captain Noah Wiswall, took down the old house, and in 1744 built on the same site the front part of the house which still stands here. Here was the first home of the Baptist faith in Newton; and in the Wiswall living-room the church received its effective organization. Oftentimes, of a summer's day, the adherents of this belief assembled under the great trees before the homestead, and listened to the deep doctrinal counsels of their elders, or the spiritual sermons of visiting pastors. At different times we see our Wiswall deputed by the town to carry out important public trusts,— to gather up the arms of the Indians; to treat with the authorities of Cambridge; or to copy the ancient records. When the Newton minute-men marched off to the battle of Lexington, three of his sons and several of his sons-in-law were in the ranks, and the venerable captain, then seventy-six years old, started after them on foot, saying: "I want to see what the boys are doing." During the *mêlée* of the retreat, three of the King's soldiers came upon him, and he quickly told the two or

RESIDENCE OF MARSHALL O. RICE.
Centre Street, opposite Homer Street, Newton Centre.

three armed farmers near him to fire on the middle one, so as to be sure of a shot. The doomed red-coat fell in his tracks, and the others fled in panic, while the old captain, binding up his hand, through which a royalist musket-ball had torn its way, went forward and took the gun of the dead regular, as a trophy of the day.

When Dr. John King, a veteran of the Revolution, rode into Newton, to succeed to the practice of Dr. John Cotton, the people at Mitchell's Tavern recommended him to board at Captain Noah Wiswall's. But Miss Sarah Wiswall, the captain's daughter, took great displeasure thereat, and exclaimed: "*Everybody* is sent to our house." Perhaps it was to get sufficient opportunity to punish the intruder that she married him, and lived with him for thirty-seven years, until Death came to call her away, leaving five stout boys. The Kings dwelt in the old Dr.-Cotton house, on the site of the home of Deacon Gustavus Forbes; and the doctor's son, Henry, was one of the guards at the execution of Major André.

Deacon Luther Paul bought the old Wiswall place, and became a local magnate and selectman, and held here his rural court. It was he who set out the noble avenue of elms that extends from the Baptist church to the ice-houses, about the year 1830, to the subsequent joy of thousands who have enjoyed their grateful shade. Some fragments of the ancient house are still preserved in the Paul mansion, which is nobly secluded under tall elms, just south of the railway, on Centre Street.

At the north-west corner of the pond was the home of the younger Samuel Hyde, who bound himself that a rod-wide way "shall be free to bring hemp or flax to the pond, and sheep to washing, or such like necessary occasions to come to the pond." His successor in the house was Francis Blanden, a far-wandering and sporadic French-Canadian, in whose memory the road afterwards called Pond Street bore the name of Blanden's Lane for a full century. In still later days, Joseph White dwelt here.

John C. Parker, the son of Samuel Parker, was brought up in the old farmhouse a quarter of a mile southeast of Baptist Pond. In 1809 he left Newton, to return no more, becoming captain of an Indiaman, and settled at Hawaii, in the Sandwich Islands, in 1815, where for fifty-three years he owned a vast grazing farm, of many thousand acres, exercising a baronial sway and a noble hospitality, and maintaining a Hawaiian clergyman and chapel for the spiritual culture of his people. And when he died, in 1864, the chief dignitaries of the island kingdom assembled at his funeral.

There has always been something congenial to letters in the aspect of this sylvan water, sequestered among the quiet highlands. It was in Jepson's house, on the south, that Dr. Carl Siedhof long carried on his well-known Classical Institute, on the German system; and in later days there was a school kept here by J. W. Hunt and later by Jonathan Tenney, who had a girls' school here in 1866. In the basement of the old Baptist church, Moses Burbank wielded the master's ferule from 1848 to 1852; and one of the brightest of his pupils was William Francis Bartlett, the Bayard of our army during the Secession War.

Among the handsome residences in the vicinity of Crystal Lake, along and near the charming boulevard of Lake Avenue, is that of Stephen V. A. Hunter, treasurer of the Goodyear & McKay Welt-Sewing-Machine Company, whose home is at the corner of Lake Avenue and Crystal Street. Near Laurel Street is the home of Joseph W. Parker, head of the well-known clothing house of Boston. On Beacon Street, near Lake Avenue, stands the house of William E. Webster, connected with the great Boston dry-goods house of Joy, Langdon & Co. And on the same street near Centre Street is the pleasant home of Charles C. Barton, Esq., a prominent counsellor-at-law, very actively interested in the educational and other public affairs of Newton, and for many years a member of the School Board, of which he is at present the chairman.

The Newton Theological Institution crowns the stately hill which rises to a height of over 300 feet, just south of Newton Centre, and its buildings and tall tower are landmarks visible for many miles throughout the neighboring countryside. It contains nearly 70 students, preparing for the Christian ministry; and its faculty includes the Rev. Dr. Alvah Hovey (President), the Rev. Dr. Oakman S. Stearns, the Rev. John M. English, the Rev. Charles Rufus Brown, Rev. Ernest DeWitt Burton, Rev. Jesse B. Thomas, Samuel S. Curry, and Rev. James F. Morton (Librarian). The course of study covers three years, and includes Hebrew, Greek, Syriac, Aramaic, German, elocution, church history, philosophy, homiletics, and all departments of Christian theology. The large buildings known as Farwell Hall and Sturtevant Hall are occupied by rooms for students, comfortably furnished at the expense of the churches in and about Boston, and allotted to the young men (as is also the tuition) free of cost. There is a comfortable gymnasium on the grounds, and also a well-used reading-room. At stated hours throughout the day, the silvery bell of the chapel sends its melodious call over the plateau, and down the adjacent valleys, summoning the students to their lectures; and the young Baptist prophets go trooping over the lawns, like members of some sober Western college *De Propaganda Fide.* Much intellectual quickening has resulted from the introduction of some twenty-five elective courses, in addition to the required and usual lines of study.

The site of the seminary has been likened to Andover's plateau and elegant shades, or the delightful crests of Amherst. Dr. Hackett used to compare the western view to that from the Acropolis of Athens. On the horizon rise Monadnock and Wachusett, with many a town and village between, the long valley towards the dome of Dedham, the rolling Blue Hills of Milton, the garden-like suburbs of Boston, and the far-away blue sea. Hereabouts stood the homestead of Joseph Bartlett, over 200 years ago. Of his great-grandsons there were six who went out into the wilderness and colonized the site of the present beautiful village of Bethel, in the upper Androscoggin Valley. They made sugar, cleared the land, and planted corn, surrounded by friendly Indians, until the time (in 1781) when wild savages from Canada made a destructive foray upon the little settlement, and carried away several of its people to their cold Northern fastnesses, hard by the St. Lawrence. Another early settler near the seminary was John Cheney, who came hither as early as 1681, and became the first miller in Newton.

Nearly a hundred years ago, this hill was bought by John Peck, of Boston, who had been so fortunate as to marry a wealthy lady, and endeavored to construct here a country-house after the old English manner, with a spacious park and domain. The mansion was founded in 1798, with the intent of making the finest private house in this region; and the present Institution Avenue was laid out, at great cost, and lined with trees; while great masses of rare flowers flamed from the sloping lawns. The money of the estate melted away in these costly outlays; and, when the War of 1812 broke out, and the price of wool rose to a fancy figure, Mr. Peck bought 500 sheep, and pastured them along the slopes of his far-viewing hill. This speculation also failed, and the family lost its estate and disappeared in the distant West. The high-cupolaed house on the hill had been facetiously entitled "the Mill"; and the people of the plains below with great humor averred that at last it had ground a Peck.

The Massachusetts Baptist Education Society was founded in 1814, and at an early date began to consider means to establish a divinity school; and in 1825, at a meeting in the First Baptist Church of Boston (then on Salem Street), the assembled clergy and laymen resolved "that it is expedient to establish a theological institution in the vicinity of Boston." As a result, the Education Society purchased the Peck estate, a large dwelling-house and 85 acres of land, for the sum of $4,250. The school was incorporated in 1826, with the Rev. Irah Chase as Professor, to whom, later in the year, the Rev. Henry J. Ripley was added, as Professor of Biblical Literature and Pastoral Duties, having been brought up from the lowlands of Georgia. Not long after the school moved up here from its temporary quarters on Ward Street, Farwell Hall was erected, its expense being met, like that of the original purchase, by subscriptions. In 1832 the Rev. J. D. Knowles became Professor of Pastoral Duties; in 1835 the Rev. Barnas Sears was elected Professor of Christian Theology; and in 1839 the Rev. H. B. Hackett became President and Professor of Biblical Literature and Interpretation.

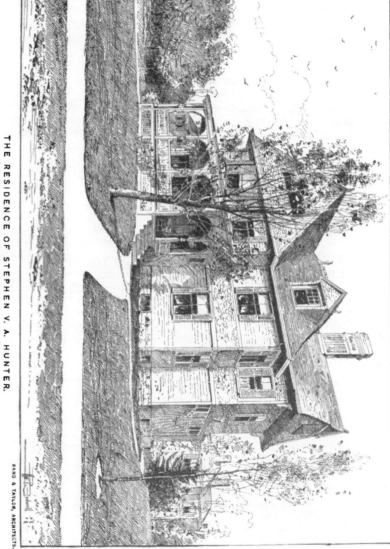

THE RESIDENCE OF STEPHEN V. A. HUNTER.
Lake Avenue, corner Crystal Street, Newton Centre.

RAND & TAYLOR, ARCHITECTS.

When the Colby-Hall building received its dedication, on a lovely autumn day of 1866, the participants were the Rev. Doctors Samson, Hovey, Stow, Caswell, Hague, Smith, and other fathers of the Baptist Church; and the President said, in his address, that "here, on this beautiful spot, prepared by the Architect of Nature for such a use, will flourish, through the ages, a 'school of the prophets,' acknowledging the Bible, and the Bible only, as the standard of Christian doctrine and duty."

The father of the library, in a large sense, was the Rev. Professor Henry J. Ripley, who in his old age for nineteen years spent his life among these books, saying: "The Library is my idol now. If I can only see it increase in scope and authority, the crowning wish of my life will be secured." His careful catalogues bear witness to his skill and accuracy; and the long line of books that issued from his pen equally attest his industry and faith. His Commentaries on the New-Testament books have been the help of thousands.

On this classic hill we may see the venerable Irah Chase, pondering over the foundation of Acadia College, or reading the tall old black-letter tomes of Irenæus and Origen, or outlining the plans of "The Christian Review"; or Horatio Balch Hackett, with his Thiers-like head and face, who had studied for many years in Europe, and was a member of the American Committee of Bible Revision, besides preparing a Chaldaic grammar, and writing a dozen or so of other books; or Barnas Sears, D.D., LL.D., a man of Massachusetts birth, and a graduate of Brown and of Newton, who studied also in Germany from 1833 to 1835, and took a prominent part in the great Baptist movement there, himself administering the rite of baptism to many persons, including some of the German clergy. From 1835 to 1847 he was a Professor in the Newton Theological Institution; from 1848 to 1855, Secretary and Executive Agent of the Massachusetts Board of Education (succeeding Horace Mann); from 1855 to 1867, President of Brown University at Providence; and, from 1867 to 1880, agent for the distribution of the George-Peabody Educational Fund in the Southern States. His edition of "Roget's Thesaurus," his "Life of Luther," his articles in "The Bibliotheca Sacra" and "American Cyclopædia," and other literary monuments attest the iron diligence of this man of God.

In a lonely grave on the Institution grounds was buried at midnight, May 29, 1838, the body of Professor J. D. Knowles, who died of confluent smallpox, after serving for six years as a teacher here, and writing several well-known books.

Among the students of the Institution have been the following: —

John Taylor Jones, D.D., for 18 years a missionary to Siam.

Francis Mason, D.D., for 44 years a missionary to Burmah, translator of the Bible into Sgau Karen, and author of several books on Burmah.

THE RESIDENCE OF WILLIAM E. WEBSTER.
Beacon Street, near Lake Avenue, Newton Centre.

William G. Crocker, who died after preaching for 9 years to the Bassas, of Liberia.

Joseph Goddard, for 16 years a missionary to China, and translator of the New Testament, etc., into the Chinese popular dialect.

Josiah R. Goddard, son of the above-mentioned, and also a missionary to China.

John W. Johnson, for 25 years a missionary at Hong Kong and Swatow.

Benjamin C. Thomas, for twenty years a Christian laborer in Burmah, and author of many hymns in the Karen language.

Isaac M. Wilmarth, missionary to France.

Albert N. Arnold, D.D., missionary to Greece.

Nathan Brown, D.D., for over 20 years preaching in Assam, and later in Japan.

Edward A. Stevens, D.D., for 40 years on the Burman mission.

Edward O. Stevens, his son, also a bearer of light to Burmah.

Joseph G. Binney, D.D., President of Columbian College, and for 24 years head of the Theological Seminary among the Karens.

Durlin L. Brayton, for 40 years a hero in the mission-field.

Lyman Jewett, D.D., the evangelist of the Teloogoos.

Arthur R. R. Crawley, for a quarter of a century laboring in Burmah.

Joel S. Bacon, D.D., President of Columbian College.

John S. Maginnis, D.D., of Rochester Theological Seminary.

David N. Sheldon, D.D., President of Waterville College.

John L. Lincoln, LL.D., Professor of Latin at Brown University.

D. A. W. Smith, D.D., for 24 years a missionary in Burmah, and President of the Karen Theological Seminary at Rangoon.

Basil Manly, D.D., President of Georgetown College, Kentucky.

Artemas W. Sawyer, D.D., President of Acadia College.

Samson Talbot, D.D., President of Denison University.

Henry C. Robins, President of Colby University.

Joseph Banvard, D.D., author and pastor.

William Hague, D.D., pastor of many churches and writer of many books.

Elias L. Magoon, D.D., one of our most prolific authors.

George D. B. Pepper, D.D., President of Colby University.

Galusha Anderson, President of Chicago University and later of Denison University.

Elisha B. Andrews, D.D., President of Denison University.

Seth J. Axtell, President of Leland University, Louisiana.

Eli B. Smith, D.D., President of the New-Hampton School.

Barnas Sears, D.D., President of this Institution and of Brown University.

James Upham, D.D., President of New-Hampton Institute.
Ezekiel G. Robinson, D.D., President of Brown University.
George W. Samson, D.D., the Orientalist, President of Columbian College.
Martin B. Anderson, D.D., President of Rochester University.
Henry G. Weston, D.D., President of Crozer Theological Seminary.
Ebenezer Dodge, D.D., President of Madison University.
Kendall Roberts, D.D., President of Kalamazoo College.
Samuel L. Caldwell, D.D., President of Vassar College.
Heman Lincoln, D.D., and many another leader in the American churches, and in the evangelization of Asia.

Several acres of the original Peck estate have been laid out for building purposes, including the streets named for the first three professors, Chase, Ripley, and Knowles.

In this pleasant region are numerous pretty houses. And among them is that owned and occupied by Mellen Bray, on Institution Avenue, near Chase Street.

Station Street runs from the railway up over the shoulder of Institution Hill, past the green and velvety lawns of the theological school, and over a far-viewing crest, to the hamlet of Thompsonville, which straggles along the cross-roads a half-mile east of Newton Centre, and is partly occupied by German families, living in small and prosaic houses. This was the region in which the New Lights appeared, in 1750, under the efforts of Jonathan Hyde. Thompson was a laboring man, who lived in these woods as a hermit for several years, and as a reward had his name attached to the region. The little cross-roads chapel was built by the First Baptist Church, as a mission station, in 1867, and is the scene of religious services every Sunday, when 30 or 40 persons are present. A quarterly collection is taken up in the parent church for its support. The Thompsonville region is rich in mica, milky quartz, crystals, and other interesting minerals; and in 1877 a deposit of silver was found near by, in the beautiful and romantic Hammond's-Pond Woods. Not far away, around Glen Avenue and Station Street, is the neighborhood long known as *Johnsonville*, after Jerry Johnson, once a large property-owner here.

There is a vast inspiration in the view from this eminence over the valley of the Charles, and the blue highlands of Canton and Milton, Stoughton and Sharon, the wide horizons beyond the Dedham dome and Highlandville spire, the country-side for hazy leagues dappled with golden grain and emerald meadows and dark-green forests. And just over the fine shoulders of Institution Hill from Newton Centre you may enter the beautiful and rural southern part of the city, which is more fully described in the chapter on Oak Hill. And it is hardly a half-hour's brisk walk, along the patrician Beacon Street, to the charming semi-English suburb of Chestnut Hill, with its plain and unpretending country-houses, each in its broad environment of park-like grounds. It will not take many years for the electric railways and other nineteenth-century devices of the West-End Railway Company to advance from Boston and Brookline along this line into Newton, and open wide new areas for development as homes.

Until that day, this region shall remain, as it has been for centuries,

"A land
In which it seemed always afternoon."

Chestnut Hill.

THE ESSEX COLONY.— A GROUP OF VILLAS.— THE CHAPEL.— WABAN HILL.— HAMMOND'S POND.— ANCIENT WORTHIES.

Chestnut Hill is approached from one of the handsomest little railway stations in the world, a gem of Richardson's architecture, worthily surrounded by beautiful landscape gardening. The structure is of light-colored granite, trimmed with brownstone; and its graceful ivy-draped arches and *porte-cochère* and chapel-like timber roof make a fitting portal for one of the most charming suburbs of Boston. For many years, this

Chestnut-Hill Station, Boston & Albany Railroad.

notable community was known as "The Essex Colony," since its chief families derived their origin from the noble old Massachusetts county of Essex, the Lees and the Saltonstalls coming from Salem, and the Lowells (like the Longfellows) being of Newbury origin.

The grounds about the station were arranged to the best possible advantage by Frederick Law Olmsted, the architect and chief engineer of the Central Park at New York, and show how much can be accomplished by refined taste and judicious outlay, within a limited area. The building itself has the usual sturdy and massive character of Richardson's work, and appears as if it grew up out of the surrounding ground rather than that it was piled upon it.

Close to the station a beautiful private driveway diverges to the right from Hammond Street, and ascends Chestnut Hill, passing through a long park of lawns and trees, which forms a delightful piece of landscape-gardening. On the left of this road is the Saltonstall mansion; and on the right is the dark-red house of Mr. Saltonstall's son-in-law, Dr. George W. West, with its quaint diamond windows.

The Saltonstalls are a very ancient and honorable family, of great distinction both in the Old World and the New. Sir Richard Saltonstall was Lord-Mayor of London in the year 1597; and his nephew, Sir Richard, one of the original patentees of the Massachusetts Charter, came to New England with Winthrop in 1630. He founded the plantation at Watertown, across the river from Newton, and left two of his sons there, when he went back to England with his two daughters and his oldest son, Richard, a graduate of Emanuel College, Cambridge, who afterwards returned and settled at Ipswich with his young wife (born Muriel Gurdon), and was such an ardent champion of liberty that he warmly befriended Goffe and Whalley, the regicide judges. He was also the first to oppose negro slavery in America; and, when a sea-captain brought in two slaves from Guinea, he had him fined, and compelled to carry back the African captives to their own land. His son, Nathaniel Saltonstall, was appointed one of the special judges for the trial of the Salem witches, but refused to serve.

Judge Nathaniel's son, Gurdon, held the governorship of Connecticut from 1707 to 1724; and had a son, also named Gurdon, who was a general in the Continental Army. Thence came the Connecticut line of the family. The Massachusetts line passes down from Sir Richard by Richard of Ipswich, Judge Nathaniel, Richard, and the fourth Richard, a scientific and practical farmer of Essex North, who held a judgeship in the Superior Court from 1736 to 1756. This gentleman's son, Richard, a heroic officer in the French and Indian wars of 1756–60, when the War of the Revolution broke out was unwilling to draw his sword against the flag under which he had fought in so many strenuous battles; and, finding it equally impossible to join the Royalists against his American brethren, he went to England, where he died two years after the close of the war. His brother, Dr. Nathaniel Saltonstall, of Haverhill, became an ardent patriot, and served the cause of the new-born States with all his heart. His son, Leverett Saltonstall, LL.D., became a prominent lawyer and mayor of Salem, and Member of Congress from 1838 to 1843. The present Hon. Leverett Saltonstall is a son of the last-named; a graduate of Harvard in the class of

1844 (and now one of its Board of Overseers); and a life-long friend of his classmates, William Morris Hunt, the great artist, Francis Parkman, the historian, Benjamin Apthorp Gould, the astronomer, and other famous men. He is one of the best of after-dinner speakers and *raconteurs*, a ruddy and vigorous gentleman of the old school, with a love for his pleasant library. One of his daughters married Dr. George W. West, the other Louis A. Shaw, Professor Agassiz's grandson. His oldest son, Richard Middlecott, who graduated from Harvard College in 1880, represents the eighth generation, in lineal descent, receiving a degree from this ancient University. The estate passed into the hands of Joseph Lee, of Salem, nearly half a century ago, being then of little value, a wind-swept pasture-

Gate at Waban-Hill Reservoir, Chestnut Hill.

field, in a thinly-populated region. The present Mr. Saltonstall was connected by marriage with the Lee family, having married the grand-niece of Mr. Joseph Lee; and so, about the year 1855, both he and Francis L. Lee moved to this barren domain, and built houses. The otherwise bare and bleak ridge was adorned on its north slope with a grove of aged chestnut-trees, and for this reason the new-comers named it CHESTNUT HILL. The beautiful trees that now enrich the fair hillsides with their lines and masses of foliage, evergreen and deciduous, were nearly all planted by Leverett Saltonstall, and the great size to which they have grown, and the incalculable increase in scenic value thus added to the estate, should encourage skilful tree-planting in many other places of our deforested New England.

Here, since his retirement from the bar, Mr. Saltonstall has led the quiet life of a country gentleman, devoted to agriculture and landscape-gardening, and cherishing and extending the liberal, scholarly, and democratic principles of his ancestors. During the Cleveland administration, he served as Collector of the Port of Boston, the chief United-States office in New England.

The crest of the hill is occupied by the estate of Ralph H. White, the Boston dry-goods merchant. He pulled down the old house of Daniel Sargent Curtis, on this site, in 1886; and since then has erected a new and spacious mansion, after plans drawn by William Ralph Emerson, the chief outward features being an encircling veranda of great length, a massive *porte-cochère*, and many picturesque gables. The view from this locality is of wondrous beauty, and includes much of Boston and its suburbs, with the Chestnut-Hill Reservoir as its chief feature, gleaming in the fair and garden-like foreground. Points in a score of towns and cities are visible from this eminence, with the pale blue disks of Wachusett and Monadnock in the distant west. The road that leads up to the house of the merchant-prince curves around and returns by Mr. George C. Lee's house to the foliage-enarched aisles of Hammond Street.

Passing northward along Hammond Street from the station, the diversified shrubbery of the Francis L. Lee estate (now occupied by Louis Agassiz Shaw) is seen on the left, with the yellow front of Hon. Leverett Saltonstall's house far back among the trees on the right. Colonel Lee was one of the best landscape-gardeners in America, famous for his love of natural effects and the delicacy of his combinations of tints and forms of shrubbery. Born to wealth, and a graduate of Harvard, he devoted himself to this profession out of pure love, and left the impress of his exquisite taste on many park-like estates around Boston. He was a classmate at Harvard with Judge Lowell and C. C. Perkins. He became commander of the 44th Massachusetts Infantry in the Carolina campaigns, and a zealous officer of the State in organizing and forwarding troops. He died in 1886. Colonel Henry Lee, one of the prominent graduates of Harvard, and one of the well-known financiers of State Street, is his brother. The father of these brothers was Henry Lee, an eminent East-India merchant of Boston, who at one time stood as candidate for the Vice-Presidency of the United States, on the free-trade platform, with John C. Calhoun at the head of the ticket. The domain contiguous to Mr. Shaw's pertains to Ernest Winsor; and nearly opposite stands the quaint little building erected for the local chapel and school-house which was given in 1861 by Thomas Lee to the families of Chestnut Hill, with the proviso that, if it ceased to be used for religious or educational purposes, it should be sold, and the proceeds devoted to charity. The pastors have been three Harvard men of the elder classes, the Rev. Messrs. William A. Whitwell (1861-65), A. B. Muzzey, and John A. Buckingham. Some years ago, the Unitarian services were abandoned, the population of the region being too small to warrant their continuance. Charming concerts and other musical and literary entertainments are often held in the pretty school-house annexed thereto, under the patronage of the cultivated ladies of the neighborhood.

The Episcopal Church of St. Andrew, sometime under the charge of the Rev. Arthur Wentworth Eaton, succeeded to the place once occupied by the Unitarians, and is now laboring to erect here a permanent parish, with dreams of a handsome stone church amid the trees and ivies, at some dis-

The Kingsbury House, Hammond Street, Chestnut Hill.

tant period. The present rector of St. Andrews is the Rev. Henry S. Nash, of the Episcopal Theological School, at Cambridge.

Beyond the chapel, and higher up the hill, stands the brick mansion of George C. Lee (of the Union Safe-Deposit Vaults, of Boston), almost hidden by groups and skirmish-lines of handsome trees. The second house beyond the chapel, on the same side, was built in 1887 by Charles H. Burrage, on the site of the very ancient Pulsifer mansion, the birthplace of the late Colonel Royal M. Pulsifer, of the Boston *Herald*.

A little way beyond the Lee place, Kingsbury Street diverges to the left, with the great modern houses of two Boston lawyers, Morris Gray and Heman M. Burr, looking over the wide valley to the south. Mr. Burr was elected Mayor of Newton for 1889. The home of Colonel Isaac F. Kingsbury, for some years the popular and efficient city clerk of Newton, and a brave veteran of the Secession War, is on Hammond Street.

Farther along on Hammond Street is the picturesque old Kingsbury house, a gray colonial building with huge chimneys and broad contiguous barns and a famous old elm in its yard. This was the homestead of John Parker, an English carpenter, who, after living a few years at Hingham, came hither in 1650, and settled among the quiet forests and high hills of Newton. Part of the landed estate afterwards passed (in 1700) into the possession of the Hon. Ebenezer Stone.

At the corner of Beacon and Hammond Streets is the large and handsome brick mansion of Dr. Daniel Denison Slade, richly draped with ivy, and commanding a pleasant view down towards the Chestnut-Hill Reservoir. Dr. Slade was a classmate with Leverett Saltonstall, in the famous Harvard class of 1844, and has been professor and lecturer on zoölogy, at Harvard University. He is the President of the Newton Horticultural Society.

When Dom Pedro II., the Emperor of Brazil, visited the United States (in 1876), he made a visit to this family. The Slade mansion is kept open all the year round, and is the seat of a delightful and refined hospitality, which includes in its charmed circle many well-known families of the neighboring metropolis. Longfellow and Tom Appleton and Dr. Holmes have also been entertained here.

On the opposite corner stands the old Hammond house, turning its back contemptuously upon the modern Beacon Street, and with its dark roof running down almost to the ground. It is still a farmhouse, environed with orchards and great barns, and looking out far down the sloping countryside to the dark woods that environ Hammond's Pond. Taking it for all in all, it is one of the most picturesque and interesting of old New-England homesteads. It was built in 1730, and is the only house in Newton illustrated in Whitefield's "The Homes of our Forefathers."

Hammond Street runs away across Beacon Street, and up through a miniature Pass of Thermopylæ, where the road lies between sharp little cliffs of rock. This locality is known to the Chestnut-Hill people as "The Gap," and to old Newtonians as "Gibraltar." On the right-hand side is the stone house formerly occupied by Charles Francis; and on the left is the home of J. Herbert Sawyer, the treasurer of a great manufacturing corporation in Boston. The farmhouse of the Sawyer estate, on Beacon Street, half a century or more ago was used as the district school-house, standing back on Hammond Street. Then the street winds away, past two or three pretty country-houses; curves under the shadow of long maple avenues; and comes out on Ward Street, close to the reservoir on Waban Hill. At the corner of Hammond Street and Ward Street is the charming country home of Albert D. S. Bell, a well-known Boston merchant.

Near the end of Hammond Street is Waban Hill (sometimes also called Prospect Hill), rising to a height of 313 feet, and supporting on its side the smooth green embankments of the Newton reservoir. Higher up, the road reaches the grassy summit, from which is outspread a view of amazing grandeur, including Wachusett and Monadnock in the blue distance, with scores of less-familiar mountains of Massachusetts and New Hampshire, and the Prospect range across the valley, and Waltham, Watertown, Arlington Heights, Mount Auburn, Cambridge, and the great Memorial-Hall tower. Farther around extend the long brick vistas of Boston, with the conspicuous towers of Trinity and the Old South, and the glittering State-House dome;

Albert D. S. Bell's Residence, Hammond and Ward Streets, Chestnut Hill.

and beyond stretches the wide blue plain of the open sea, flecked with white sails. The Blue Hills close the magnificent panorama on the southeast; and the fair foreground is dotted with the villas and estates and villages of Newton. This view has been pronounced by travellers the finest in all the suburbs of Boston, so famous for their rich hill-top prospects of sea and cities and mountains.

The venerable garrison-house that stood in this vicinity was taken down in 1821, after standing 170 years and sheltering seven generations of Newton lads and lasses. It was built probably by John Ward, an English turner, who married Edward Jackson's daughter Hannah, and became the town's first representative to the General Court, the year after Sir Edmund Andros was overthrown. The old house descended to his son, Deacon Richard, and his grandson, Deacon Ephraim, his great-grandson, John, and his great-great-grandson, Samuel.

South Street is a beautiful curving avenue, that wanders from Beacon Street off into Brighton, between Waban Hill and the Chestnut-Hill Reservoir, commanding most charming views of the broad lawns on the left, and the Amos-Lawrence farm on the right. Early in the century this great domain passed into the hands of Deacon Thomas Hyde, and from him it went to Deacon Nathan Pettee. Afterwards, the estate was acquired for a small sum by Amos Lawrence, in the year 1864; and part of its meadow-land is now occupied by the western basin of the Chestnut-Hill Reservoir.

The great tunnel of the Sudbury Water-Works penetrates the Chestnut-Hill ridge from Newton Centre to the Reservoir, a distance of 4,635 feet, most of which is through hard conglomerate rock, where the bottom is covered with a floor of concrete, and the rest is left as excavated. It took from September, 1873, to November, 1875, to cut this great tunnel, with several engines, drilling machines, and powerful explosives, air being driven in by machinery, and the débris removed by mule-cars.

Just south of the railway, not far from the Chestnut-Hill station, and opening toward Hammond Street, stands the fine old homestead of Judge John Lowell, brother of Augustus Lowell, and for 20 years judge of the United-States District Court. Mrs. Lowell was a daughter of the Hon. George B. Emerson, the eminent educator; and her gracious hospitalities are as freely exercised here as at the Lowells' sea-shore residence at Winthrop, or their great town-house on Commonwealth Avenue. The house now occupied by Judge Lowell was erected by one of the Hammonds in 1773, and remained in that family for over eighty years, passing to the Lowells after 1850.

The Hammond's-Pond Woods are one of the most interesting and beautiful forests in New England, rich in every variety of ferns and lichens, and abounding in rare plants and brilliant flowers. Rank and luxuriant lowland glades alternate with rocky hills, and everywhere the beauty of the trees arches over the scene. There is a delightful path a mile and a half long, leading south from Beacon Street, nearly opposite the Bishop estate, and traversing the entire forest; and the same path may be found more readily where it crosses the railway, perhaps half a mile west of Chestnut-Hill station. Another (and still easier) mode of entrance is by an ancient and abandoned wood-road which turns to the north from Boylston Street, a few rods west of the Hammond's-Pond ice-houses. Amid this rich and picturesque woodland the Newton Natural-History Society, the Appalachian Mountain Club, and other lovers of nature have enjoyed their field-days, in the blue and fleecy days of summer. On one side is a broad and solemn amphitheatre, defended by walls of shattered cliffs and crags, carpeted with fragrant besoms, and studded with vast and stately hemlocks, whose murmurous branches make a perpetual twilight beneath. Elsewhere there are walls of conglomerate rock, as tall and straight as castle-bastions, crowning the hill-tops, and menaced by storming-parties of trees, whose green banners have been planted in the crevices far up their mighty steeps. On the crest of one silent ridge is a marvellous rock formation, where cliffs a score of feet high surround three sides of a little grassy court, open on the fourth side to the long perspective of the forest, and entered by a narrow pass hardly a yard wide, and many feet long, leading between huge upright ledges. Through this portal, embroidered with delicate ferns and live-green mosses and gray lichens, the woodland wanderer enters the rock-walled chamber, fit audience-hall for Titania herself. Strolling down the grassy paths, — remnants of long-forgotten farm-roads, — one sees gorgeous orange and canary-colored fungi, delicate sprays of sassafras clambering above the shattered rocks, luxuriant ivies mantling the glacier-scarred ledges with living green, and magnificent ferns, now waving in broad sweeps of tropical luxuriance, and then nestling down among the bowlders in tiny sprays of the most exquisite grace and delicacy of outline. So broad and sequestered and unfrequented is this lovely forest that no sounds of prosaic human life invade its cloisters, and nothing disturbs the saunterer's reflections but the low songs of the birds, or the scampering of an occasional gray squirrel over the dry leaves. Instead of spending some hundreds of thousands of dollars for public parks, as the Newtonians occasionally try to compass, it would be wiser to publish, at the city's expense, a few little tracts setting forth the glories of her forests and hills, and telling how to find and recognize them.

In old times this forest was known as the "Slate-Rock Woods," after the great pile of slate now visible near the railroad between Newton Centre and Chestnut Hill. It was also called "Coonville," on account of the game abounding in the vicinity. Otis Pettee writes: "Washington Street in Boston, in colonial times, extended out over the Neck to Roxbury and thence by a circuitous route to Brookline — then known as 'Punch Bowl'; and when the Worcester turnpike was built, it was simply an extension of old Washington Street. After Tremont Street was opened to Roxbury, that part of Washington Street towards and beyond Brookline lost its identity, and has since taken another name [Boylston Street]. I well remember, when driving to Boston in my younger days, meeting hunters and trappers, with their guns and hounds, on their way to these woods for game."

Deep in the woods, between Judge Lowell's house and the little German hamlet of Thompsonville, is Hammond's Pond, a lonely lakelet of twenty acres, where in old times the farmers' lads used to catch eels and pout, with occasionally a lively two-pound pickerel. The natural outlet of the pond flowed through the rivulet which traverses the western part of Brookline, and thence along Bald-Pate Meadow, and down into the Charles River. But about forty years ago an artificial channel was made from the westerly shore, by which the overflow of the lakelet descends into Smelt Brook, and so wanders off into the Charles, by Waltham. The pond has for more than two centuries borne the name of Thomas Hammond, one of the three wealthiest pioneers (the others having been John and Edward Jackson) of the twenty original settlers of Newton. He came here in 1650, from Hingham, where he had settled in 1637, and where his four children were born and baptized. The clan of Hammond is now a numerous and widely disseminated one in Eastern Massachusetts.

Another of the pioneers of this fair land was Vincent Druce, who in 1650 bought a great expanse of woods with Thomas Hammond, and held them in common with him until 1664, when they divided them, the line running over the great hill. It was his son John who was mortally wounded while Prentice's cavalry fought against King Philip. At Swansey, Vincent's great-granddaughter Nancy was still alive as late as the year 1853. Vincent Druce built the mansion since known as the Crafts house, on the Denny place, about the year 1695, and in its modernized and newly-painted form it looks like some comfortable old village-inn, strayed away into these lovely rural uplands. Before King Philip's War this locality also became the home of Thomas Greenwood, the weaver, and town clerk, who gave a son and a grandson to Harvard College and the ministry.

While contemplating the groups of beautiful and costly homes, along the slopes of Chestnut Hill, one can scarcely realize that in the year 1800 there were but three houses in all Newton valued at above $1,000; and that the entire valuation of the 175 houses then in town was but $72,900. Up to the year 1850, nearly all the Chestnut-Hill region was occupied by the market-gardens of Kingsbury, Hammond, Woodward, and the Stones. The roads were narrow grassy lanes, bordered by barberry and burdock bushes, and other wild plants, and always wrapped in an atmosphere of peace and tranquillity. Then several patrician families from Boston moved into the neighborhood, and established a delightful and refined social life amid these scenes so highly favored by nature. More recently, however, several of the chief families have migrated into Boston every winter, to their town-houses on the Back Bay, leaving the younger branches of their clans to remain here through the inclement season. During the delicious days of spring and early summer and autumn, lawn-tennis parties are all the vogue; and Hammond street is lively with dog-carts and village-carts and the heavily-rumbling family carriages.

Oak Hill.

A LAND OF HIGHLANDS AND FORESTS.— THE OLD-TIME FARMERS.— MODERN COUNTRY SEATS.— OAK HILL AND BALD PATE.— HOLBROOK HALL.— KENRICK'S BRIDGE.

The southern part of the city of Newton, covering perhaps four square miles, is by nature the fairest of all her districts, and the most abundant in the varied charms of hill and glen, upland and meadow, long and placid river-reaches, and high-arched forests. Its comparative remoteness from the railways has retarded the inflowing of population, the cause of the erection of such great villages elsewhere in Newton; and the inhabitants are mainly devoted to agriculture, as in the old days of the Stuart dynasty. The infrequent roads that wind picturesquely over and around the hills lead by low and broad-based old farmhouses, with their clusters of weather-stained barns, overarched by trees of venerable age and glorious and majestic size. Here are gnarled and bent orchards, looking as ancient as the olive-trees around Jerusalem; broad fields smiling with abundant crops; and grassy pasture-lands, slanting toward the sun, and bounded by picturesque walls of field-stone. It is a land of brooding peace, in which it seems always afternoon; and the roar of the great metropolis of New England, within a long cannon-shot, is as unheard and unrealized as if it were as far away as Bombay or Buenos Ayres. And for two hundred and fifty years past, nothing but the Gospel of Peace has been known here, and generation after generation of industrious yeomen has tilled the fields without alarm.

The chief features of the natural scenery are Oak Hill, which rises to a height of 296 feet, and is crowned by the Bigelow villa; and, not far away, the shaggy Bald Pate, whose heavy crowning forests make a *chevelure* which belies its title. This noble eminence reaches an altitude of 318 feet, and is the highest of the many hills of Newton. Pleasant forest-paths connect the two highlands, skirting ancient farms and lonely upland pastures, and leading past vistas finer than those of any metropolitan park. One of the loveliest views in this (or any other) region is that gained from Dudley Street, a little way south of Boylston Street, whence one looks out and down upon the heavy forests of Bald Pate, the long slopes of Oak Hill, and over the far blue distances to the dreamland plains of Norfolk County, the Italian dome over Dedham, and the noble outlines of the Milton hills.

Old Goody Davis lived in this sequestered and pastoral region until her death, in 1752, at the age of 117 years. She had 3 husbands, 9 children, 45 grandchildren, 200 great-grandchildren, and above 800 great-great-grandchildren before she died. This noble mother in Israel cultivated with her own hands the sterile acres of her little farm, as skilful with the scythe as the hoe, and was often seen, after her hundredth year, at work in the fields. Later, she was supported by the town, retaining her faculties until she had passed 115 years, and living through the reigns of Charles I., Oliver Cromwell, Charles II., James II., William and Mary, Queen Anne, George I., and George II. Governor Dudley visited her little farmhouse, in 1750; and Governor Belcher had a portrait painted of her, which is now owned by the Massachusetts Historical Society. "From her great age, the face is wrinkled and rugged; the features are strongly delineated, the eyes blue and smiling, the lips full and rosy, the forehead honest and open; and a white, plain cap surrounds the head, face, and chin, which gives a death-like look to the picture, as though it had been taken from some living being who had already entered the valley of the shadow of death."

The Oak-Hill country is a region beloved of the sunshine, amid whose perfumed quietude flourish the feathery blooms of the golden-rod, constellations of white and purple asters, pungent yellow blossoms of tansy, the bearded purple balls of burdock, gray-green pods of milkweed, the golden rosettes of mullein, catnip and motherwort and spikenard, sage and thyme and mayweed, and all the glorious company of New England's floral regalia. Along the brooks bright elecampane blooms, and floating lilies star the still waters; and even the lean upland pastures are enriched by the pale-blue pennyroyal blossoms, and fair marigolds, and fragrant junipers. On every side appear

"The long, green meadows, wet with dew,
The daisies springing white and new,
The scent of fresh life in the air,
The flying birds adrift in song."

Here and there, by the quiet roadsides, are gray old barns, with their great lofts crammed with hay, close under the mossy roofs. The ancient trees, coeval with the Georgian era, make rich masses of shade over the clustered farm-buildings, and dreamy amber lights rest upon the broad stretches of field and forest. And the orchards bring to the springtime their wealth of perfumed blossoms, and to the Indian Summer its largess of golden and crimson fruitage.

On the quiet Bald-Pate Meadow, where his father-in-law, Edward Jackson, had bequeathed him a hundred acres of land, Thomas Prentice made his home, back in the seventeenth century, and brought up a family of sturdy and valiant sons. Another of the pioneers was Captain Jeremiah Wiswall, son of the famous Noah Wiswall, who settled here in 1750, and had a great family. This valiant yeoman was a captain of minute-men at

RESIDENCE OF LEVI C. WADE.
Dedham Street, near Parker Street, Oak Hill.

Lexington and at Dorchester Heights, but escaped the angry bullets of our British brethren, waiting on earth until the year 1809, when he passed away, at the venerable age of 84. Hither also came the Longleys and Murdocks and Woodwards, and other broad-shouldered farmers, compelling the soil to produce them abundance.

The pioneer of the Stone family in this region was John, son of the Hon. Ebenezer Stone, who bought a part of the Rev. Nathan Ward's farm, and built a house here in 1724, which thirty years later passed to his son Deacon and Captain Jonas Stone, who lived until 1804. His son Ebenezer inherited the mansion, and bequeathed it to his son Samuel, who lived until 1849. The Stone neighborhood was along Dedham Street, about a mile from Newton Highlands, across the valley, and not far from the Wade chateau; and one or two of their quaint old farmhouses may be seen there to this day.

The great house of this region pertains to the Hon. Levi C. Wade, who has subdued a broad domain of rocky ridge and hillside, and erected a large country-house, with great chimneys and gables. The estate covers over 200 acres, and is called Homewood.

Mr. Wade graduated at Yale College, and taught school in Newton while fitting himself for the profession of the law. He entered practice in Boston in 1873, and in 1877, with Hon. J. Q. A. Brackett, now Lieutenant-Governor of Massachusetts, formed the law firm of Wade & Brackett. Mr. Wade represented Newton in the General Court for four successive years, and in 1879 was Speaker of the House of Representatives. Refusing a re-election, he has ever since devoted himself to railway law and management. He was one of the four original projectors and owners of what is now included in the property of the Mexican Central Railway Company; and is President and General Counsel of that Company, having held those offices for the past five years. He is also associated with President John S. Farlow in the directory of the Cincinnati, Sandusky & Cleveland Railroad.

Not far distant from the Wade place, on the noble crest of Oak Hill, stands the new mansion of Dr. Henry J. Bigelow, commanding from its generous verandas a prospect of idyllic beauty, extending from the high Blue Hills of Milton around over the Dedham meadows and the valley of the upper Charles, and including many a famous mountain-peak in the far west, Monadnock and Wachusett and all their famous company.

Near the southern base of Oak Hill is the little Oak-Hill school-house, the successor of the one founded in the year 1701, nearly a generation before the birth of George Washington. From this locality it is about a mile to Kenrick's Bridge; 2 to West Roxbury, 4 to Dedham, Brookline, or Jamaica Plain, 6 to Hyde Park or Readville, and 7½ to Boston.

A country lane leading off Dedham Street to the southward, near the Oak-Hill school, enters the baronial domain of Holbrook Hall, the manor of William S. Appleton, of Boston. This estate covers 340 acres, bounded for a long distance by the Charles River, and beautifully diversified with wide lawns, sequestered glens, and bits of forest. The house is a spacious Gothic building, on a broad and sunny upland, with park-like surroundings of great symmetry and grace. Mr. Appleton is a half-brother of the late Thomas Gold Appleton, the wit and author; and a brother-in-law of Henry Wadsworth Longfellow. He has resided in Europe for some years past.

Oak Hill School, Dedham Street.

The celebrated Oak-Hill Stock Farm of E. D. Wiggin on Dedham Street, a mile and a quarter from Newton Centre, is modelled after the famous institutions of this kind in the Blue-Grass region of Kentucky, with paddocks and a half-mile trotting-track, and separate places for stallions and brood-mares, colts, and fillies. Some very celebrated racing-horses have been brought up here, including the well-known mahogany-colored stallion, Charley Wilkes. In this pastoral region, between Winchester Street and Dedham Street, and south of the brook, is the long ridge formerly known as Winchester Hill, from a farmer who dwelt hard by.

This pastoral region should be the field of operations of the Jersey Stock Club, whose membership includes many of the foremost Newton men. But wherever the scene of its victories may be, the goodfellowship and fraternity of this association cannot be excelled, even among professedly social clubs.

The road to the westward crosses into Needham by Kenrick's Bridge, one of the oldest pontifical works in Newton until 1886, when the ravening river swept it away. A new bridge of stone was erected in its place.

The Tuckerman estate, near the river, north of Nahanton Street, was formerly the home of the father of the Rev. George H. Hepworth, whose mother was organist of the First Baptist Church in 1841-42. Amid these pleasant fields passed the boyhood of that famous Unitarian divine and author, so long pastor of the Church of the Unity, in Boston, and the Church of the Messiah, in New York. Some years ago the Roman-Catholic church acquired this estate, and a broad domain of rocky hills between Winchester and Nahanton Streets and the river, with the intention (yet unfulfilled) of founding a school in these salubrious solitudes. The subsequent erection of the theological seminary at Brighton renders it unlikely that this tract will be put into use by the Church authorities. The two famous trees near the bridge are among the oldest in settled New England.

We have taken our confiding traveller on a long and arduous journey "through the Newtons" (as the phrase goes), from where we found him at Newton station, looking blankly out on Centre Street, to where we abandon him, in the last stages of exhaustion, down among the lonely woods of Needham. And to comfort him, withal, let us leave two final sentiments pertinent to the subject, one of them being drawn from the ancient Greek, and another from the English of the classic period.

It has often been said, *Vede Napoli e poi mori*, "See Naples and then die"—as if after that crowning pleasure life could have nothing more worth living for. But Naples was only the Greek *Nea*, "new," *Polis*, "town," or, in fact, the New town, or Newton, of the Mediterranean. And since we cannot all go beyond the Pillars of Hercules, some must be content to see their Naples in the vernacular, in Newton of the Massachusetts. Nor need they then die, but live in great content.

As to our Englishman, we shall not insist too strongly upon his evident meaning, or attempt to demonstrate what at this length of time may not be demonstrable. Look, therefore, upon these lines by Alexander Pope, and judge for yourselves: —

"Nature and Nature's laws lay hid in night,
God said 'LET NEWTON BE'—and all was light."

Noteworthy Boston Firms.

MACULLAR, PARKER, & COMPANY.

The most noted house in its line in this country.

MACULLAR, PARKER, & COMPANY'S name must always be included in a list of eminent Boston firms, for their great clothing and piece-goods establishment at No. 400 Washington Street is one of the most noteworthy examples of progressive and creditable industry to be found in any city in America. It is only a little less than forty years ago that the business was started in a very small way; and yet to-day the firm give employment constantly the year round to upwards of 600 hands, men and women, in one of the neatest manufacturing establishments in the world, — one, too, in which all reasonable provision is made for the comfort and health of all the employés. The magnificent and commodious building fronts on two streets, — on Washington at Nos. 398 and 400, and on Hawley at No. 81.

Macullar, Parker, & Company's Entrance.

No adequate idea of its size can be had from a view on the street. Only by passing from one end to the other on all the many floors can the visitor form a correct impression of its magnitude and attractiveness. The floor surface alone amounts to 80,000 square feet, including the space occupied for the engines, boilers, pumps, ventilating apparatus, and carpenter's and machinist's shops. The building is used solely for the manufacturing and retailing of clothing for men, youths, and boys, and the importing and jobbing of piece-goods. The clothing made is sold at retail only by this firm, and in cut, style, trimmings, finish, and goods

MACULLAR, PARKER, & COMPANY.
Nos. 398 and 400 Washington Street

ranks equal to that made by the leading merchant-tailors. No person is likely ever to enter into this establishment without being able to find a proper fit in thoroughly trustworthy clothing; and every one who patronizes this firm knows that the "one-price" system is positively invariable under all circumstances. It is the constant aim of MACULLAR, PARKER, & COMPANY to furnish the best and most satisfactory garments that can be furnished for the amount charged for them. It is an inviolable rule of the house to satisfy a person, or else not to take his patronage. No false or misleading statement in any particular is ever allowed to be made. People who visit or patronize this firm are never importuned to make purchases, nor is any one ever inveigled into buying things that are not wanted; the constant aim being to find out what the people want, and to supply them accordingly. The

Hawley-Street Front of Macullar, Parker, & Company.

custom department of MACULLAR, PARKER, & COMPANY constitutes the largest merchant-tailoring establishment, and the department for the importing and jobbing of woollens and other piece-goods also forms the foremost house in its line, in New England.

SPRINGER BROTHERS' CLOAK ESTABLISHMENTS.
Their Sumptuous New Branch House.

MESSRS. SPRINGER BROTHERS, who are recognized as the foremost fashionable cloak makers of America, have recently opened an entirely new establishment at the corner of Washington and Bedford Streets. It is called a branch house; but this so-called "branch" is a whole establishment in itself, and while it is small in comparison with the other great places of the Springer Brothers, it is nevertheless a very large place, consuming almost three whole buildings. This establishment is not a branch in the sense of an agency, but it has been opened by the Springer Brothers to show some of the choice goods for which they are so famous throughout this country. The three buildings have been remodelled throughout, both inside and outside, and form one of the handsomest places of business to be found anywhere in this country or in Europe, and have already become one of the noted sights of Boston. The furnishings, the decorations, the arrangement, and the conveniences are all designed and executed in the best taste.

Springer Brothers' Cloak Bazaar, Washington cor. Bedford.

The main establishment of the Springer Brothers is the conspicuous block five stories high, built of sandstone, fronting on three thoroughfares, Essex and Chauncy Streets, and Harrison Avenue,—the site of the former home of Wendell Phillips. The factory buildings are on Green Street, near Bowdoin Square. The firm in busy seasons give employment to nearly one thousand operatives. Besides the establishment in Boston, they have also a wholesale house in San Francisco and purchasing agencies in London, Paris, and Berlin. They manufacture every variety of outer garments for ladies, misses, and children, and their goods are unsurpassed by those of any manufacturers in the world; and the trade everywhere look to Springer Brothers of Boston for the introduction of the most stylish and most acceptable garments in their line.

JOHN C. PAIGE'S FIRE INSURANCE AGENCY.
The Leading Agency in New England.

JOHN C. PAIGE is the leading fire-insurance agent in New England, doing the largest business, and representing the greatest amount of capital. Moreover, his offices, occupying the entire building at No. 20 Kilby Street, are unsurpassed for their elegance, convenience, and arrangement. Seventeen years ago Mr. Paige was recognized by the profession throughout this country as a skilful adjuster of fire-losses, and as an experienced general agent. Duties incident to the Great Fire of 1872 brought him to Boston, where he subsequently decided to establish a local insurance-agency in connection with his general agency business; and to-day, by reason of his great ability, varied experience, extreme popularity, and indomitable energy, he has placed himself in the foremost rank of the underwriters in the United States. The companies he represents are the "Imperial Fire of London, Eng.," "City of London Fire of London, Eng.," "Orient of Hartford, Conn.," "Fire Association of Philadelphia," "Mechanics Fire of Philadelphia," and the "Niagara Fire of New York." The gross assets of these companies amount to almost fifty million dollars, and the losses they have paid amount to an enormous sum. This agency's business extends throughout the United States; for Mr. Paige is the American resident manager for the City of London Fire, and the Imperial Fire, two great London companies. In the Boston office are about one hundred male and female employees. John C. Paige personally is one of those genial, whole-souled men with whom it is always a pleasure to do business. "Nothing mean about him," never was more fitly applied to any man; and this characteristic is evidenced by his every action in public and private life.

John C. Paige's Insurance Building, 20 Kilby Street.

SMITH & ANTHONY STOVE CO.,

48, 50, 52, and 54 Union Street, Boston,

Manufacturers of the Celebrated Hub Stoves, Ranges, and Furnaces.

THE ANTHONY STEEL PLATE FURNACE has had a large sale in Newton, and is indorsed by our patrons as being the highest development of Sanitary Heating. Below we show two Newton residences heated by this Furnace: —

Residence of J. H. Sawyer, Chestnut Hill, Newton, Mass. Andrews & Jaques, Architects, Boston.
Heated by two Anthony Furnaces.

Mr. Sawyer's testimonial is as follows: —

Messrs. Smith & Anthony Stove Co.

Gents, — The two Anthony Furnaces for my house at Chestnut Hill, Newton, have proved very satisfactory; and the experience I have had with them so far has been all that I could wish. At present I am running but one furnace, which gives ample heat, reserving the two for the coldest weather. I selected the furnaces on their merits, and have had no reason to regret the choice.

Yours truly,

J. H. SAWYER.

Residence of J. R. Prescott, Linwood Park, Newtonville, Mass.
Heated by one Anthony Steel Plate Furnace.

Carpets and Oriental Rugs.

Joel Goldthwait & Co.,

163 to 169 Washington Street,

Boston,

Show . a . large . stock . for . fine . furnishing.

Established 1857.

F. G. BARNES & SON,

Real Estate, Mortgage, and Insurance Brokers,

AUCTIONEERS AND APPRAISERS,

EDWARD F. BARNES, { 27 State Street, Boston.
Brackett Block, Newton.

WEDDING GIFTS
SELECTED AT   CRAWLEY'S   ARE ALWAYS APPRECIATED.

They are odd, seldom duplicated, and always admired.

ADVANCED NOVELTIES FROM EUROPEAN MARKETS
A SPECIALTY.

TABLE AND EXTENSION FLOOR LAMPS.
WROUGHT IRON AND BRASS ANDIRONS, FENDERS, FIRE SETS, etc., in Large Variety at

CRAWLEY'S, 171 TREMONT ST.,
BOSTON.

D. P. ILSLEY & CO., - No. 411 Washington Street, Boston.
The most magnificent and best stocked fur and ladies' hat establishment in **America**.

Cooked, Boned, and Truffled Dishes. ICE-CREAM and OTHER ICES. Charlotte Russe, Jelly, etc. Silver, China, and Glassware.

Also, EXPERIENCED COOKS. Polite and Attentive Waiters Furnished. SPECIAL ATTENTION to Wedding and other Parties.

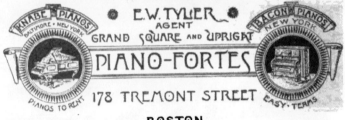

OLDEST AND BEST

SOLD BY LEADING DEALERS.

The Partelow Riverside Boat-house at Riverside, on the Charles (River).
The Largest and most Complete Boat and Canoe Livery in New England.
Boats, Canoes, and Steam Launches can be rented by the hour or day.
Take cars for Riverside Station, B. & A. R.R.

H. V. PARTELOW & CO., Proprietors, - - Auburndale, Mass.

H. V. PARTELOW & CO.,
Manufacturing Boat, Canoe, and Steam Launch Builders,
Oars, Paddles, etc. Adirondack Boats, etc.
Warerooms, 424 ATLANTIC AVE., BOSTON. Factory at AUBURNDALE, MASS.

GEORGE W. BUSH,
BOARDING, LIVERY, AND HACK STABLE,
WARD 7,
ELMWOOD STREET, NEWTON.

Having made many additions to my former stock, by the purchase of New Horses and Carriages, I am better prepared than ever to furnish the Best Horses and Carriages for Business and Pleasure Driving. Carriages may always be found in waiting at the Newton Depot on the arrival of all trains. Parties called for at their residence to take trains. We have the best facilities for **BOARDING HORSES**. Having a large **BRICK STABLE**, the risk by fire is lessened on the loss of Horses or Stock. Best of care given. None but competent men employed.

ALSO,
FUNERAL AND FURNISHING UNDERTAKER.

Caskets, Coffins, and everything suitable for the business kept on hand. This branch of the business will be under the supervision of WM. H. PHILLIPS, who has had an experience of Twenty-nine years in Newton, and who will attend to all calls personally. All orders by Telephone or otherwise promptly attended to, Day or Night.

TELEPHONE 48-3.

"HALFTONE"
Engraving made direct from a photograph by the
BOSTON PHOTOGRAVURE COMPANY,
27 BOYLSTON STREET.

Send drawing or photograph for estimate.

Boston Safe Deposit and Trust Co.,

87 Milk Street, Post-office Square,

Assumes the care of Invested Property and Collection of Incomes. Accepts Trusts created by will or otherwise. Allows Interest on Deposits.

Acts as Transfer Agent for Railroad and other Corporations.

Certificates of Stock registered at small expense.

Rents Safes in its vaults at from $10 to $150 a year, according to size.

Receives Bonds and other Securities and Valuables for Safe Keeping.

CAPITAL,	$600,000.
SURPLUS,	$400,000.

FREDERICK M. STONE, *President.*   **FREDERIC W. LINCOLN,** *Vice-President.*

EDWARD P. BOND,   **FRANK C. MILES,**
Secretary and Manager of Safe Deposit Department.   *Treasurer.*

SOLOMON LINCOLN, *Solicitor.*

HERBERT NICKERSON.   PAUL ASKENASY.

337      337

Paul Askenasy & Co.

MEN'S OUTFITTERS,
SHIRT MAKERS,
FINE LAUNDRY WORK.

No. 337 Washington Street,   -   -   Boston.

We make a specialty of fine Custom Shirts.
Our laundry work is done daintily and promptly.
Our stock includes a complete line of gentlemen's furnishings.

ESTABLISHED 1872 — INCORPORATED 1888

Moses King Corporation

Manufacturers of "King's Handbooks" Guides and Maps

Boston, Mass.

MOSES KING, President. **CAPITAL, $250,000.**

THIS . CORPORATION . IS . THE . ONLY . ONE . IN . THE . WORLD . DEVOTED . EXCLUSIVELY . TO . THE . PUBLISHING . OF . GUIDE . BOOKS . AND . MAPS. . . . .

IN MAKING
THE SERIES OF KING'S HANDBOOKS . . . .

for all of the larger American cities, it has been the invariable policy to produce for each city a book in which all residents will take pride, and all visitors find pleasure. . . . .

ALL OF
KING'S HANDBOOKS ARE PROFUSELY ILLUSTRATED, . .

many containing upwards of 300 specially engraved views, showing all the important features of the respective cities. The books necessarily vary in size, each containing from 60 to 500 pages, exquisitely printed on super-fine calendered paper, and bound in beautiful and substantial cloth and gilt covers. . . . .

EVERY ONE OF THE ENTIRE SERIES . . . .

will be found accurate, readable, and handsome. Every one of these books is revised, enlarged, and improved in the successive editions. . . . . .

THESE BOOKS
ARE ALWAYS OBTAINABLE AT ANY BOOKSTORE, ...

and at all the leading news-stands and prominent hotels. They may also be obtained direct from the publishers. . . . .

The price is uniformly one dollar, in cloth binding.

For . a . complete . list . of . "King's . Handbooks" . send . for . catalogue.

CHAS. A. SMITH & CO.,
MERCHANT TAILORS,
18 and 20 School Street, - Boston, Mass.,

HAVE ALWAYS A COMPLETE ASSORTMENT OF EVERY VARIETY OF FINE CLOTHS FOR DRESS OR BUSINESS PURPOSES. . . . . . .
. . . . GENTLEMEN ARE INVITED TO CALL.

ESTABLISHED 1838.

W. E. HODGKINS.   C. G. BEAL.

Established 1873.

ELECTROTYPES

L. W. ROGERS, Proprietor.

Telephone, 2833.

BOOK AND JOB WORK OF ALL KINDS FURNISHED IN BEST MANNER.

Among the books we have electrotyped in 1887 are: —

"ENOCH ARDEN," For E. P. Dutton & Co., New York.

"BUNCH OF VIOLETS," For Lee & Shepard.

"SONG OF THE RIVER," For Estes & Lauriat.

Electrotyped in 1888: —

"FAIRY LILLIAN," For Estes & Lauriat.

"DAYS SERENE," For Lee & Shepard.

"OUR LITTLE ONES." For Russell Pub. Co.

TYPE COMPOSITION, PROCESS, AND WOOD ENGRAVING FOR ELECTROTYPING.

FINE CUT WORK A SPECIALTY.

165 Devonshire and 26 Arch Streets,   -   -   Boston.

☞ Please send for estimates.

Artists' Materials,
AND
Drawing Instruments
OF EVERY DESCRIPTION.

DECORATIVE NOVELTIES,
ART STUDIES, ETC.,

FROST & ADAMS,
IMPORTERS,

37 Cornhill,

BOSTON, MASS.

Send for Catalogue and mention "King's Handbook of Newton."

PERMANENT CARBON PRINTS.

PHOTOGRAPHS OF EVERY KIND.

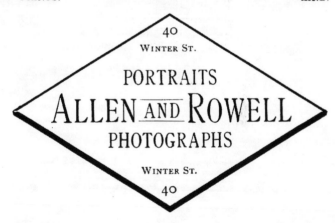

40 Winter St.

PORTRAITS

ALLEN AND ROWELL

PHOTOGRAPHS

Winter St. 40

AMATEUR PHOTOGRAPHERS' SUPPLIES.

PRINTING FOR AMATEUR PHOTOGRAPHERS.

NEW ART GALLERIES,

75 Boylston Street, Boston, cor. Park Square.

Noyes, Cobb & Co.

(Formerly at 127 Tremont St.)